S0-BQZ-210

# SUBURBS UNDER SIEGE

# SUBURBS UNDER SIEGE

## RACE, SPACE, AND AUDACIOUS JUDGES

*Charles M. Haar*

PRINCETON UNIVERSITY PRESS   PRINCETON, NEW JERSEY

SCCCC - LIBRARY
4601 Mid Rivers Mall Drive
St. Peters, MO 63376
WITHDRAWN

Copyright © 1996 by Princeton University Press
Published by Princeton University Press, 41 William Street,
Princeton, New Jersey 08540
In the United Kingdom: Princeton University Press,
Chichester, West Sussex
All Rights Reserved

*Library of Congress Cataloging-in-Publication Data*

Haar, Charles Monroe
Suburbs under siege : race, space, and
audacious judges / Charles M. Haar.
p.   cm.
Includes index.
ISBN 0-691-04444-9 (Cl : alk. paper)
1. Discrimination in housing—Law and legislation—
United States.   2. Land use—Law and
legislation—United States.   3. Courts—United States.
4. Race relations—United States.   5. Social justice—
United States.   I. Title.
KF5740.Z9H3      1996
344.73′0636351—dc20
[347.304636351]      95-37263

This book has been composed in Sabon

Princeton University Press books are printed
on acid-free paper and meet the guidelines
for permanence and durability of the Committee
on Production Guidelines for Book Longevity
of the Council on Library Resources

Printed in the United States of America
by Princeton Academic Press

10   9   8   7   6   5   4   3   2   1

**To Suzanne** _____

WITH LOVE AND APPRECIATION

# Contents

# Illustrations _____

## Preface

THIS BOOK springs from a deeply felt desire to understand and ameliorate the racial and ethnic divisions that stubbornly continue to polarize our public life. I seek, in particular, to comprehend—and to help that mythic person, the general reader, comprehend—our legal system's response to these divisions as they affect the modern American metropolis. My focus is on the intersection of two realities of post-modern society: segregation by race in metropolitan settlements, and the role the courts play in responding to the ensuing inequalities.

No domestic issue is more troubling to American society today than the economic and social division between the races. While a cleavage along class and racial lines runs through many and diverse aspects of American life, nowhere is the partition more glaring or inescapable than in the gulf between the poverty and despair of central cities and the wealth and opportunity of suburbs. The exodus of jobs and mostly white middle- and upper-income people from our urban centers to suburban enclaves has split this country into two nations: one reserved for the haves, the other entrapping the have-nots.

What is to be done? As a student of urbanism at a law school, heir to the Holmesian precept that the life of the law is, fundamentally, experience, I have sought to translate general concepts into concrete actions. In public service at national and state levels, I have joined with many others in efforts to bridge the gap between rhetoric and reality so as to emerge from the shadow that falls between the democratic ideal and the sober reality.

Gunnar Myrdal, whose classic *An American Dilemma* set the terms of discourse and public policy on race relations fifty years ago, anticipated the impending patterns of metropolitan segregation. He could not, however, foresee the judicial response to that geographic divide as it became ever more ensconced and harder to budge. In the decades since Myrdal wrote, it has become evident that the growth of suburbia is not merely a physical or demographic development but an indicator of what our society values.

Since chairing President Johnson's Task Force on Suburban Problems in 1967, it has been clear to me that the growth of suburbia and the movement of capital and other resources away from the cities—patterns rarely considered in the formulation of policies concerning race relations and poverty—are key points that must be addressed if we aspire to solve the paradox of great wealth and great poverty coexisting in our metropolitan areas today. For as decentralization accelerates, the concentration of poverty and the segregation of minorities into the geographically isolated islands of inner cities will inexorably exacerbate racial tensions and associated ills. As the schism between suburb and central city worsens, obstacles to equality of educational opportunity threaten to become insurmountable. As suburban occupations become increasingly inaccessible to inner-city residents, due to the spatial-job mismatch, unemployment—often for life—becomes the grim prospect for too many of our citizens.

Enter the courts, and the famous Mount Laurel Doctrine, named for a typical New Jersey suburban community that found itself a defendant in a lawsuit originally brought on behalf of current and future African-American residents of that township. Over a twenty-year period, the New Jersey Supreme Court chose to counteract the dangerous metropolitan split through a series of ever-expanding judicial interventions. The court's pathbreaking stance is the central focus of this book. The history of this long judicial process is an engrossing showcase for a new approach to adjudication, as well as a powerful instance of a court attempting to provide relief denied by executive and legislative branches. Given the politically explosive nature of any directive for opening up the suburbs, the proper role of the judiciary in implementing public policy, especially in the face of the most recalcitrant organizational resistance, becomes a central issue.

Desiring to maintain their distance from unwanted land uses and populations, suburbs have long invoked a variety of land-use ordinances known as "exclusionary zoning" to erect legally accepted gates at their borders. Thus, it was to their astonishment when this long-accepted practice was challenged and invalidated by the courts. In a pioneering interpretation of the state's constitution, the New Jersey Supreme Court barred the exercise of local regulatory power to exclude low-income groups and furthermore decreed that localities must assume a fair share of the regional need for affordable housing. Not surprisingly, this anti-majoritarian stance precipitated a fierce political battle that tested the power of judges to carry out unpopular policy decisions.

Rejecting the traditional adversarial mode of litigation, declarative judgments, and injunctions, the New Jersey high court chose instead an ongoing program for reform supervised by specially selected judicial agents. Affirmative remedies, rather than the finding of liability, became the focus of attention as judges and special masters developed and monitored individual plans for the creation of low-income housing in the suburbs. While parties to a lawsuit normally control and define the issues presented to the court, in this instance trial judges modified the customary adversary system, undertook their own fact-finding, devised innovative administrative machinery, and in the middle of a major conflict within society fashioned innovative remedial formats. Their administrative techniques and novel procedural approach are applicable nationwide to other instances of judicial restructuring of failed governmental institutions, such as schools, public housing, state mental hospitals, and prisons.

In rendering constitutional principles operational, echoing Holmes's nostrum, the New Jersey courts literally transformed the suburban landscape and along with it the social consciousness of the population. For what this extensive, drawn-out legal process reveals is that, in this last decade of the twentieth century in the United States, meaningful access to economic, social, and public infrastructure is indispensable to survival. Without such access, there is scant opportunity either for full citizen participation or for mutual respect and dignity. As a legal matter, then, equality of access to such fundamental human resources as housing, schools, employment, credit services, and social networks has become arguably as important as other constitutionally guaranteed freedoms.

Though not ignoring philosophical arguments over application of the formal separation of powers doctrine or the ideal scope of exercise of judicial discretion, I chose to pursue a more pragmatic course by going directly to the principal actors in this legal drama: judges, special masters, lawyers, public officials, and administrators. Lengthy interviews illuminated a fascinating evolution of ideas and conduct. On the basis of this exploration, supplemented by my personal experience as special master in the Boston Harbor and other institutional litigation cases, I reached a conclusion not widely shared by the population at large or even commonly held by members of my profession: at the present juncture of class and race relations in the United States, an aggressive posture on the part of the third branch of government is indispensable to the achievement of economic and social equality.

It is my hope that the general reader will find this examination of the activist role of the courts (in a society both drawn to and repelled by the primacy of law) enlightening and persuasive. If judges are compelled to act by the failure of public institutions to carry out the missions entrusted to them, then society must be concerned about the way judges formulate the issues, decide within the institutional constraints of their office how to proceed, and sometimes even reconstruct the very system of which they are an integral part.

More broadly, individuals may wish to reflect on the consequences of transforming public policy issues, such as the metropolitan opportunity structure, into legal issues, and ultimately on the wisdom of converting judges from adjudicators to agents of social change. For as gridlock becomes a metaphor not only for city street traffic but for the inaction of contemporary political bodies, the courts may be summoned increasingly to help—or push—society to restructure itself. In the Mount Laurel cases, the courts not only coped with the fragmentation of government powers over land uses within metropolitan areas, but in their constitutional role as the last resort for the voiceless and disadvantaged, became the standard-bearer for an egalitarian vision so often promised, yet less often realized, in American life.

The courts' piecemeal decisions requiring the provision of affordable housing in the suburbs opened up avenues that, one hopes, will lead to more equitable and efficient metropolitan communities. Only a deeper understanding by citizens of the complexities, pitfalls, and potentialities of the judicial role in a constitutional democracy can begin to bestow on court activism the necessary legitimacy for continued long-term results. Born out of a singular mandate to interpret and guarantee the constitutional rights of all Americans, the judicial vision represented by the Mount Laurel experience offers a signal lesson for reducing the economic and social chasm arising from the isolation of the poor in the central cities of this land of plenty.

# Prologue

## A NATION OF SUBURBS

# I

## Breaking New Ground: The Role of the Courts in Social Change

IN APRIL 1974, Ethel Lawrence launched a lawsuit destined to dominate the suburban agenda of the country for the next two decades. The forty-one-year-old homemaker, a part-time practical nurse, could not find a house she could afford in her hometown of Mount Laurel, New Jersey. Heeding her minister's advice, she and her daughter, Thomasene, invoked the help of young legal service attorneys in their search for an affordable home.[1] This simple action would become a flashpoint in the nationwide debate over exclusionary zoning and the destiny of American metropolitan areas. One immediate consequence was that the New Jersey Supreme Court undertook the boldest and most innovative judicial intervention ever to countermand exclusionary zoning: in the landmark Mount Laurel trilogy of cases, the court identified and enunciated a constitutional right for all people—rich or poor, black or white—to live in the suburbs. It went to extraordinary lengths to break down the legal fences raised against affordable housing in the suburbs. Mount Laurel I also represented an attack against the skewed spatial distribution—by race, ethnicity, and income—of metropolitan populations. It set the tone for all future legal encounters with discriminatory local land-use regulatory barriers.[2]

The Mount Laurel cases constitute a historic judicial intervention. The political system had malfunctioned: suburban communities were operating on behalf of their neighborhoods—providing open spaces, preserving home values, keeping property taxes down—at the expense of the larger society. But if law was the willing handmaiden of malignant intention, it could and would also be its palliative. If the legislative and executive branches would not provide a constitutionally mandated fairer society, then the state judiciary would. No other public body was willing to secure the constitutional rights of *all* individuals to the benefits of an open and mobile society. No other government institution in the prevailing political and social climate was motivated to represent the interests of the metropolitan area as a whole. Yet, surprisingly, the Mount Laurel decisions have barely entered the mainstream of discussion, and few have sought to extract their deeper meaning, despite the intense immediate controversies that flared up around them.

## The Walled Suburbs

Ancient themes underlie the long struggle over how to allocate regional responsibility for low- and moderate-income housing. A parcel of land for oneself, free of any tenurial restraints, is the promise the United States has held out to its citizens and all newcomers ever since the American Revolution. From the dwelling of the colonial era to the homestead of the post–Civil War era to the home in surburbia in the modern era, this yearning for a place of one's own has endured. Access to land, the capacity to appropriate space and thereby gain a sense of belonging, an almost mythical attachment to a personal stake in the soil—these sentiments persist even in the age of the electronic superhighway. Crucial to understanding the exclusion of minorities from this commonly shared goal and the ensuing struggle over suburban turf is an awareness of the new urban form that has emerged in the past few decades: the fragmentation and stratification of metropolitan areas into inner cities and proliferating suburbs.[3]

The United States, by all accounts, is the first and premier suburban nation. Beginning in earnest after World War II, a great migration transformed the American metropolis. This exodus featured a dizzying rush from the cities to the suburbs: during the postwar baby boom, the net population gain by the suburbs was thirty million people—more than double that of the rest of the country; while central city populations increased by 14 percent in that period, suburban areas increased by fully 79 percent. The 1990 census officially acknowledged this metamorphosis: 46 percent of the total U.S. population now lives in the suburbs and but 31.3 percent in the cities.[4]

## Suburban Dominance (Population, 1990)

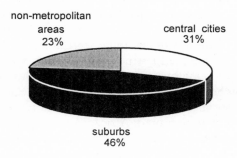

non-metropolitan
areas
23%

central cities
31%

suburbs
46%

Suburbanization, as a distinctive aspect of urbanization, recast not only the center of gravity of the population but also patterns of investment and technology: the suburb is now the country's broadest new frontier. For example, in 1970 central cities contained 71 percent of the nation's office space; ten years later more than half the office space was located in suburban areas. National and state elections are now decided by the choices of suburbanites. Increasingly, services once considered truly characteristic of the city—hospitals, cultural centers, financial facilities, for instance—are located in the suburban belt.[5]

It is in suburban settings that the American sense of success—both symbolic and physical—is made most manifest, through the metaphor of home ownership. And minorities are substantially excluded. Indeed, for partisans of democracy, the most disturbing characteristic of the metropolitan scene is surely the high degree of racial and ethnic separation in the new spatial pattern. The nearly complete residential separation of the races is widespread; at every income range, minorities are far less likely than their white counterparts to live in suburbs.[6] Furthermore, when minorities manage to reach suburbia, they tend to cluster in racial enclaves, continuing the separatist tendencies of the older urban ares.[7]

The spatial polarization of poor and affluent is equally striking: in the hundred largest central cities, the percentage of the population living in census tracts with poverty rates greater than 40 percent more than doubled between 1970 and 1990.[8] The old central cities were hollowed out as white upper-income households moved to the detached, single-family homes in the suburbs. Two worlds loom up—residentially segregated minority areas with poor-quality schools, inadequate public facilities, few job opportunities, and high crime and delinquency rates, and a suburban sphere whose housing, infrastructure, densities, and ways of life are more expensive and expansive, safer, and more conducive to sound individual development. In Benjamin Disraeli's words describing another country and another century, this gulf divides the citizens of metropolitan areas "as if they were dwellers in different zones, or inhabitants of different planets."[9]

Contrary to the assertions of those who attribute segregation to economic and market forces or to long-term structural trends in the decentralization of population and employment, neither affordability nor preference of individual households explains the high levels of segregation. Economists, like other social science investigators, maintain that very little of the serious underrepresentation of African-American households in suburban areas is explained by low income or by other socioeconomic characteristics alone.[10] Instead, racial discrimination in the operation of housing markets appears to be the most powerful factor. Interpreting the essential conditions of modern urban life as dangerous interdependency, many Americans have moved to the suburbs to find a safer and more congenial environment. By choosing to insulate themselves from the worrisome quandaries posed by problems spanning unemployment, dilapidated housing, teenage pregnancy, and crime, they have created a division between the black central city and the predominantly white suburbs, a geographic partition that has undermined efforts to find a common solution to the most volatile domestic problems of the day.

The distorting and baleful effects of housing discrimination are as well documented as they are painful to their victims. Segregation defeats free operation of the real estate market and prevents minority families from competing equally in their search for housing. Since most American individual wealth is positioned in residential real estate, enforced physical segregation blocks minorities from what has become a major route to wealth by denying them the vehicle for capital accumulation. Separation facilitates redlining, a major barrier to access to mortgage and credit facilities. Forced segregation condemns minorities to localities with inferior facilities and services, creating a de facto apartheid that few Americans would willingly endorse or deliberately create.

Isolating neighborhoods by race and class contributes to the desperate condition of inner-city schools and flouts efforts at equalization of educational opportunity. The partition of metropolitan areas—with bands of wealth ringing poor communities—has converted many public schools into institutions overwhelmed by poverty-related problems. Lack of integration in housing also necessitates the hated move to school busing. The years of futile efforts expended on improving the American school system have finally alerted practitioners and scholars to the significance of the central city–suburban schism, and racial and economic housing segregation is now the major theme sounded in the latest wave of lawsuits seeking to integrate the inner city's public schools with those of their suburban neighbors.

The higher rates of unemployment and the lower incomes of African-Americans and Hispanic-Americans may be traced to the spatial mismatch of home and work in the metropolitan area.[11] Unable to move to neighborhoods with the greatest opportunities for economic mobility, minorities must incur high commuting costs to reach the jobs increasingly located outside the central city.[12] More than half of these jobs, especially in the new outer suburbs, are inaccessible by public transportation. And the flow of information regarding job openings is a trickle: enforced segregation isolates blacks, whites, and Hispanics, inhibiting the personal connections and friendships that can lead to employment.

The economic geography of whole regions has permanently shifted as the cities no longer function as employment hubs; the bulk of new office construction, service job creation, and retailing expansion has dispersed to suburban settlements.[13] From 1980 to 1986, for example, the total job growth for the inner city of Los Angeles was but 13,000 as against 279,000 in its suburbs; Philadelphia gained 25,000 jobs, while its suburbs gained 205,000; Washington, D.C. added 29,000 jobs compared to 301,000 in its suburbs; Chicago lost 40,000 jobs against a gain of 212,000 by its suburbs; Detroit shared a similar fate, losing 57,000 jobs, while jobs in its suburbs increased by 120,000.[14] The largest share of jobs lost in each city were manufacturing, clerical, and blue-collar employment, the traditional entry level for the urban working class.

These employment statistics and others like them were available to the Mount Laurel judges.[15] Moreover, the courts' jurisdiction had suffered similar losses: in New Jersey, the adjoining townships of Edison, Franklin, and Piscataway support as many jobs—115,129—as Newark, which has only half the total number of jobs it had forty years ago.[16] Central Newark lost nearly 80,000 jobs between 1970 and 1988, and the area within two miles of the central city lost 40,000 more; areas six miles or more from downtown Newark, however, gained jobs steadily, with the greatest increases recorded in areas about sixteen miles out.

The destructive and pervasive consequences of segregation, both for excluded minorities and for the society at large, call for bridges over the physical divides in metropolitan areas.[17] Housing discrimination is an especially urgent social problem not only in and of itself but also because it is an underlying cause of other pressing ills in American society.[18] Concentrated poverty in the inner city creates social pathologies different in magnitude and in kind from those associated with individual low incomes, and the problems of crime, increased dropout rates for high school students, drug addiction, and other asocial behavioral patterns in the inner cities are self-perpetuating.[19] Thus the more promising urban policies are not incentives for housing or employment initiatives for central city neighborhoods but those fostering the redistribution of minority households into the suburban areas. Deconcentration—facilitating the movement of poor families from inner cities to suburbs—becomes an urgent social strategy for breaking the grip of concentrated poverty.[20] Permanent exclusion from mainstream society, graphically visible in the structural configuration of metropolitan areas, bears with it dire consequences for all: deprivation for the excluded and the grimness of a fortress mentality for the excluders.

## The Activist Court

Ironically, the law has been a major player in the pattern of segregation and housing discrimination. Indeed, to a large degree, it makes exclusionary conduct possible. The state confers on localities the sovereign power to regulate land use as they see fit. And although local geographical boundaries are increasingly artificial as today's metropolis spreads out across counties and districts, suburbs, as separate legal municipal corporations, deploy exclusionary zoning in its many forms to keep out "undesirables"—both uses and people. Law has become a surrogate for physical walls. Minimum lot and room sizes, setback rules, and discretionary procedures for multifamily developments—familiar argot to the zoning specialist—become dependable weapons in the exclusionary zoning arsenal. Providing relatively few dwelling units affordable to low-income people and using local land-use regulatory ordinances to raise the cost of other housing beyond their reach keeps up property values and produces villages that conform to the images of their existing residents.[21]

Until the 1940s, there was legal acceptance of private exclusion through restrictive covenants; even the mortgages guaranteed by the Federal Housing Administration contained racial restrictions, and the administration's underwriting manual advocated their use. Finally, after years of complicated and difficult litigation, the courts ruled such restrictions unconstitutional. But institutional discrimination through pervasive local systems of exclusionary land-use ordinances went unchallenged. Moreover, as inherited policies, they allowed individuals to deny responsibility for their actions.

Outlawing local restrictive land-use controls is the latest skirmish in the century-long battle to let the market operate freely in the allocation of metropolitan land. Implicit in the Mount Laurel decisions is a ruling that zoning bylaws prevent minorities from gaining a foothold in the locality in the same way that private restrictive deeds did; hence exclusionary zoning, and the land-use patterns it produces, should be similarly outlawed. The court could not disregard the mass of physical evidence illustrating the inequity between the separate worlds of inner city and outer suburb. Disparity in living conditions, following the lines of the new urban spatial patterns, was too obvious a daily reality, too glaring a manifestation of prejudice, to be shunted aside.

What makes the Mount Laurel dilemma so poignant is that the court's crafting of one principle—the ideal of equality of opportunity regardless of race, ethnicity, or income—clashed with another highly valued article of faith: people's deeply rooted belief in their right to defend bastions against would-be invaders. The suburban enclave is a continuation of the old idea—strong in American tradition—of the preeminence of the local community. Home rule, grass roots, the right of association, and neighborhood invincibility are basic building blocks of local government arrangements. The Mount Laurel Doctrine, with its emphasis on the fairness of equal sharing of the burdens of metropolitan existence and equal access to the suburban lifestyle, challenges all these tenets. Not surprisingly, then, the institutional reordering undertaken by the New Jersey courts thrust them into confrontation with the state legislature and local municipalities. The political dialogue weighing hopes against fears—a society's conversation with itself—continues to this day.

The Mount Laurel cases and the exclusionary zoning debate in general must be considered in the context of the broader trend to use the judicial system to redress national wrongs through litigation. Over the past two decades, courts have been drawn more and more into the reorganization of public institutions that are failing in their designated missions. When judges must step in to repair abuse of mandate and systemic flouting of legal norms—whether in relation to segregated schools, overcrowded jails, or environmentally degraded rivers—their expanded role arouses intense opposition by the majority. Complaints against judges (the imperial judiciary) as agents of social change are many and, at times, seemingly overwhelming: inadequate judicial resources; the courts' innate incapacity to initiate, maintain, and supervise long-range plans; adverse (albeit unanticipated) impacts on the operations of challenged institutions; and most seriously, subversion of the separation of powers. In the end, the indictment runs, by expanding its role the judiciary undermines the very legitimacy of its own authority by intruding in what are deemed inherently political and for that reason volatile affairs.[22]

## The Promise of Mount Laurel

The New Jersey experience shows what extraordinary resources—moral, intellectual, legal, and political—dedicated people need to effect social change. It is all too easy to be satisfied with a pious statement of equal access entered on the statute books. Results on the ground are too often disappointing. Profound resistance from challenged institutions threatens to stalemate the courts' efforts. And the fervent, frequently personal nature of their attacks may stop many state courts and communities from embarking on reform. Yet through trial and error, the judicial system in New Jersey ultimately structured a process that combined what were conventionally understood as legislative and executive functions with its traditional equity jurisdiction so as to address—with remarkable effectiveness—the dilemmas raised by its Mount Laurel Doctrine. By devising new procedural mechanisms that expedited the preparation and monitoring of remedies, the New Jersey Supreme Court called society back to its fundamental and abiding precepts. The judicial system, not without an intensive struggle, proved itself up to its assigned task and also stirred the legislative and executive branches into action in a most sensitive area—right where people live.

In a society dedicated to equality of opportunity, the Mount Laurel decisions must be understood as among the most significant judicial opinions of our time. While still too soon to be equivalent in stature, they are on a par with *Brown v. Board of Education,* that great judicial breakthrough on educational equality, if only because of the sweep of their mandate to enhance life chances. In a sense, in fact, Mount Laurel is the more ambitious, in that it regulates the use of the very space where humans must live not just where they may go to school. The New Jersey judges grappled with the idea of the Inclusionary Society. Their opinion was the first of its kind, taking into account the need for access to suburban space in the larger metropolitan area. The Mount Laurel Doctrine recognizes that in the current urban-suburban setting, the search for freedom and equality is still tied to land, that the age-old connection continues, in the modern version of suburbia, to be vital and indispensable. Mount Laurel's rules govern entry to that land. By deepening our understanding of the potential (as well as the limitations) of institutional restructuring it can aid trial judges struggling to give voice to the majestic guarantees of due process and equal protection found in the federal and state constitutions.

Discrimination and exclusion from land violate the nation's professed beliefs in social responsibility. Making affordable housing in suburban areas a reality in the lives of minorities is thus a battle to define the character of a society; and restoring to excluded populations the possibility of land ownership and the web of goals it furthers—independence, dignity, civil peace, and democracy—is Mount Laurel's singular achievement. The New Jersey Supreme Court's interpretation of the general welfare clause of the state constitution infuses its opinions with a grander vision of group relations. The tortuous history of the cases—their ups and downs, their cycles of hope and despair—reveals much about society's capacity for justice and empathy.

Metropolitan fragmentation grows worse. The democratic system is unable to act. In the search for a bridge across the racial and ethnic divisions of the metropolitan area, to end the isolation and immobility that reinforces the culture of poverty in the central cores, the courts emerge as the one government agency able to act. This may be the larger significance of the Mount Laurel experience. By their decrees, judges can change both the legal and physical landscapes of metropolitan areas. In seeking to assure the availability of land in the suburbs to all, by meeting head-on the problems of concentrated poverty and racial isolation in the territorial framework of metropolitan areas, the courts call us back to the original charter of the American society.

# Part I

CHALLENGE AND RESPONSE

# II

## Launching the Mount Laurel Doctrine: "Pack Up and Move to Camden!"

IN THE 1970s, following a decade of soaring residential growth, New Jersey burst on the developers' firmament as the most desirable state for real estate investment. With the expansion of U.S. Route 1 and the migration of industry, offices, and population out of the New York City area to the north and Philadelphia to the south, New Jersey land values skyrocketed. Housing production surged to record levels; shopping centers and industrial parks sprouted up from Princeton north to the Lincoln and Holland tunnels. There seemed an insatiable demand for land to develop. And in response to this runaway market, many suburban communities, desiring to maintain their original character and protect their tax bases, prescribed acreage minimums, frontage or lot width requirements, and other forms of growth control. The exclusionary zoning ordinance was the suburban weapon of choice, though resort was made even to selective or total moratoriums on development.

In an early case, the New Jersey Supreme Court sustained the power of local communities to prescribe minimum floor areas for new residences in order to avoid the impacts of "the next onward wave of suburban development"; it upheld the ordinance on the basis of both aesthetic and health considerations.[1] The decision was widely hailed as a vindication of the public interest over voracious speculators. Home rule sentiment was strong in all legal circles. Yet all the while, with little public recognition or comment, the noose was being drawn tighter and tighter around the Newarks, Trentons, Camdens, and other major urban centers in the state experiencing economic and social problems of increasing severity.

## The Common Law of Zoning

What did the New Jersey state court consider to be within the proper scope of local regulatory power under the state legislature's grant of police power to municipalities? In case after case, the state judiciary handed the suburbs carte blanche. From the first major post–World War II case, *Lionshead Lake v. Township of Wayne*, which upheld a minimum building size ordinance, through *Fischer v. Township of Bedminster*, which found a five-acre minimum not excessive, and continuing with *Vickers v. Township Committee of Gloucester Townships*, which validated a ban on trailer parks, the New Jersey Supreme Court found virtually nothing to controvert localities' power to zone for their public health, safety, morals, or welfare.[2] Although it paid lip service to the doctrine that the validity of zoning was not fixed "like the law of the Medes and Persians," the reality was a constant reaffirmation of local authority.[3]

For a full decade, Justice Frederick Hall was the only dissenting voice on the New Jersey Supreme Court. He persisted in arguing that land-use regulations, which held back the poor from realizing the American dream of living where one chooses, were exclusionary and unconstitutional. His convictions derived from a sense of the overall unfairness of this type of restrictive regulation. His legal analysis was more particular: certain local restrictions went beyond the pale of the state zoning authority delegated to the municipalities. Here he was building on the traditional doctrine that the power to regulate land use resides at the state level and devolves to local governments only through the specific terms of the state zoning enabling act. According to Hall, municipalities that enacted exclusionary restrictions acted solely from the perspective of local well-being.[4] Such local legislatures, he argued, failed to recognize that the state legislature implicitly imposed on them a requirement to enhance the overall welfare of the state as a condition precedent to their exercise of land-use control.

Although Justice Hall's arguments were prescient, for years they failed to persuade or deter his colleagues. He remained a lone dissenter on the court in cases dealing with the shaping of human settlements, a voice crying in the wilderness. In fact, however, Justice Hall was not so lonely a figure. There was creeping awareness in New Jersey of the intensity of the crisis arising from the expanding division between the city and the suburb. And it was as a culmination of a long process of educating his brethren that, to a surprised citizenry, a unanimous court handed down the Mount Laurel decision in 1975.

## The Lawsuit

In 1969 Ethel Lawrence, who lived on Elbow Lane Road in the Springville section of Mount Laurel, a largely rural area of the township that was home to much of Mount Laurel's African-American population, helped found the Springville Action Committee. The committee's plan to build about a hundred units of low-income housing near Hartford Road ran into Mount Laurel's minimum half-acre zoning ordinance, which the township refused to change. A group of ministers eventually referred the committee to legal service organizations willing to take the case—the Southern Burlington and Camden chapters of the National Association for the Advancement of Colored People (NAACP) and the Camden County Congress on Racial Equality. By April 1974 Ethel Lawrence, together with her daughter, Thomasene, who had moved in with her after living in a converted chicken coop in the Springville section, and her niece, Mary Smith, who had moved to nearby Moorestown because she could not find low-income housing in Mount Laurel, were instrumental in bringing a class-action lawsuit against the town, in which Ethel was one of the name plaintiffs. Lawrence never dreamed, she reported later, how extensive the lawsuit would be, how much was involved, and how society would react.

Aided by fervently abolitionist Quakers, blacks had settled in the Mount Laurel area in the pre–Civil War days of the underground railroad. Ethel Lawrence was born and raised in the township; her family had lived there for seven generations, and an ancestor had helped found one of the town's churches in 1859; the cemetery behind the church known as Jacob's Chapel contains the graves of soldiers who fought with the colored regiments in the Civil War. Yet Lawrence recalls sitting in church in the late 1960s and listening to a town councilman (who had not lived there more than five years) outline the official view: "If you can't

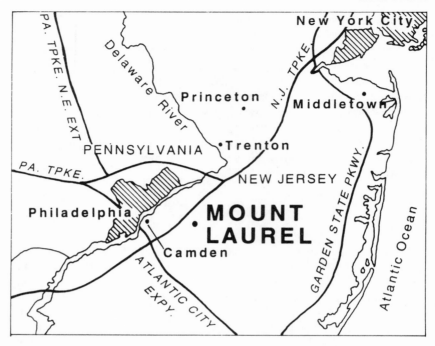

afford to live in Mount Laurel, pack up and move to Camden!" As one of the leaders of the township's small group of poor, mostly minority people, she was taken aback but undeterred. As she later eloquently explained to a questioner, "God meant us to live in harmony on earth, or else he'd have made rich and poor communities in the hereafter."

At the time of the initiation of the suit, Mount Laurel was a relatively small rural municipality of twenty-two square miles with a population of some 11,000. (Newark's twenty-three square miles, by contrast, wrapped in a population of about 382,000).[5] Sixty-five percent of the land was vacant or used for agriculture, and 29 percent was zoned exclusively for industrial use. The town's ordinance zoned the remainder for single-family detached housing with minimum lot sizes of 9,300 square feet and up, and minimum house sizes of 900 to 1,100 square feet and higher.[6] Attached town houses, apartments (except on farms, for agricultural workers), and mobile homes were not allowed anywhere. Very much a bedroom suburb, the town was close to the city of Camden and within easy driving distance of the Benjamin Franklin Bridge crossing the river to Philadelphia.[7]

Mount Laurel's landscape was dominated by orchards, farms, woods, and back-country roads. In many ways it was a typical small suburban community, made up of individual housing and without a main street, a shopping center, or even a supermarket. Indeed, Mount Laurel's first post office was not built until 1983. To reach the busy shopping malls in surrounding towns required a car since there was no public transportation. By the town's own estimate, it still had nearly six thousand acres of developable land.

## The Decision

On March 24, 1975, after years of well-argued dissents that consistently failed to persuade his colleagues not to uphold municipal exclusionary regulations, Justice Hall finally brought them around to his view of the land-use universe. Mount Laurel I, as it is usually referred to, Hall's final major decision, was an extraordinary vision of social justice and a fitting memorial as he bade his farewell to the New Jersey bench.[8]

The initial elaboration of the Mount Laurel concept required a careful sifting and inspired selection of legal principles. Justice Hall's reasoning can be fairly characterized as a doctrinal free-for-all with a minimal linkage to prior case law. He addressed major issues, all discursively, not head-on but on cat's feet, drawing arguments from all quarters in support of the conclusion he strove to reach. The opinion was at once careful and sweeping, subtle and many-sided, as it unlocked many issues and established a sweeping judicial mandate for land-use reform.

It was shaped by two fundamental strategic moves that insulated the court from reversal or second-guessing by other institutions. First, Justice Hall apparently crafted the decision on constitutional rather than legislative grounds in the hope of avoiding a reversal by the state legislature. Although he could not make the Mount Laurel Doctrine as a whole immune to change, he could fashion it so that its constitutional groundings could not be altered except by the drastic and time-consuming method of constitutional amendment. Second, by basing the decision firmly on New Jersey constitutional law, on which the state supreme court has the last and final word, Justice Hall was able to avoid review by the federal judiciary. In fact, he had no choice but to go this way: the federal judicial interpretation of the applicability of equal protection clauses to land-use controls had been far more deferential to local decision making than he was about to be in his pathbreaking opinion.[9]

The Mount Laurel Doctrine flows directly from the way Justice Hall chose to define the issues. As he posed it, the question before the court was whether a developing municipality could validly enact a land-use regulation making physically and economically impossible the provision of housing for low- and moderate-income families within its borders.

Article 1, paragraph 1, of the New Jersey Constitution provided that "all persons are by nature free and independent, and have certain natural and unalienable rights, among which are those of enjoying and defending life and liberty, of acquiring, possessing and protecting property, and of pursuing and obtaining safety and happiness." Justice Hall interpreted this provision as requiring every municipality, through its regulation of land use, to "presumptively make realistically possible an appropriate variety and choice of housing."[10]

Once Hall had framed the issue so that it hung on a solid constitutional hook, he had only to add a simple elaboration: local regulations, he wrote, must affirmatively make preparations for low- and moderate-income housing "at least to the extent of the municipality's fair share of the present and prospective regional need therefor."[11] In other words, localities cannot foreclose opportunities for affordable housing to entire classes of people, most especially those of low and moderate income. Instead, Hall specified, they were required to permit multifamily housing (without restrictions on number of bedrooms) as well as "small dwellings on very small lots," low-cost housing of various types, and high-density zoning "without artificial and unjustifiable minimum requirements as to lot size, building size and the like."[12] The amount of land removed from residential use by zoning for industrial and commercial purposes had to bear a reasonable relation to the anticipated present and future needs for such purposes. And without exactly specifying compliance mechanisms, Hall emphasized that the mere elimination of negative restraints would not suffice to meet the constitutional requirement of breaking down barriers to low-income families seeking shelter in the suburbs. With this shot across the bow, Justice Hall laid down the Mount Laurel Doctrine, which was to generate almost two decades of lawsuits, reforms, and controversy.

The flavor of the contending positions is best revealed in excerpts from the oral arguments. A township attorney argued that to require local zoning codes to meet regional low-income housing needs "just moves the ghetto around." Madison Township attorney Richard Plechner said, "I don't see how you can compel a community to provide any kind of housing."

Lois Thompson, attorney for the Suburban Action Institute, an opponent of the zoning ordinance, contended that "the issue is whether zoning is going to be used by a private club to determine who is going to live in a community, or for the public welfare."

Plechner observed that if the court upheld the trial court's ruling of invalidation, "then the court becomes a great zoning board in Trenton . . . when the solution belongs rightly in the Legislature." He continued, "We've got everything but ratables. . . . Striking down the ordinance only aggravates the problem without offering us a solution."

Thompson replied that every community has a responsibility to do its "fair share" in providing housing for the poor. Her assertion brought this question from Chief Justice Joseph Weintraub: "By fair share you mean a responsibility for a community that welcomes industry to provide housing within the means of its workers, or in other words, providing the bedrooms for your own enterprises?" Thompson agreed, and the chief justice commented that it would be hard for the court to determine what a community's "fair share" would be. "Send us a proposal," Weintraub told her.

Justice Hall asked the attorney for Mount Laurel whether he felt the township had any responsibility to meet the housing needs of the area outside the community. The reply was no, and Hall commented, "That's really what this case is all about."[13]

The Mount Laurel Doctrine sought to unite the public and private sectors—including developers, who ordinarily would not be expected to argue on the same side as public interest groups—in a joint effort to produce housing for low- and moderate-income families in suburban portions of metropolitan areas. In effect, it constituted a warning to New

Jersey municipalities and their public officials that they could use neither their land-use and growth controls nor the other fruits of the regulatory powers delegated to them in ways that would splinter the state's metropolitan areas through exclusion or discrimination. Obviously, the decision was destined to have its most immediate impact in the lower courts of New Jersey, especially at the trial level. Its effects, however, extended much farther.

## Expanding the Equal Protection Claim

The due process clause of the Fourteenth Amendment provides that no one shall be deprived of life, liberty, or property without due process of law and no one shall be denied equal protection of the law. The U.S. Supreme Court of Earl Warren had recalled the equality norm from constitutional exile and in the process had unleashed an ethical and constitutional force not easily confined. Traditionally, litigants assert a constitutional claim under the equal protection provision of the due process clause by demonstrating a substantial disparity in the government's treatment of similarly situated individuals. The judicial outcome depends on the stringency of the standard that the reviewing court employs in weighing the difference in treatment against the proffered excuse. The standard "minimum" review is confined to "loose" testing for a rational excuse or reason for the difference and usually ends up sustaining the legislation. If plaintiffs can bring themselves within the "strict scrutiny" criterion, however, their chances for success are overwhelming. Under the microscope of heightened scrutiny, the disputed legislation can be upheld only if the differential treatment is necessary to serve a compelling state interest. Thus, in a quite real sense, the standard for judicial review that is applied determines the outcome.

Throughout Mount Laurel I, federal judges' minimalist reviews of cases under the equal protection clause, which tended to uphold local authorities' actions, were the unacknowledged stumbling block. A desire to skirt their applications of the federal equal protection doctrine must have motivated Justice Hall's decision to impose the then relatively novel two-pronged strict scrutiny analysis of the equal protection rule. Accordingly, Hall formulated a tight scrutiny standard for the state, one far more rigorous than the federal standard requiring a classification to be arbitrary, capricious, or unreasonable for it to be struck down. Two possible claims could trigger imposition of the strict scrutiny standard: that discrimination was predicated on a suspect classification or that it encroached on a fundamental personal interest. Any exclusionary local ordinance that met either condition was subject to a judicial review that would be hard—no, impossible—for a municipality to counter.

Justice Hall began by discussing suspect classification. For the purpose of determining the correct standard of review, the federal courts and federal constitutional theory had determined that whereas race was a suspect classification calling for intensified review, a distinction based on economic grounds was not.[14] This meant that if a group of poor people mounted a federal constitutional assault on restrictive zoning ordinances by alleging discrimination in access to suburban land solely on the basis of economic status, their claim would be held to lie outside the refuge of strict scrutiny, and the garden-variety rational basis test would apply. This would be true even if the complaining class was composed of racial minorities, as long as they did not also claim race to be the source of the invidious classification.

The contrarian position that Justice Hall developed displayed ingenuity and audacity. Although the case was brought by the Southern Burlington and Camden chapters of the NAACP and evidence of racial discrimination had been introduced at the trial, Hall refused to use the racial handle as the basis for his reasoning. In fact, he made no reference to the racial composition of the disadvantaged class, going out of his way to set a broader precedent. As a result of Mount Laurel I, economic classification, at least as far as the state of New Jersey is concerned, is an alternative suspect criterion that triggers intensive judicial reexamination. Furthermore, under Hall's interpretation, economic discrimination could be invoked as an inherently suspect basis of classification not only by those of low and moderate incomes excluded from a community by virtue of local zoning regulations but also by all those who were poor in the sense that they paid too large a proportion of their incomes for shelter.[15]

Under Justice Hall's analysis, the court found that Mount Laurel operated an invidious system of land-use regulations that excluded classes that he defined as constitutionally protected. The township's regulations, declared the unanimous court, were an illegal, indeed an unconstitutional, use of the police power that the state had delegated to local governments via the state zoning enabling act.

In applying the second prong of the new equal protection clause—that of fundamental personal interest—Hall pitted himself once more against the federal line of construction, albeit without citing specific federal cases or directly attacking federal practice. Federal courts held that access to housing did not rise to the dignity of a fundamental interest requiring heightened judicial scrutiny. "We do not denigrate the importance of decent, safe and sanitary housing," the U.S. Supreme Court, in an opinion by Justice Byron White, had ruled, but it was not such a fundamental interest that the government may encroach on it only if it can demonstrate that the differential treatment is attributable to a compelling interest.[16] Carefully avoiding the use of terminology that would signal too clearly his divergence from federal rules, Hall took a tack that appears to be purposefully evasive, employing synonyms that convey the same import as "fundamental interest," referring to the "basic importance" or the "indispensability" of shelter to human existence. Using such circumlocutions, Justice Hall spelled out that in New Jersey jurisprudence, low-income housing was imbued with the degree of high interest that triggers the equal protection standard of strict scrutiny and intervention. Never invoking the talismanic phrase *fundamental personal interest*, the opinion nevertheless noted that "there cannot be the slightest doubt that shelter, along with food, are the most basic human needs."[17] By this means, Hall established a direct route to a demanding judicial standard of review by identifying the quest of the poor for land on which to construct or rent a house as the pursuit of something akin to a fundamental right.

Under Mount Laurel I, when plaintiffs bring themselves within the protective mantle of a suspect classification or a fundamental interest, the only acceptable rebuttal by the defendant municipality is a showing of a "compelling governmental interest" as justification for the disparate treatment. Here, taking the next step in the logical analysis, Justice Hall proceeded to examine the typical excuses advanced in the various state courts for restrictive zoning ordinances. These boiled down to three interrelated reasons: to avoid increased taxation, to minimize the expenditure of government resources for newly required infrastructure, and to forestall undesirable environmental impacts. Each of these Hall refused to accept as a compelling state interest justifying a restrictive classification. As he tersely (and perhaps too simply) put it in overruling the defense of conservation of the government fisc, zoning is for people, not for property.[18] Relief from the heavy burden of local taxation has to be furnished by other branches of government; fiscal needs cannot be invoked to exclude low-income housing. On more subjective terrain, such as quality of life, environmental impacts, and the aesthetics of a town setting, Justice Hall's discussion is limited; his balancing of interests is primarily on the surface, simply and solely restating the already determined conclusion.

Before proceeding with his determination, Justice Hall had to clear some preliminary underbrush by addressing the jurisprudential debate over whether to evaluate the existence of governmental discrimination by intent or by effect. Hall did not hesitate for a moment, making it immediately clear that he considered it irrelevant whether Mount Laurel actually intended its zoning regulations to be exclusionary; discriminatory impact, he concluded, was sufficient to prove the case.[19] Significantly, this holding ran counter to the doctrine of the U.S. Supreme Court, which elevated intent over effect and held that evidence of unequal results alone did not invalidate a law; rather, a purpose to discriminate must be shown.[20] Hall's interpretation meant that good intentions in the exercise of governmental responsibilities could not controvert a prima facie showing of a discriminatory result, thereby denying municipalities an important defense, since a pattern of practice or an effect is far easier to prove than sinful motivation, which demands a probing of intent and an understanding of the legislative heart.[21]

### Broadening the General Welfare Claim

The Mount Laurel decision, in a tangential manner, consistently links its fundamental interest discussion to the basic legal concept of general welfare. It is a longstanding principle (and one embodied in the Standard State Zoning Enabling Act, which was drafted by a national government committee in 1926 and serves as the model for most states, including New Jersey) that when local governments exercise their police powers to regulate land use, the regulation must be in pursuit of the general welfare. Over time, this term has come to signify the welfare of the enacting municipality and, almost by self-definition, to be limited to the interests of those living within the corporate boundaries of the legislating locality.

Perhaps the major doctrinal advance in Mount Laurel I—one destined for increasing significance in future zoning legislation and litigation—is Justice Hall's expansion of the meaning of the term *general welfare*. Conceding the earlier history and the weight of precedent where prior decisions of the New Jersey courts had spoken only in terms of the interest of the enacting municipality, the New Jersey Supreme Court characterized this set of precedents as creating a misleading impression by fostering the idea that local politicians need only consider welfare from a parochial perspective. In Mount Laurel I, the court intended to clear up this misunderstanding once and for all.[22] Arguing that modern changes in transportation modes and the relentless shifts in industrial and residential concentrations brought into question the exclusive reliance on municipal boundaries in local regulatory matters, Justice Hall stressed that "the universal and constant need for . . . housing is so important and of such broad public interest that the general welfare which developing municipalities like Mount Laurel must consider extends beyond their boundaries and cannot be parochially confined to the claimed good of the particular municipality."[23]

Exactly what kind of obligation does Mount Laurel I place on localities? An educated guess is that it requires municipalities, at a minimum, to consider the regional general welfare. The court stated flatly: "The presumptive obligation arises for each such municipality affirmatively to plan and provide, by its land use regulations, the reasonable opportunity for an appropriate variety and choice of housing including of course low and moderate cost housing, to meet the needs, desires, and resources of all categories of people who may desire to live within its boundaries."[24] Furthermore, according to the court, "when regulation does have a substantial external impact, the welfare of the state's citizens beyond the borders of the particular municipality cannot be disregarded and must be recognized and served."[25]

## Framing the Remedy

Having found no adequate societal justification for the Mount Laurel ordinance that would stand up to strict scrutiny, Justice Hall turned to remedy. Naturally, this proved to be the most difficult portion of the opinion, and Hall did not meet it head-on. In fact, he faltered, and not surprisingly: Mount Laurel was truly the first postwar suburb-versus-city crisis that a state supreme court had been called on to resolve, and everyone involved was a novice. New Jersey was on a course where surprises lurked around every corner.

Either overlooking the need for detailed requirements or wishing to postpone unpleasantness, Hall refused to mandate a step-by-step course of municipal and trial court conduct in implementing the new duties he was enunciating. The method for eliminating the use of local zoning power for improper exclusionary purposes was to be left to the discretion of localities. The "municipality should first have full opportunity to itself act without judicial supervision," he wrote. He added, somewhat as an afterthought: "We trust it will do so in the spirit we have suggested."[26] While the opinion did declare parts of the ordinance invalid and granted the town of Mount Laurel ninety days to correct the ordinance's other deficiencies, the details of the process were, as Hall put it, "the local function and responsibility in the first instance."[27] On his remand to the trial court, Justice Hall simply ordered that plaintiff and defendant together prepare a plan to meet the fair share of the present and prospective regional housing needs and submit it to the court for approval, noting that preparing such a plan would require attention to a series of questions bearing directly on the public policy issues of metropolitan areas. At a minimum, it involved a determination of what constitutes a region, a calculation of various types of current and prospective housing needs for the region, and then an assignment of these needs among the constituent municipalities on a case-by-case basis.

In a concurring opinion, Justice Morris Pashman worried that nothing in the record warranted Hall's optimism and faith in local government and that justice delayed would in fact become justice denied. He would have upheld the quantification remedy for affordable housing framed by the trial court, which would have required municipalities to commit themselves to precise numbers in defining and meeting their fair share obligations.[28]

The issue of remedy—rather than the question of liability—remained the burning controversy at the trial court level until in 1983 *Southern Burlington County NAACP v. Township of Mount Laurel*, or Mount Laurel II, detailed the nature of the relief. Justice Hall, if cornered, would no doubt have admitted that, as a product of his generation of judges, he was reluctant to break an inordinate number of eggs to prepare his omelet. It was simply not timely to demand anything else; he did not wish to jar local officials more than was absolutely necessary. The court considered the other options available—such as directing the municipality to provide mechanisms for the building of low-income housing, or ratifying the trial court's requirement to make studies and present a plan of affirmative public action, or mandating incentives and bonuses to help private builders—and rejected each as too extreme to impose at this early date. About affirmative action programs, Hall would say only that the court hoped the town would pursue them "both by appropriate zoning ordinance amendments and whatever additional action encouraging the fulfillment of its fair share of the regional need for low- and moderate-income housing may be indicated as necessary and advisable." An overall reluctance to specify a remedy was obvious. The court did, however, explicitly invite the plaintiffs to come right back if Mount Laurel did "not perform as we expect."[29]

Caution—and perhaps the need to hammer out a unanimous majority—made Hall reject Justice Pashman's call for more stringent requirements to be placed on the town. Pashman's concurring opinion warned that the "experience of the nation over the past twenty years must serve as a caution that, however much we might wish it, we cannot expect rapid voluntary reversal" of the desire of towns like Mount Laurel to maintain themselves as enclaves of affluence or of social homogeneity. Pashman, without the responsibility attending a majority opinion, enriched the ideological possibilities of the decision. He would have the court move much more quickly: "It will not do to approach such problems gingerly; they call out for forceful and decisive judicial action." Finding exclusionary zoning to be abhorrent as well as repugnant to the ideals of pluralistic democracy, he added that he "differs from the majority only in that I would have the Court go farther and faster in its implementation of the principles announced."[30] But while making a most remarkable judicial advance, the Mount Laurel I court struck a lower chord.

## The Underlying Justification

Mount Laurel I remains a lightning rod for criticism. Detractors feel the court exceeded its appropriate role in a constitutional democracy. Others, while recognizing its accomplishments, believe that the Mount Laurel holding is too easily manipulable, the work of a doctrinal Hamlet. Still others think that the doctrine should have received a forceful and principled elaboration right from the outset, which might have set a new political tone and brought intractable municipalities into line. Such a detailed administrative mechanism would not appear until 1983, when Chief Justice Wilentz modified and expanded Mount Laurel I in the light of subsequent frustrating experiences; however, even this later opinion leaves gaps between the logic and the experience.

Moral considerations shaped the Mount Laurel propositions. In the original case, Justice Hall introduced the doctrine in fundamentally ethical terms, explaining it as a self-evident philosophical principle embodied within the state constitution. In Hall's vision, shelter was a basic human need, and "it is plain beyond dispute that proper provision for adequate housing of all categories of people is certainly an absolute essential in promotion of the general welfare."[31] Developing municipalities that practice exclusionary zoning act out of "selfish and parochial interest[s]," zoning for the benefit of the local tax rate rather than for the "living welfare of people." More specifically, the court found it clear that "when a municipality zones for industry and commerce for local tax benefit purposes, it without question must zone to permit adequate housing within the means of the employees involved in such uses." In response to his opinion, Hall expected that municipalities would recognize "at least a moral obligation to establish a local housing agency . . . to provide housing for its resident poor now living in dilapidated, unhealthy quarters." The end result, he believed, would be the growth of "better communities for all," communities that provide "good living and adequate services for all their residents in the kind of atmosphere which a democracy and free institutions demand."[32]

With all the questions that may be raised about consistency of doctrine and lack of adherence to precedent, and whatever one's beliefs regarding the appropriate role of the judiciary in social change, the fact remains that Justice Hall, in Mount Laurel I, succeeded in evoking the conscience of the people: could a society that claims to provide justice for all condone such obvious disparities in living conditions and in opportunities for a better life? Could a nation tolerate such manifest differences in housing conditions between inner-city concentrations and outlying suburbs? Rather than upholding the fragmentation of the metropolitan area by legal barriers, the Mount Laurel I court saw law as a means to link buildings, neighborhoods, and regions that had become disconnected. Thus on March 4, 1975, the New Jersey Supreme Court raised the level of judicial scrutiny for American society's overriding goals of community; standing in welcome contrast to the hesitant and weary legal pronouncements found elsewhere, Mount Laurel I marked a dramatic turn for future doctrine, for judicial interpretation of land-use law, and for the relations among the different branches of government. Today, during a time of federal judicial retreat from asserting jurisdiction over local land-use controls, the decision assumes even greater pertinence.

# III

## The View from the Mount

THERE WAS perhaps a certain inevitability to the second pronouncement from Mount Laurel. For nearly a decade the New Jersey Supreme Court chafed under a municipal resistance that made a near mockery of its much-heralded ruling in Mount Laurel I. In outlawing exclusionary zoning, the court had run smack into the dedication to home rule that dominates American land-use control law. American municipal law entails a delicate balance between the powers that reside in municipalities and those that the state has delegated, between those functions inherently local and those whose implementation must be statewide.[1] Of all the powers held by the local sovereign, that of land-use control is deemed most sacred by its citizens. Property law has always been regarded as the province of local government, and interference in the daily zoning of land kindles towering passions and stirs fierce protest meetings. Everyone is caught up in the dispute—asking, challenging, doubting, puzzling, proposing. For the New Jersey Supreme Court, from the distance of an ivory tower in Trenton, to dictate how a tree should be planted at a street corner or how land should be most appropriately developed in a small neighborhood seemed an outrageous affront to voters.

In one sense, having set the state constitutional standard, Mount Laurel I could be read as an open invitation to the body politic to take charge of the issue through its legislative and executive processes. Time and experience, however, would demonstrate the citizenry's overwhelming unwillingness to accept such a challenge. Such recalcitrance required the court's forceful return to the fray. The major contribution of the Mount Laurel II court, as it surveyed the alignments that followed Mount Laurel I at the local level, was its revisitation and elaboration of the Hall opinion to bring to full effect that noteworthy judicial advance. Naturally, Chief Justice Wilentz's opinion benefited from a deeper awareness of the strengths and limitations of Hall's doctrinal leaps as they played themselves out on the municipal stage. But the lapse of time between Hall's and Wilentz's opinions, which resulted from the accepted judicial ethos of caution, was taken for indecisiveness; moreover, the interval left an opportunity for the opposition to maneuver and for hostile reactions to flare. Courts and legislature clung to their positions as litigation over the Mount Laurel Doctrine waxed and waned, both sides seemingly content with the barrage of words from the courts meeting legislative inaction on behalf of the local suburbs.

## The Aftermath of Mount Laurel I

The cause of housing reform at first received a boost from developers anxious to move into New Jersey's burgeoning real estate market. Their role remained largely peripheral, however: on the whole, they were inclined to finish their deals, make concessions while retaining the option to litigate, receive their building permits, and move on. Soon enough suburban planning boards in New Jersey rendered it increasingly difficult for them to come in at all. Among the ingenious devices they fashioned to prevent unwanted low-income housing from entering their precincts were large-lot zoning and minimum-size houses, as well as the absolute exclusion of apartments, prohibition of extra bedrooms, and a ban on mobile homes; some even went as far as to place extraordinary fees on new development. In laying this exclusionary grid over the land, local officials simply built on the permissive precedents of early New Jersey Supreme Court decisions. To take but two prominent examples, *Duffcon Concrete*

*Products, Inc. v. Borough of Cresskill* allowed a town to exclude a use as long as it was permitted elsewhere within the region, and *Bedminster Township* approved a five-acre minimum lot size.[2] Justice Hall's dissent in *Vickers*, in which he protested the exclusion of that most feasible form of affordable housing, the mobile home, was one of a long line of warnings he uttered in vain during the years leading up to his groundbreaking opinion in Mount Laurel I.[3]

The immediate impact of the decision, with its reversal of existing precedent, put the courts very much on the defensive, reacting to virulent public opinion and local opposition. The crisis was fueled by an internal division within the judiciary itself, most notably between the infantry of the trial courts and the strategic headquarters of the supreme court. The fate of the original Mount Laurel remedy—a remand back to the trial judge—highlights this schism. The Mount Laurel parties found themselves before Superior Court Judge Wood in 1978. This time the plaintiff challenged the township's compliance with the supreme court's decision. Stating that it was "unable from the plethora of figures and formulae produced and propounded by the witnesses to make a determination of Mount Laurel's 'fair share' of housing needs," the trial court continued to defer to the town's judgment on regional fair share, exonerating the town's revised regulatory ordinance as a bona fide attempt to provide for the requisite fair share of housing responsibilities.[4] That, it thought, was all the situation required. The fact that the town, in response to the supreme court's sweeping opinion, had grudgingly mapped three new zones for low-income housing—substandard and expensive to develop, isolated from utilities and residences, surrounded by undesirable industries, and one, indeed, in the path of a proposed extension of a highway—made no difference to the trial judge.[5]

In further obeisance to local sentiments, the judge went along with the idea that planned unit development (PUD) projects, a form of zoning that permits mixed uses on a large scale and allows developers to mingle office development with residential, could be the means to provide needed low-cost housing units. However, the PUD approach, in and of itself neutral, would be more likely to serve market uses desired by well-to-do consumers and paid for at market rates than the type of housing contemplated by Justice Hall's Mount Laurel I.[6]

The net result was that the lower court, in essence, deferred to the wishes of the local population, despite the shove from the upper court. The Mount Laurel local legislature's grudging and microscopic changes in its rezoning made little land realistically available for moderate- and low-income housing.

Nor did matters improve with time. As described by one reporter, there was but little change over the years in the township's underlying factual pattern:

> The 33 acres set aside years ago remain as they did then. One plot of 13 acres is a field on the fringe of an apple orchard. . . .
>
> Another plot has 13 acres of idle land at the rear of the Moorestown Shopping Mall. Another Philadelphia company, the Binswanger Management Corporation, which plans and manages office buildings, owns it. Binswanger has never proposed construction of housing on the site . . . although Binswanger attempted to win approval for an industrial park on adjacent land it owns. . . .
>
> The third designated low-income housing plot, with seven acres, has for years been a farm for Christmas trees owned by Alfred DiPietro, an engineer for RCA, who lives in Guam. His nephews run the farm.

The report goes on to cite one of the interviewees: "Mr. Godfrey, the owner of the country store and a friend of Mr. DiPietro, said, 'Until he gets a fortune for the land, he'll never sell it for any housing.' "[7]

Other signs of a judicial schizophrenia could also be noted. The period between the two Mount Laurel decisions featured a revelatory line of cases paralleling those of Mount Laurel. For two decades, for example, from 1950 to 1970, the town of Madison had struggled to adopt a master plan and zoning ordinance that would curb growth and stabilize the tax rate. The land-use plan and policies finally promulgated called for one- and two-acre lots on most of the remaining vacant land. The evidence presented in the trial court indicated that only households with incomes in the top 10 percent nationwide could afford the housing built on such lots. Furthermore, the zoning ordinance limited the rate of new multi-family units to two hundred per year.[8] At the same time, unaware of the inconsistency, the township was encouraging new industry, with its attendant jobs, to settle within its borders.

When *Oakwood at Madison, Inc. v. Township of Madison* reappeared before the New Jersey Supreme Court in 1977, the court beat a retreat from the position it had enunciated in Mount Laurel I.[9] It balked at demarcating regional boundaries or specifying what constituted "fair share." It adopted what might be deemed a simplistic direct approach to the complicated question of what constitutes a region: for the previous, more precise regional standard of Mount Laurel I, it substituted the concept "substantial area." Although the introduction of the word *substantial* created a loophole through which an attorney could drive a truck, it succeeded in moving the discussion of regionalism from a technical to a more abstract plane, thus relieving the court from a level of precision that would have called for experts to argue, debate, and split hairs. Stripped to its bare bones, the holding of *Madison Township* indicated that if a definition—any definition—expanded consideration of zoning beyond local parochial concerns, the court would uphold it as an appropriate measuring rod. Thus the *Madison Township* decision put a judicial stamp of approval on any approach that could be said to provide roughly for an appropriate physical area to accommodate extralocal needs.

In addition to withdrawing its judicial troops from what loomed as a losing battle in the definitional war—the task of delimiting a region, calculating a fair share, and allocating need to each of the municipalities in the region—the supreme court executed a distinctly sharper retreat on another front: it replaced its original Mount Laurel requirement of low- and moderate-income housing with that of "least cost housing." The duty it now imposed on municipalities was to provide land appropriate for the least expensive housing that could be built. Such a concession could easily conjure up a price tag for shelter higher than low-income people could bear.

Read between its lines, the *Madison Township* opinion virtually avowed that the complex technical, political, and economic difficulties inherent in determining a "region," quantifying "need," and ascertaining "fair share" were beyond judicial competence.[10] The court simply stepped back from Justice Hall's requirements in Mount Laurel I—and certainly from concurring Justice Pashman's notion of a specific, quantitative remedy. The *Madison Township* test substituted for the requirement of a regional fair share of affordable housing a minimum demonstration by the municipality that there was "some opportunity for either lower income or least cost housing" and that "bona fide efforts had been made to minimize cost-generating requirements in a reasonable area of the municipality."[11] (Judge Furman, the trial judge in the lower court decision, had similarly equivocated, even though he had a specific model and allocation of need in the Middlesex County Interim Master Plan that was used extensively elsewhere in the case and could have provided him with the wherewithal to apply a quantitative formula.)[12]

In yet another case, *Pascack Association Ltd. v. Mayor of Washington*, the New Jersey Supreme Court distanced itself once more from a major concept propounded in Mount Laurel I. In explicit terms, it limited the Mount Laurel rules to "developing communities," which reduced the number of communities subject to the fair share requirement. A benign consequence of the court's downscaling of its original goals was that developed communities—those already densely populated by low-income people—did not have to provide any more land for affordable housing units. On the other hand, the "developing communities" revision rendered rural areas—areas that the market for development had not yet reached—immune from the exclusionary zoning prohibition of Mount Laurel.

Naturally, the *Pascack* limitation contributed a new array of difficulties that led to considerable litigation. The injection of a new term into the lexicon of zoning disputes created one more topic for expert testimony and technical differentiations. Furthermore, the doctrine tended to reward towns with histories of exclusionary zoning: never having developed, they reaped the benefit of earlier regulatory barriers and were able to stay as they were. Lawyers argued over whether "developing" was an issue of fact, hence not reviewable by an upper court, or an issue of law, meaning that appeal to the scrutiny of the upper court would always be available, or a mixed question of fact and law.

The split of opinion was even wider outside the court system. Rarely has a judicial opinion produced as explosive and immediate a reaction from so wide a range of citizens as did Justice Hall's Mount Laurel Doctrine. Not only had it attacked the privileges of powerful interests, but it had also enunciated a revolutionary doctrine in the world of land-use planning: that local zoning ordinances must provide a realistic opportunity for the building of low- and moderate-income housing. As a consequence, Mount Laurel became the subject of front-page headlines, editorials, and news stories around the country; it also provoked excited discussions and heated debates among citizen groups. The opinion became famous and infamous. Naturally, any governmental action with the potential for drastically affecting housing values, changing the character of towns, and bringing an influx of minority populations into formerly white enclaves had the potential to shake up the entire political system of the state and set off sympathetic shock waves from coast to coast. Inevitably, the Mount Laurel Doctrine placed the courts under a glaring spotlight (not all that friendly) of publicity and scrutiny.

Thus it was with a mixture of indignation and determination that a grim Chief Justice Wilentz ascended the mount once more on January 20, 1983, this time to announce the unanimous opinion of the New Jersey Supreme Court reaffirming the Mount Laurel Doctrine.

## The Counterattack

In evaluating the situation at the time that six cases were consolidated into what was to become Mount Laurel II, the court was sharply aware of the uneasy aftermath of its Mount Laurel I decision: the major reluctance of the municipalities to correct the wrongs detailed by the court, the tidal wave of litigation, the ensuing confusion at the trial court level, the split in the judicial system as individual judges worked with their own appraisal of the wisdom or foolishness of the New Jersey Supreme

Court decision, and the almost universal conclusion that the prescribed remedies were not working. A new approach was needed. And this was to be found in the judgment the New Jersey Supreme Court was about to render. When the chief justice began to read in open court from the extensive Mount Laurel II opinion—virtually a treatise on planning law and practice, running nearly 250 pages in its initial typewritten form—the experience of years of litigations and political repercussions colored even the phrasing of the resolutions.[13]

The Mount Laurel II decision's immediate background was curious. A series of somewhat mysterious delays dogged the entire enterprise. In the late 1970s the New Jersey Supreme Court consolidated six major lawsuits challenging local zoning policy as unfair and exclusionary, the suits having slowly wended their way up to the court following the first Mount Laurel decision in 1975. In 1978 the court announced that it would hear the cases together. Then nothing happened. To some degree, this inaction stemmed from changes in the composition of the court; judges had died or retired, necessitating redeliberations and rehearings by their successors. Then, in May 1980, the court issued what can only be characterized, for students of the appellate process, as an unusual request. When a trial court's opinion is appealed to a higher court, the attorneys generally first submit their arguments in written briefs, and then both sides appear before the court for oral argument. But in this instance, in a rare attempt to guide the proceedings, the court sent out a set of twenty-four written interrogatories—resembling most closely in form the questions a law school professor might include on an examination in a land-use course—and asked that the lawyers focus on answering them in their oral arguments. The interrogatories' breadth was extensive—for example, two of them read, "Discuss the wisdom of limiting the reach of Mount Laurel to developing municipalities" and "Discuss the function of expert planners in exclusionary zoning cases"—with each calling for an answer of considerable length.

Once the attorneys had filed their responses, the consolidated cases were put down for oral argument in October 1980. The arguments lasted an unprecedented three days (oral arguments generally last only a matter of hours). Some details will give an indication of the scope of the cases: twelve communities were parties in the action; another twenty-one municipalities were "officially interested" parties; four developers were involved; five interested entities, including the state legislature and the city of Newark, submitted briefs as amici curiae (friends of the court), as did four nonprofit public interest groups representing minority groups ranging from the NAACP to the Urban League. Once again nothing happened. Finally, over two years later, on January 20, 1983, came Chief Justice Wilentz's delivery of the unanimous opinion.

## A Sweeping Opinion

Whatever the speculations of anxious municipalities and hovering property developers or the shivering expectancies of academic experts on judicial functioning, the long-awaited reappraisal was forthright and clear: the court affirmed, in the strongest possible terms, its adherence to Justice Hall's original Mount Laurel Doctrine.

Beginning with a blasting critique of the response of New Jersey's local governments to the court's 1975 decision, the decision did not mince words. The chief justice expressed considerable impatience with the failure of the state's suburban communities to comply with the rulings of Mount Laurel I. "We are far from where we had hoped to be," he complained, "and nowhere near where we should be with regard to the administration of the doctrine in our courts."[14] He pointed out the waste of judicial energy, the length and complexity of trials, the overwhelming cost of litigation. Above all, he scolded, the Mount Laurel case, so heavily pondered and elaborated by the court, had ended not in the production of low- and moderate-income housing in New Jersey that was its goal, nor in the fulfillment of the constitutional obligation that a "fair share" of such housing be built within the state's suburban areas, but only in a costly excess of paper, a crop of new litigation strategies, and a complete stalemate in the operations of public policy. Litigation—not housing—the chief justice lamented, had become the dominant product of the Mount Laurel Doctrine.

In Mount Laurel II, the New Jersey Supreme Court revealed that it was "more firmly committed" than ever to the correctness of the original doctrine. In a ringing reaffirmation of its earlier opinion, it grounded the regional constitutional obligation in basic concepts of fairness. As a reinforcement of this argument, the court added: "The basis for the constitutional obligation is simple: the State controls the use of land, all of the land. In exercising that control it cannot favor rich over poor. It cannot legislatively set aside dilapidated houses in urban ghettos for the poor and decent housing elsewhere for everyone else."[15] The Mount Laurel II opinion confirmed that a sense of concern for the welfare of the underclass and of fairness and hope for the future, rather than any express textual or theoretical considerations, inspired the decision: "It would be useful to remind ourselves that the doctrine does not arise from some theoretical analysis of our Constitution, but rather from underlying concepts of fundamental fairness in the exercise of governmental power."[16]

What was Mount Laurel II made of? Needing a comprehensive strategy to bring its substantive goals to life, the court laid out major holdings that dramatically modified previous case law. Faced with the recalcitrance of localities and the abdication of responsibility by the legislative and executive branches, the court also set forth a new procedural system intended to make the administration of its revamped land-use policy more judicially manageable.

## Substantive Innovations

ZONING FOR REGIONAL WELFARE

A key starting point for the court's opinion is the idea that municipalities must exercise the constitutional power to zone delegated to them by the state legislature for the general welfare of the state—over and beyond the municipality's own boundaries. Broadly conceived, the court's definition of "regional welfare" includes the housing needs of those residing outside the municipality but within the surrounding region. Therefore, according to the court, every community has a constitutional obligation to provide a realistic possibility for decent housing for lower-income people, and its land-use regulations must create an affirmative opportunity for the construction of its fair share of the present and prospective regional need for low- and moderate-income housing.

JUDICIAL DETERMINATIONS TO INCORPORATE THE STATE PLAN

The Mount Laurel I opinion had adumbrated, and later cases had spelled out, the regional housing obligations brought about by growth. Interestingly, in sketching the new obligation, the Mount Laurel I court had brought into play the expertise of the state planning agencies. As the sequel, Mount Laurel II incorporated New Jersey's State Development Guide Plan (SDGP) into its calculations, ingeniously placing the onus of refining technological and numerical requirements on the executive branch of government. The obligation of providing a realistic opportunity for a fair share of the present and prospective low- and moderate-income housing now ran to every municipality containing within its boundaries territory that the plan designated as a "growth area."[17] No longer would borderline communities be uncertain as to whether the fair share obligation applied to them; now they could look to what the state planners had wrought.

Chief Justice Wilentz was careful to point out "that the judiciary will not contribute to irrational development, discordant with the state's own vision of its future, by encouraging it in areas that the state has concluded should not be developed . . . or by inadvertently leading municipalities to encourage lower income housing in such areas."[18] Mount Laurel II thus made a key contribution by linking the obligation to provide a fair share of affordable housing to sound comprehensive planning undertaken by the executive branch of government. As if to illustrate its commitment to this pledge, the court mandated that housing, even low- and moderate-income housing, not be sited in prime agricultural lands, open spaces, or areas of scenic beauty or environmental quality. This new sensitivity to sound planning principles was a cooperative hand proffered to the other branches of government engaged in the heavy labor of planning realities. Moreover, the reservation underlined the court's awareness of its inter-connectedness with its sister branches of government by stating that municipalities' efforts to fulfill the Mount Laurel obligation, as a matter of "sound judicial discretion reflecting public policy," should be consistent with the state's regional planning goals.[19]

## LEGAL IMPACT OF THE PLAN

Deference to state planning was not absolute, however. The court emphasized that the plan should be presumed correct only if it were kept current—that is, revised every three years in accordance with sound planning principles.[20] Should the state take seriously its obligation to ensure that the plan reflected the real world, the court added, a litigant challenging its restrictions could overcome the presumption of correctness only by showing arbitrary, capricious, or significant changes since a particular area's designation as a growth area; furthermore, the court made clear, this burden would be a heavy one for a municipality to sustain.[21]

In giving such significant legal import to the SDGP, the court was going beyond—considerably beyond—the original legislation establishing the framework for municipalities' exercise of the state's zoning power, by which municipalities were not required either to plan or to zone in conformance with the state plan.[22] One significant curlicue: the state's executive branch saw the plan more as a means of coordinating state capital investments than as a tool for planning the uses of land or allocating the constitutional obligation to provide a fair share of low- and moderate-income housing. No doubt, the same was true for the state legislature. That the court embraced the first SDGP was a matter of high strategy, in which it recast the plan for its own purposes. And by giving the plan true bite in the world of land development—by making it a force that directly affected the allocation of housing in New Jersey—the judiciary put itself directly at odds with the policy fashionable with other branches of government at that time.

In its argument, the court seemed to recognize the political dangers its opinion might encounter. Perhaps it recalled the movement in the legislature to overturn the first Mount Laurel decision by statute or, at the extreme end of the political spectrum, by constitutional amendment.

Fearful that the legislature might greet Mount Laurel II by withdrawing the state planners' authority to prepare their plan (either by revoking authorization or withholding appropriations), the court put the governor and legislature on notice (albeit, respectfully, only in a footnote) that should the legislature take this tack the trial courts would be asked to revert to the "developing municipality" test that was so expansive of judicial power. In other words, to forestall an obvious legislative rejoinder, the court announced that it was ready to take over the broad functions of land planning should the legislature make that step necessary.

### EARLIER RETREATS REVERSED

A major hurdle to bold action was the court's own earlier vacillations. In *Madison Township*, the court, yielding to the importunities of the town, had placed as its gloss on the doctrine the rule that fair share allocations need be neither "precise" nor based on "specific formulae."[23] Six years later, in evaluating the results of that approach, the court concluded sadly that it had "underestimated the pressures that weigh against lower income housing."[24] Municipalities too easily succumbed to the temptation of ignoring the obligation or, only slightly better, providing an absolute minimum of realistic opportunity, assuring, at most, only a trickle of lower-income housing.[25] Moreover, litigation had become an end in itself. Cases concluded without anyone knowing with any certainty what constituted a municipality's fair share. And to the disappointment of the planning community, despite its simpler requirements, the *Madison Township* ruling did not make Mount Laurel–type litigation more manageable. Parties continued to present long and complicated proofs of region, need, and share with little idea of exactly what was persuasive or relevant. Wilentz observed that "*Madison* has led to little but a sigh of relief from those who oppose Mount Laurel."[26]

This step backward had to be canceled. So in Mount Laurel II the New Jersey Supreme Court restored the original specificity of the Mount Laurel Doctrine and, what's more, changed its tune: after Mount Laurel II, good faith efforts by a community to remove exclusionary barriers would no longer suffice; the community could discharge its fair share obligation only by presenting numerical proof that it had provided its share of low- and moderate-income housing. Moreover, these numbers had to square with the totals determined to be the regional need for a reasonable time in the future. Litigants would have to provide specific numbers showing present need and prospective need as well as the specific proportions of those numbers of units required to meet low-income (as distinguished from moderate-income) housing needs. Municipalities would be obliged to design their ordinances to meet clearly specified goals; a numberless approach to planning would no longer be acceptable.

The court also indicated a preference for formulas linked to employment and tax base, thereby expressing its disdain for criteria that had the effect of reinforcing past low-income proportions or exclusionary practices. During its excursion into land-use planning theory, the court also justified its new approach by arguing that while specific numbers would not always be perfectly accurate, they were nonetheless essential because a definitively formulated and stated objective would be more likely to achieve Mount Laurel goals than an indefinite standard with no targets or timetables, such as characterized the *Madison Township* adaptation of Mount Laurel I.

Mount Laurel II also put an end to the wave of lawsuits—with different trial courts deciding cases according to diverse definitions and varying standards—over what constitutes a "developing" municipality.[27] The *Pascack* decision was reversed, and Justice Hall's original limitation of the Mount Laurel obligation to developing municipalities was lifted.

An interesting aside showing the sweeping range of the opinion was the court's overruling of another earlier decision, the *Vickers* case.[28] In *Vickers*, the court had upheld a zoning ordinance that completely banned mobile homes from the town's borders. It was one of those occasions where Justice Hall had glimpsed exclusionary zoning's ugly face behind the mask of regulatory structure, and he had issued a ringing dissent. Now that view, submerged in past protests, was made the ruling law: in overruling *Vickers*, the court stated unequivocally that "municipalities that cannot otherwise meet their fair share obligations must provide zoning for low-cost mobile homes as an affirmative device in their zoning ordinances."[29]

## AFFIRMATIVE REMEDIES

Once it had explained its renewed faith in the necessity of numerical proof, the court felt free to adopt a drastic course of remedies; it proceeded to require local government to adopt all affirmative measures necessary to fulfill the Mount Laurel obligation.[30] Recognizing that realistic opportunities required more than eliminating the negative, unnecessary restrictions that increased costs, for example, the court declared that "affirmative governmental devices should be used to make that opportunity realistic, including lower income density bonuses and mandatory set-asides."[31] Inclusionary zoning's palette of density bonuses and mandatory set-asides, it added, were both constitutional and within the New Jersey Zoning Enabling Act. Most revealingly, in order to reach this conclusion the court openly disagreed with the Virginia Supreme Court, which had held that inclusionary zoning measures were an impermissible socioeconomic use of the zoning power, since they were not related to the physical and spatial aspects of land use.[32] The New Jersey Supreme Court even went out of its way to say that it found the Virginia court's argument "particularly inappropriate," stating flatly:

> The very basis for the constitutional obligation underlying *Mount Laurel* is a belief, fundamental, that excluding a class of citizens from housing on an economic basis (one that substantially corresponds to a socio-economic basis) distinctly disserves the general welfare. That premise is essential to the conclusion that such zoning ordinances are an abuse of the zoning power and are therefore unconstitutional.
>
> It is nonsense to single out inclusionary zoning (providing a realistic opportunity for the construction of lower income housing) and label it "socio-economic" if that is meant to imply that other aspects of zoning are not.

The court went on to explain:

> Detached single family residential zones, high-rise multi-family zones of any kind, factory zones, "clean" research and development zones, recreational, open space, conservation, and agricultural zones, regional shopping mall zones, indeed practically any significant kind of zoning now used, has a substantial socio-economic impact and, in some cases, a socio-economic motivation. It would be ironic if inclusionary zoning to encourage the construction of lower income housing were ruled beyond the power of a municipality because it is "socio-economic" when its need has arisen from the socio-economic zoning of the past that excluded it.[33]

This conclusion was founded on an important perception. Because controlling physical use of land is solely a means to an end—in this case, promotion of the general welfare—there is no reason why a municipality cannot directly require a developer to construct low-income units rather than be forced to resort to elaborate, ingeniously designed regulations purportedly tied to physical use in order to obtain that same end. Cutting through the smokescreen of fine distinctions enabled Wilentz again to remove an intellectual barrier to the effective deployment of remedies.

The court further stated that "the municipality should cooperate with the developer's attempts to obtain federal subsidies." From the experiences of those communities that had sought to comply with Mount Laurel I, the court learned that novel forms of financing, as well as innovative planning development techniques, were necessary to build the housing low-income families could afford. This meant that municipalities had to take those actions necessary to qualify for subsidies, such as adopting local "resolutions of need" spelling out the basis for the request for public housing and funding, and providing tax abatements to subsidize housing development.[34] "It was never intended," the court declared, "that this awesome constitutional obligation, designed to give the poor a fair chance for housing, be satisfied by meaningless amendments to zoning or other ordinances." Thus, while a municipality was free to choose the specific means of achieving compliance, the court clearly stated that a trial judge could ask it "to institute any or all affirmative measures in order to redress a violation of constitutional right."

## GENEROUS LOW-INCOME DEFINITIONS AND
## REALISTIC OPPORTUNITIES FOR AFFORDABLE HOUSING

In a long footnote, the Mount Laurel II court established what it meant by the terms "low" and "moderate" income.[35] Although it took its cue from the definitions of the U.S. Department of Housing and Urban Development (HUD), it cast its net wider into the sea of potential beneficiaries than does the federal government. The court's definition of a moderate-income family corresponded to HUD's definition of a lower-income family, and its low-income family to HUD's very-low-income family. In addition, the court deemed housing "affordable" only if a family paid no more than 25 percent of its income for the housing, even though HUD went as high as 30 percent.

The court also recognized that a great deal turns on whether low-income housing opportunities are realistic. On this difficult point, the inexperience of the judges became apparent even to them. Still, they struggled to lay down a standard that would be workable in practice. According to the court, a realistic opportunity is one that creates a "likelihood— to the extent economic conditions allow—that the lower income housing will actually be constructed."[36] Perhaps not satisfied with this vague encapsulation, the court elaborated: "For an opportunity to be 'realistic,' it must be one that is at least sensible for someone to use."[37] Even after the Mount Laurel II opinion, extensive economic forecasting and expert testimony from the market regarding whether opportunities are "sensible" and actual construction a "likelihood" continue to be features of Mount Laurel litigation. Because localities carry the burden of demonstrating by a preponderance of evidence that they have provided their fair share of low-income housing and created realistic opportunities, a substantial advantage continues to lodge with the developers.

## *The Administrative Machinery*

### JUDICIAL MANAGEMENT AND EXPEDITION OF
### INSTITUTIONAL LITIGATION

Mount Laurel II's approach to judicial management and the framework the court devised to fulfill its aspirations constitute a most remarkable contribution to institutional litigation as a whole. A striking and completely novel aspect of the Mount Laurel II opinion was the structure it created for the internal regime of the state's lower courts and for the trial and appellate processes as a whole. Recognizing that the "doctrine is right but its administration has been ineffective," the New Jersey Supreme Court took major ameliorative steps so that a Mount Laurel case could be handled completely with one trial and one appeal.[38]

This ambitious plan for making doctrine an ongoing reality at trial had three primary components. First, the court divided New Jersey into three judicial areas, in each of which a trial judge would be selected to specialize in Mount Laurel cases. Future Mount Laurel litigation would be assigned to these three judges. As the only judges presiding over exclusionary zoning cases, they would become experts and, it was hoped, actively foster the policies laid down by Mount Laurel II.

Second, the court promulgated a detailed set of rules governing how the specialized trial judges should handle their cases, covering the process from the beginning of a case through the fashioning of remedies to final judgment and appeal. The chief justice emphasized the need for both early and frequent pretrial conferences and the continued use of experts to dispose of questions of regional need, fair share, and compliance that lie at the heart of Mount Laurel–type litigation.

Third, Mount Laurel II established a number of procedural devices intended to expedite litigation and settlement. For example, it liberalized the standing-to-sue requirements so that "any individual demonstrating an interest in, or any organization that has the objective of, securing lower income housing opportunities in a municipality will have standing to sue such municipality on Mount Laurel grounds."[39] It provided, moreover, that if successfully sued, a municipality had only ninety days to revise its ordinance. The court also authorized each trial court to appoint a special master (paid for by the municipality) to facilitate the revision of the ordinance. Unlike the typical master, who acts more as a generalist administrator than as an expert who becomes intimately involved in the details, the Mount Laurel special master's power, flowing directly from the trial judge, often turned out to be enormous.

THE BUILDER'S REMEDY

In one of its bolder and most politically savvy moves, the New Jersey Supreme Court authorized what came to be known as the builder's remedy, thereby marrying public interest to private profit. Under the builder's remedy, an incentive aimed at the private sector, if a builder successfully demonstrates that a municipality's land-use regulation is exclusionary, and promises to deliver a substantial number of low-income housing units, that builder is granted permission to build additional market-priced units over and above the nominal number permitted by the zoning ordinance.

In the earlier *Madison Township* case, the New Jersey Supreme Court appeared to discourage these types of extraordinary remedies, observing that "such relief will ordinarily be rare."[40] Again, however, experience revised this reasoning. By affording a remedy valuable enough to make worthwhile the expenditure of money, time, and effort needed to challenge a municipality, the builder's remedy turned out to be a powerful tool for reform—indeed, one that came to dominate the New Jersey litigation scene. Because it promised a reward for bringing a successful lawsuit—the economic benefit of a change in an ordinance going directly to the developer initiating the regulatory challenge—it proved to be an effective way to engage the private sector in the enforcement of the public policies driving Mount Laurel II. A flurry of legal actions by the for-profit sector ensued.

It should be noted, however, that the builder's remedy narrowed the scope of latent solutions, and once unleashed, it was potentially powerful enough to distort the impact of the Mount Laurel Doctrine. Certainly, antiexclusionary litigation became extensive, but it often served chiefly to benefit the affluent. Income from the private market-rate units, rather than financing from the public sector (except for municipal services and infrastructure), became the driving force behind expanding the housing market for lower-income groups. The Mount Laurel II court had foreseen potential abuses and attempted to limit them by imposing the remedy only if the litigating developer proposed "a project providing a substantial amount of lower income housing." In a long footnote that would exert profound influence on future land development in New Jersey, the court suggested 20 percent of any development as an appropriate proportion for low- and moderate-income housing in a typical builder's remedy situation.[41] This hopeful recommendation for a minimal floor in practice functioned as a ceiling: profits from the more expensive units subsidized the losses on the affordable housing units, with the result that builders limited the proportion of low-income housing in order to maximize earnings.

The court planted further hedges about a remedy so powerful. Foreseeing that builders would use the threat of the remedy in their negotiations with municipalities as a lever to obtain approval for density increases or higher-income developments that would do nothing to meet local fair share obligations, the court sought to convert this strategy into a losing gambit: "Proof of such threats shall be sufficient to defeat Mount Laurel litigation by that developer." As a further comfort to defendant municipalities, the court urged the trial courts to cushion the impacts of the builder's remedy by phasing the timing of development.[42]

OTHER REMEDIAL INNOVATIONS

Perhaps most extreme among the procedural mechanisms was the response to municipalities that failed to submit revised ordinances within the proper time or whose submissions proved inadequate. The court's earlier tentativeness, partly attributable to the very newness of the Mount Laurel Doctrine, gave way to a steady resolve that compliance be ensured as far as possible. Mount Laurel II set out a whole range of potential remedial orders, broadening by far the scope of what courts previously had authorized. Specifically, a trial judge faced with noncompliance could issue orders:

* requiring that the noncomplying municipality adopt every ordinance—including particular amendments to its zoning ordinance and other land-use regulations—necessary to enable it to discharge its Mount Laurel obligations;
* delaying development or construction elsewhere within the municipality—even those projects unrelated to the challenged ordinance—until the municipality satisfactorily revises its ordinance;
* voiding zoning and other land-use regulations in whole or in part to relax or eliminate building and use restrictions in all or selected portions of the municipality; and/or
* deeming as approved particular applications to construct housing incorporating lower-income units.

Furthermore, any noncomplying municipality was to remain under the supervision of the trial court with no right of appeal pending a final judgment of compliance. Noncompliance was a serious matter, and the court would no longer permit municipalities to defer implementation of the goals underlying Mount Laurel I while they dragged their feet with dilatory actions, motions, and appeals. This was judicial process but speeded up far past its usual deliberate pace.

As a sop to the suburban communities, to induce their cooperation while still underlining the importance of compliance, the court put in place a guarantee of finality for judgments of compliance: once a trial court found a municipality in conformity, it became immune to suits under the Mount Laurel Doctrine for a period of six years—even if community circumstances changed.[43]

## A Missed Opportunity

Massive procedural recasting was the court's response to the slow, meandering, and frustrating course of land-use reform in New Jersey after

Mount Laurel I. The court's extensive and precise attention to detail reflects its undeniable exasperation with the aftermath of the original Mount Laurel decision. At the end of the opinion, Chief Justice Wilentz summed up by stating his sincere desire for closure:

> We hope that individualized case management, the constant growth of expertise on the part of the judges in handling these matters, the simplification and elimination of issues resulting both from our rulings and from the active involvement of judges early in the litigation, and the requirement that, generally, the matter be disposed of at the trial level in its entirety before any appeal is allowed, will result in an example of trial efficiency that needs copying, not explaining.[44]

This was the order of the day.

Crucial as the procedural innovations were, the court faltered in the equally critical task of expressing its opinion in a manner calculated to educate and persuade. A telling aspect of the decision, aside from its sheer length (and who but a dedicated devotee could digest a 250-page opinion in this era of the ten-second sound bite?), is the difficulty of condensing its thesis into a cogent, dramatic argument. Almost deliberately, it seems, the chief justice refused to take his case to the people and convince them of the legitimacy of his point of view at the most basic level. The lengthy and technical legal argument stripped the issues of their emotional appeal and obscured the essential link between local administrative actions and the rule of law under the constitution.

The hostile and touchy environment of land-use reform demanded a Gettysburg Address of sorts, a powerful statement sustained by the noble American rallying cry of fairness and equality in the exercise of governmental powers. That local zoning exclusion is a crippling condition that, left unattended, would so distort the structure of metropolitan areas as to rob New Jersey's next generation of its birthright was a theme unsounded. This was the court's last clear chance, for the written opinion is the major tool through which the judiciary exercises its role as moral persuader. At its most inspired, judicial prose can win over public opinion. At a minimum, it should provide grist for editorial mills, certainly when a case of Mount Laurel II's importance comes along. Yet, somehow, the persuasive power of the New Jersey Supreme Court's ideas is lost in the myriad of doctrinal details supporting the legal edifice.

The propelling idea behind the chief justice's conclusions—the notion that local regulatory barriers are dividing the United States into two nations, a nation of poor people forced to live in the deteriorating tenements of inner-city slums and a nation of suburbanites living in attractive homes surrounded by well-manicured lawns—could have been formulated in vivid language meant to sway as well as to instruct. It is unfortunate, therefore, that such a clutching image is submerged in a vast sea of text and evoked through a tedious examination of legal doctrines. Even had it been brightly outlined, however, the Chief Justice's startling message, too painful in its prescience, probably would have failed to move property owners and local officials preoccupied with visions no less wrenching to them: the loss of their property value and suburban exclusivity.

In part, the lack of explanatory material is attributable to the mind-set of the third branch of government. The judicial endeavor is inherently cautious, and judges tend to pepper their rhetoric with appeals to tradition and precedent, even when they are making radical public policy through their pronouncements. In addition, bridging the gap between the judicial understanding of social justice and popular beliefs is especially difficult when a court is reshaping precedent and setting a new course. In Mount Laurel II, the court may also have decided that attempting a direct appeal to the public was too risky, given how fickle, frightened, and prone to manipulation it can be and given further that many suburbanites share the same prejudices as local officials. The court's articulation of a vision of New Jersey that was obviously antithetical to the vision of many, if not most, suburban residents was bound to create intense controversy no matter how it was couched.

As dry as it is, the opinion clearly reflects a deep desire, imbued with traces of hubris, to lead rather than follow in the tracks of the other branches of government. Mount Laurel II does make a modest bow to the separation of powers, but not without reserving a special note for its own role: "As we said at the outset, while we have always preferred legislative to judicial action in this field, we shall continue—until the Legislature acts—to do our best to uphold the constitutional obligation that underlies the Mount Laurel doctrine." By far, the court's major emphases are on shouldering the burden of reform and forging the various weapons for its armory. While some olive branches are extended, the dominant message is that the court is ready to declare war on its own. "We have learned from experience," it emphasized, "that unless a strong judicial hand is used, Mount Laurel will not result in housing, but in paper, process, witnesses, trials and appeals."[45] The challenge by local authorities had been direct and unmistakable, and the court was ready to muster all available forces to rebuff it. Of course, the danger of casting the terms of the debate in this way was that it could foster division more than solidarity.

Although understandable after eight years of municipal recalcitrance, the tone of the opinion nonetheless grates. Mount Laurel II's complex remedial edifice and the court's determination to show independent force overwhelm the opinion's genuine concern for local initiatives—a concern that might have provided a hook for public sympathies. Notes of reassurance to municipalities scattered throughout the opinion read as perfunctory afterthoughts and fail to make a clear case for judicial action that well-intentioned citizens and opinion molders at least could grasp, even when they did not entirely agree. Nor did the opinion articulate its underlying ethical base—especially its concern with fair sharing of the burden—in a way that appealed to the average suburbanite whose home and community the court was requiring to bear the burdens that having a different class, a different income group, and a different racial composition in a neighborhood impose. The chief justice could not find quite the right words to embody the power of his ideas.

Attempts at sophisticated and subtle leadership were made in the opinion, but they were peripheral and did not wholly succeed. In its attempt to win over environmentalists, for example, the court declared more than once that the Mount Laurel Doctrine did not leave natural resources and open spaces hostages to developers. Put more bluntly, Mount Laurel would not create wall-to-wall low-income housing in the state; development would be phased according to the growth plan of the State Development Office. Specifically, the court added, the Mount Laurel obligation "does not extend to those areas where the [SDGP] discourages growth—namely, open spaces, rural areas, prime farmland, conservation areas, limited growth areas, parts of the Pinelands and certain Coastal Zone areas." Even a developer armed with a builder's remedy would have to locate and design the project in accordance with sound planning concepts, "including its environmental impact."[46]

In a pitch to local politicians intended to take bruised feelings into account, the court spoke of its respect for the decisions of localities: if they were to meet the Mount Laurel obligation, the court conceded, they ought to be allowed wide-ranging freedom to plan and to zone. Choice of remedy, where an ordinance was found to be exclusionary, was left to the discretion of the municipalities. Safe harbor would be furnished to those that complied. But these assurances were scattered throughout the opinion, rather than in sequence, and nowhere were articulated in a clear, spirited, crisp fashion.

Overall, the court missed the opportunity to emphasize that its remedies were not intrusions of public power into spheres of activity formerly reserved for private decision making but rather intended to correct abuses of local regulatory power that raised barriers to movement—of capital as well as of people. In fact, the point could have been made that instead of bestowing power on the public sector, the Mount Laurel decisions, in their reliance on incentives such as the builder's remedy to move the private branch, reinforced the market-based approach to land development as opposed to a command-and-control regulatory model. The Mount Laurel opinions, in other words, invalidated improper exercises of public power by overreaching local governments. Such an argument could have countered the widespread perception that the court was promoting a developer hegemony rather than facilitating the fair sharing of a metropolitan burden.

Even the timing of the proposed change was not put in its most favorable light. By way of confession and avoidance, the court overtly acknowledged that "flexibility is needed here, for our work is partially legislative in character." "Care should be taken," the chief justice wrote, to ensure that Mount Laurel remedies did not "radically transform the municipality overnight."[47] The court gave trial courts the discretion to moderate impacts by phasing them in over a period of years. But yet again, the court cast this mollifying provision almost as an afterthought, burying it within the frequent references to the need for speed.

With the wisdom born of the litigation that followed Mount Laurel II, it is clear that the court should have focused more intensely on educating the public. In its thorough reappraisal of the experiences engendered by Mount Laurel I, Mount Laurel II strongly restated and reinforced Justice Hall's original opinion, but it did not stress the countervailing themes that would sweeten the dose: the right of municipalities to retain reasonable land-use restrictions and protections against would-be speculators seeking to benefit from the builder's remedy; an acceptance of sound growth control plans; a period of repose after a settlement. Quite the contrary: almost all the consoling messages are lost in the interstices of the opinion's longer discussions. Mount Laurel II appears unwilling to stoop to the concerns and queries of the average citizen.[48] Indeed, the most resounding chord in the opinion is not the court's desire to explain the necessity for, or the limited or temporary nature of, the judicial intervention, but a determination to put steel into its Mount Laurel Doctrine. "Our warning to Mount Laurel—and to all other municipalities," the court reiterated, "will seem hollow indeed if the best we can do to satisfy the constitutional obligation is to issue orders, judgments and injunctions that assure never-ending litigation but fail to assure constitutional vindication."[49]

By any evaluation, the dominant theme in Chief Justice Wilentz's opinion is frustration, outrage, striking back.[50] Justified as the court may have been in its disappointment, arguing to New Jersey homeowners that "the change will be much less painful for us than the status quo has been for them" was unlikely to win over people who saw their home values threatened or to prove persuasive to those to whom the issue came alive not in terms of constitutional mandate but as an influx of strangers. Almost ignored was the fairness argument that each locality would be asked to bear only an appropriate share of the pain and that all would be treated equitably, though this would have been a modulated response to vexations and an exposition the court could readily have made.

## In Sum, Success

All this said, the breadth of approach, the imaginative creation of new administrative mechanisms, the thinking through of the implications of each move, and the logic of detail of Mount Laurel II are overwhelmingly impressive. The New Jersey Supreme Court geared the judicial system for full and effective remedying of discriminatory local land-use controls. It announced a blueprint, legislative in its sweep, for conducting trials and decreed a step-by-step procedure by which a case could be settled and put to bed. It suspended the usual rules of judicial procedure and abolished interlocutory appeals for Mount Laurel cases. To fight the conservative tendencies of the appellate division, it took the even more drastic step of ordering direct appeal to the supreme court so that parties could completely bypass intermediate-level courts. The opinion segmented the state into three areas, announced the appointment of specialized judges and masters, and provided for firm judicial case management. It pondered guidelines for the definition of region, need, and fair share and created a powerful remedial framework—culminating in the builder's remedy—that mobilized the private sector. Throughout, the opinion explored potential loopholes at every stage of trial and sought to block them. In short, it transformed the abstract judicial principles of Mount Laurel I into workable instruments of social change.

Nor should it be overlooked that Mount Laurel II was a most courageous act, as deliberate a countermajoritarian measure as it was extraordinary. Given the tensions swirling around the issue of exclusionary zoning, it was a dramatic and wrenching task for the court to reaffirm its commitment to the doctrine. Mount Laurel I had run head-on into the long-standing practice of social class exclusion that dominates, indeed may be a major reason for, the existence of suburbs. "A man's home to him a castle and fortress is," Lord Coke proclaimed in the sixteenth century, marking a break with the feudal concepts of property law. And suburbanites took this analogue to heart, transferring their affections to the detached one-family house.

When Mount Laurel I put forward a right to affordable housing in the suburbs, critics of the decision saw it as a radical challenge to the American way of life. That the use of the delegated state police power to bar

low-income housing from a locality's boundaries was an affront to the
state constitution should have concluded the matter; instead, the issue
was inflated into a full-blown constitutional crisis. Deaf ears were turned
to Justice Hall's sounding of the bugle. Mayors and councils alike ignored the call for revisions of land-use regulations—as if the unanimous
opinion of Mount Laurel I was precatory language not meant to be
taken seriously in day-to-day human affairs. The court, for the sake of its
constitutional position—indeed, its very legitimacy—could not permit
public scoffing at the doctrine. A major strand, therefore, in Mount Laurel II (although not specifically so phrased) was the reassertion of judicial
legitimacy.

Mount Laurel II owes its prominence not only to the ideals it embodies
and the compliance mechanisms it developed for their effectuation but
also to the deepest social concerns of the era that produced it. The decision came at the height of the expansive real estate development that intimately affected American families in the decades following the Second
World War, a period in the history of American liberalism when preven-
tive solutions through government interventions still seemed possible and
appropriate.

A series of judicial events built up slowly in Hall's pre–Mount Laurel
dissents and then emerged in his opinion in Mount Laurel I out of a gnaw-
ing sense that the constitution would not tolerate the physical division
between families caught in inner-city despair and those enjoying suburban comfort, from an anxiety that the American dream of the melting pot
was over, and from the growing fear that the ideal of America as a classless society was fading into illusion. Suburban legal barriers (enforced by
earlier passive judicial acceptance) are deeply implicated in a way of life
dominated by privatization, enclaves, and indifference to the larger general welfare; they privatize not just individual but community space. In
Mount Laurel II, a state supreme court attempted to move people still
further toward the recognition that society could no longer isolate itself
from the evils of concentrating poverty in the urban ghettos of the metropolitan area and could no longer shirk responsibility for the future of the
nation's cities, suburbs, and countryside.

While the court was making judicial history in New Jersey, the absence
of a national forum was becoming painfully apparent. No matter how
socially and physically visible the isolation of minorities in the inner
cities, no precedent for major judicial action existed until the Mount Laurel line of decisions. In 1973 President Nixon had signed the federal
Housing and Community Development Act, which funneled entitlements
to central cities and urban counties—such as Middlesex County, the site
of the Madison Township litigation—and ignored incentives for the metropolitan units adjoining them. No federally funded inducement com-

mingled the burdens of cities and their surrounding suburbs, prompting them to form partnerships that might ease the transition to a nondiscriminatory housing market. The collapse of subsidy and incentive programs at all levels of government left the poor feeling robbed of a sense of purpose, of identity; indeed, the cities seemed no longer much of a place within the entitlement structure.

From a technical viewpoint, the long-awaited Mount Laurel II opinion promised only a resolution of the immediate litigations before the court. But it also offered something much rarer: a vision. If the public would only step back from the specific doctrinal details, it would discover that the court assumed the best about them and about society—that local municipalities, in enacting land-use regulations, could lift their sights beyond the short-term horizons that normally govern the exercise of public power. Housing discrimination divides the society along territorial lines, with minorities shunted to city cores by the surrounding fences of exclusionary land-use regulation. The urban core constitutes an island of misery that should not be allowed, by sheer concentration and internal digestion, to keep repoisoning itself. In an area minimally susceptible to consensual resolution, the New Jersey Supreme Court, pointing to the institutional ties of community and pluralism, sought to cope with the smoldering issues of segregation of race and class raised by exclusionary zoning.

Litigation usually starts at the lowest trial court level, works its way upward through intermediate appellate courts, and finally draws the ruling of the high court. In the Mount Laurel cases, however, a detailed top-down mandate from the state supreme court—twice repeated—mustered the support of the rest of the judiciary to attain reform objectives. Justice Hall, in the first Mount Laurel decision, set forth an intellectual framework with a constitutional basis for assigning to localities an affirmative regional duty to provide low- and moderate-income housing. The signal was even clearer in Mount Laurel II, in which Chief Justice Wilentz went out of his way to substantiate his directives. The point was clear. After years of local vacillation, the New Jersey Supreme Court had concluded that only by a show of force could it guarantee fulfillment of the constitutional limitations on the exercise of local exclusionary zoning ordinances. Mount Laurel II meant to impose real sanctions, dangle genuine incentives, expedite proceedings, attain a speedy determination—and bring low- and moderate-income housing into actuality in the suburbs. As the first step toward an effective judicial mechanism at the trial level to implement the court's vision of both fairness and social well-being, it foreshadowed—even made inevitable—the course of events that was to take New Jersey, after three years of progress under the trial judges, to the

SCCCC - LIBRARY
4601 Mid Rivers Mall Drive
St. Peters, MO 63376
WITHDRAWN

legislature's sharp reaction in the Fair Housing Act of 1985 and to the present administration of New Jersey's policy on affordable housing, bifurcated as it is between the trial courts and the Council on Affordable Housing.

The struggle began in earnest with Mount Laurel II and now plays on and on.

# IV

## Judges into the Fray

AND NOW for the hard part.

The battle of words had been won with Chief Justice Wilentz's pronouncement on January 20, 1983. The Mount Laurel Doctrine stood reaffirmed. If Justice Hall had been the visionary, Chief Justice Wilentz was the realist. He knew he had a huge war ahead of him, and like a field marshal preparing for battle, he needed the foot soldiers to fight in the trenches. The general chose three distinguished trial judges—Anthony Gibson, Eugene Serpentelli, and Stephen Skillman—for the special mission of bringing the Mount Laurel Doctrine down to earth and rebuffing the anticipated counterattacks from suburbanites and municipalities.

His selection process was revealing. Wilentz first put together a list of some thirty judges and interviewed them all, reducing the number to about a dozen. He then reinterviewed and ultimately cut the list down to the chosen three. What he sought in the interviews is unclear. Background familiarity with zoning and planning was secondary to energy, intelligence, managerial skills, and ability to handle public flack. But any similarity among the judges ended there: the three varied widely in background and in social and political outlooks. Perhaps the interviews had an additional purpose. While the trial judges would put their individual stamps on the doctrine, it is unlikely that, after their conversations with the chief justice, any of them would purposely misconstrue it or narrowly apply it.

Among members of the New Jersey judiciary, selection for Mount Laurel litigation was regarded as a high compliment and an important credential for career advancement. One candidate was told by a mentor, "Are you crazy? I understood that the chief has spoken to you twice about doing the Mount Laurel thing and you've said no. The next time he calls you, you tell him that you'd be happy to."

All three appointees moved quickly to sustain the confidence that the chief justice and his colleagues had invested in them. In this assignment, they succeeded beyond expectations. Observers, both within and outside the group of planning experts and lawyers assembled for the burgeoning field of Mount Laurel–type lawsuits, agree that the trial judges did a superb job of fleshing out the abstract principles proffered in Mount Laurel II, bringing them to fruition in intelligent applications and rendering them administratively effective. Indeed, the judges' problem-solving capacities removed the concerns of those who had warned that the complexities of regional land-use planning would endlessly entangle the courts as they tried to cope with complicated zoning situations.

## The Terms of the Battle

The volume of litigation already swirling around the Mount Laurel Doctrine meant that the judges' first and most urgent task was definitional and the setting of standards. Where, precisely, were the boundaries of a region? What were the standards for setting a region's need for low-income housing? What portion of that regional need should a municipality have to provide through its land-use regulations? Did the parcels of a locality, rezoned to meet Mount Laurel obligations, satisfy the regional need? Of what usefulness in bringing about adequate affordable housing were the various compliance techniques offered by the municipality? The channels of communication were clogged by the absence of contact, by the mutual suspicion bred of abrupt social change, and by the uncertainty of transition. It fell to the courts to deal with the quagmire of semantic and statistical assertions put forth by combatants hoping to gain an edge in the litigation.[1]

Take the central question of what constitutes a municipality's fair share of low- and moderate-income housing. Having reasserted the constitutional obligation to respond to regional housing needs, the court called for a numerical fair share to be elaborated in the remedy. Yet the New Jersey Supreme Court sent out only the vaguest of signals as to how it should be determined. And the proverbial devil was in the details, for until practical meaning was attached to the concept of fair share, no construction of suburban affordable housing could proceed. This potential impasse was forestalled early on by Judge Serpentelli in *AMG Realty Co. v. Township of Warren*, where he poured content into the concept.[2] By creating a logically satisfying methodology for determining a municipality's fair share, he saved the courts from years of debate and muddle.

In the major litigation sequence, in which the National Urban League sued twenty-three municipalities in Middlesex County, the plaintiff and each of the defendants engaged separate planning experts. "I remember that we were all in a state of some anxiety," one judge recalls. "How were we ever going to develop a fair share formula in one case that would fit another case, and if we couldn't, were we going to have six hundred different formulas in New Jersey, and would the formula in the central district be different from the formula in the northern and southern districts?"

Confronting this potential Tower of Babel, Judge Serpentelli took draconian measures. After a brief attempt at hearing testimony in a conventional adversarial process persuaded him that the planning community could debate for years over equally reasonable alternatives, he placed the parties' planning experts together in a conference room with the request that they work out a formula to which all could subscribe. All lawyers were excluded. If not quite as extreme as the closeting of the medieval jury, whose members were denied food until they reached a verdict, the technique still worked in this modern drama. Somehow, after breaking up into subcommittees, with back-and-forth private consultations, the twenty-one experts, representing a cross-section of the profession (and including professional planners not involved in the actual litigation), after several days succeeded in hammering out a consensus formula for prescribing regional fair share.

The new methodology was applicable not only in the immediate litigation but to all municipalities throughout the state. "I felt good about the planning profession in New Jersey," reports one of the participants, "as a result of them being able to see the need for finding common ground on a methodology that is highly complex and would affect their clients in different ways." Further testing and cross-examination by Judge Serpentelli himself—for he was genuinely seeking guidance as much as the legitimacy that would derive from professional consensus—and his occasional presence during the course of the deliberations led to the path-breaking and unified approach to fair share analysis set forth in *AMG*.[3]

The adopted quantification methodology asked three questions: What is the region in which the municipality is located? What is the present and prospective need for low-income housing within that region? And what is the municipality's proportional obligation for fulfilling that present and prospective regional need?

Mount Laurel II gave only general guidance, but numerous decisions had stressed the housing market as the demarcator: a region is "that general area which constitutes, more or less, the housing market area of which the subject municipality is a part, and from which the prospective population of the municipality would substantially be drawn, in the absence of exclusionary zoning."[4] *AMG* began by distinguishing the region it deemed proper for allocating fair shares of present need from that used to calculate fair shares of prospective need.[5] In this dual-region solution, the group of planners recommended four regions in the state for "present need." One huge region consisted of eleven counties—virtually all of northern New Jersey. Ostensibly, sheer size may engender surprise. Boundaries were drawn broadly to provide sufficient receptors to meet the housing needs of families from such major cities as Newark, Elizabeth, Jersey City, and Paterson, which possess high quantities of dilapidated housing; the definition sought to balance the high levels of need in the older urban cores with the resources—land and financial—to meet that need in the newer suburban areas.

*AMG* determined that "prospective need," generated as it is by employment growth, would be served better by another casting of boundaries; for those purposes, the opinion defined *region* as the area within reasonable commuting distance of a municipality's downtown area or, absent a functional center or municipal building, the major crossroads within the municipality. The approach identified all points that could be reached during a specified commuting time by traveling outward in all directions on existing highways; thus a separate commuter shed region was determined for each individual community.[6] Judge Serpentelli eventually settled on a thirty-minute commute as the journey-to-work standard, with the further proviso that, should the commute reach any part of an adjacent county, the entire county would be included in the prospective need region.[7]

In a later interview relating to the thinking behind the applicability of these standards, Judge Serpentelli reflected: "I recognize it is not my prerogative to define regional configurations for counties not within my jurisdiction. However, I also recognize that to determine regions within my jurisdiction without evaluating their consistency with other potential regional configurations could promote the inconsistency which the Supreme Court sought to avoid through the use of the three judge system. . . . Of course," he added politely but perhaps unnecessarily, "my fellow Mount Laurel judges will address these regional configuration issues in their jurisdictions."[8]

The consensus methodology defined *present need* to consist of two elements: *indigenous need*—need within a municipality—and the municipality's fair share of the region's *reallocated excess need*.[9] *Indigenous need* referred to the existing substandard housing—the product of past housing neglect and almost invariably concentrated in built-up communities. It was further spelled out that to be considered substandard, housing had to accommodate representatives of the income-eligible group—that is, people whose annual income was below 50 percent of the regional median income for lower-income housing and below 80 percent for moderate-income housing—and be physically deficient (lacking either complete plumbing or adequate heating facilities) or overcrowded.[10] As a science, housing quality determination has moved from the field survey, necessarily subjective, reflecting the observed condition of the housing to a utilization of surrogates of deterioration. "Surrogates" do not declare in so many words that a unit is dilapidated; what they do indicate is that if a dwelling unit has these characteristics, it most likely would be confirmed by a field survey as dilapidated.

One possible factor—referred to in passing by Mount Laurel II—was not formalized. Although that decision suggested that not more than 25 percent of income should be spent for housing costs, the *AMG* calculation does not cite standard dwelling units in which lower-income households pay a disproportionate share of income for shelter. The data was unreliable, and the proximate figures would have been unrealistically high.

*AMG* also established a method for calculating a municipality's share of the region's *excess present need*. The method first determined the total regional housing stock and identified the percentage of substandard stock within that total. Municipalities' own percentages of substandard stock relative to their total housing were then compared to the regional average, with any excesses to be redistributed among the remaining towns in the region that did not have substandard housing in excess of the regional percentage.

The final step was that of allocating regional need to individual municipalities. Allocation on a simple proportional basis offers the advantage of simplicity of calculation, but such an equal share formula suffers from treating all localities alike despite real differences in size, employment base, environmental sensitivity. *AMG* adopted a more complex formula. For distributing *present need*, Justice Serpentelli accepted an average of three factors: *growth area*,[11] the percentage created by dividing the number of growth area acres within the municipality by the number of growth area acres within the present-need region; *present employment*,[12] the percentage created by dividing the total number of jobs covered by unemployment compensation within the municipality by the number of covered jobs within the present-need region; and *median income*, the ratio of municipal median income to the present-need region median income.[13] After present need had been calculated came projections to determine future need.

Hence the next step was ascertaining future need. Under *AMG*, *prospective regional need* represented the dwelling units required to meet the expected increase in income-eligible households over the projection period. It was derived by projecting the number of households in the region in 1990, comparing that number to the number that existed in 1980, and identifying the extent to which the increase in households would involve an increase in lower-income households. Household formation and employment growth analyses were conducted individually for each county—statistics were readily available only on that basis—in the region before the county totals were aggregated to form the prospective regional need. Prospective regional need was next allocated to the municipalities within the region, using *employment growth* in addition to the three factors defined for present need.[14]

In summation, the municipal fair share is calculated by combining indigenous, surplus present, and prospective need and then using the prescribed allocation formulas to bring the obligation down to the local level. As a final mollifier for localities, Judge Serpentelli introduced a "fudge" factor of 20 percent, on behalf of a municipality that lacked adequate vacant developable land.[15]

The judicial discourse on methodology came alive with Judge Skillman's polite disagreement with aspects of the consensus formula; in *Countryside Properties, Inc. v. Mayor of Ringwood*,[16] he accepted a slightly different version of present indigenous need. The borough defending its zoning ordinance in that case was described in the SDGP as a "rugged area" that should be "considered as a significant resource to be appropriately managed and conserved by the State."[17] As a conservation area, it was required to accommodate only present need, and not the fair share of the regional need for lower-income housing. At the outset, Judge Skillman summed up the agreement of the experts at the trial. The best source of data on deficient housing units occupied by lower-income persons is the U.S. Census, which generated data relating to seven negative characteristics: whether the unit was built prior to 1940; whether it is occupied by more than 1.01 persons per room; whether it permits access only by entering through another dwelling; whether it lacks plumbing facilities for the exclusive use of the occupants; whether it lacks complete kitchen facilities; whether it lacks centralized heating facilities; and whether it lacks an elevator if located in a structure of more than four stories. The area of disagreement among the experts—therefore the primary testimony at trial—concerned which factor enumerated in the census data should be used and the weight it should be accorded in determining the number of deficient units.

Relying on the *AMG* methodology, the builder's expert naturally resorted to the three surrogates (lack of complete plumbing, overcrowding, lack of central heating) of housing deficiencies that the case employed. His calculations revealed 10 units lacking plumbing for exclusive use, 69 overcrowded units, and 63.49 lacking adequate central heating, a total of 142.49 deficient units. For the next step—the crucial one of determining the percentage occupied by lower-income households—he used the 82 percent formula of the Tri-State Regional Planning Commission, as had *AMG*. Overall, he concluded that deficient units totaled 117.

A different total was put forth by the borough's two experts. Although both relied on the methodology employed by the Center for Urban Policy Research of Rutgers University (Rutgers Report),[18] one placed the present need at 79, while the other expert (who had coauthored the report) concluded that 61 was the proper figure.

Commissioned by the League of Municipalities and the Builders Association in June 1983, shortly after Mount Laurel II was decided, the report's calculations were the only serious intellectual rival to the consensus methodology of *AMG*.[19] Unlike the *AMG* recognition of a single surrogate signifying dilapidation,[20] the Rutgers methodology required that there be at least two deficiencies, since by broadening their number it felt it should require the presence of multiple surrogates for a unit to be considered deficient. Judge Skillman deemed this multifactor approach more reliable than *AMG*'s single surrogate approach. "This court is satisfied," he wrote, "that the Rutgers methodology provides a far more reliable indication of the percentage of deficient units occupied by lower income persons."[21] A multisurrogate definition would be more likely to identify truly deficient units, he added, while minimizing the count of adequate units that may have only a single negative characteristic. Judge Skillman also thought the database sample of housing units stored on computer tapes with information on the characteristics of each unit and its occupants made the Rutgers Report's conclusions more reliable. By contrast, the most serious drawback to the *AMG* techniques was its acceptance of the assumption that 82 percent of deficient units are occupied by lower-income people.[22]

But Judge Skillman did not accept the report as a whole, rejecting the part dealing with the techniques for allocating the percentage of the regional present need to the local level. That the computer data was compiled only for subregional levels made suspect the conversion to the municipal level; to the judge, this methodology seemed inapposite, for one municipality might be populated by all middle-income households occupying adequate housing, whereas another with the same population and median household income might have significant pockets of low-income families residing in dilapidated housing. By combining, in true Solomon-like decision making, the Rutgers Report method for determining the total number of deficient units occupied by lower-income households with the *AMG* method for converting regional results to the municipal level, he arrived at a present need of 63.[23]

Judge Serpentelli returned to the debate three months later in a spirited rejoinder in *J. W. Field Company, Inc. v. Township of Franklin*.[24] At his special request, a coauthor of the Rutgers Report testified in the case. "I have therefore had an opportunity," the judge reported, "to fully re-examine the present need issue in light of Judge Skillman's opinion and the testimony of Dr. Burchell."[25] He remained unconvinced. He did agree, however, that the Tri-State's 82 percent estimate was inappropriate, and substituted for it the figure of 64.2 percent used by the Rutgers Report.[26] "In all other respects, however," he concluded, "it is my judgment that the approach adopted in *AMG* is sound."[27] Judge Serpentelli went on to question the validity of several of the surrogates of deficiency used by the Rutgers Report.[28] As a final word, he strongly endorsed the *AMG* consensus methodology because, in his judgment, it was direct and simple.

The obligation to create a realistic opportunity for the construction of low- and moderate-income housing was the ukase that the New Jersey Supreme Court had issued. But defining what this meant, as the idealistic pronouncement pounded against the realities of local homeowner sentiment, fell to the three trial judges. They had to sift through local actions, ordinance by ordinance, to test whether they met the prescribed standard. To a large extent, this was as it ought to be, for the anomaly remains that the New Jersey Supreme Court could not have understood the full implications of the Mount Laurel II opinion at the time of its delivery and thus could not have given practical content to terms such as *fair share*. Despite the past efforts of open housing advocates, experience was simply lacking on how the need for low-income units should be determined, and how they could best be designed, built, and operated in the new and hostile setting that suburbia too often offered. The planning and development professions had not yet evolved the standards necessary for working with neighborhood and community aspirations. In the grand tradition of the common law, the details of the overarching plan awaited hammering out case by case.

In *AMG*, Judge Serpentelli accepted this challenge and laid down definitions that shaped Mount Laurel–type litigation. He compromised on the forecasts generated by different computer programs, probably recognizing that there was too much room for disagreement and that, while each model sported its own bells and whistles, the key equations were remarkably similar. He noted with a sure-handed assurance that the "pivotal question is not whether the numbers are too high or low, but whether the methodology that produces the number is reasonable."[29]

## From the Dictionary to the Field

With minor variations, Mount Laurel lawsuits fell into the following pattern. Either a builder or a public interest plaintiff sued a municipality on the ground that it improperly regulated land use—for example, by excluding housing types or prescribing excessive site improvement standards. Each type of plaintiff was likely to demand a different result. The usual remedy that public interest groups sought was to force a revision in the land-use regulation in order to make it realistically possible for households to move into the offending municipality in numbers adequate to fulfill the municipality's fair share obligation. When a builder brought the suit, the remedy typically sought was permission to build at higher densities without the burden of adhering to those features of the municipality's land-use regulations that could be proven unnecessary for the preservation of health and safety.

In either case, the trial judge had to identify the extent of the municipality's fair share obligation. First, the judge had to specify the precise number of low-income units whose construction the municipality, under the Mount Laurel Doctrine, had to make realistically possible. With this number in mind, the judge then examined the municipality's existing zoning ordinance to see how many low-income units could be built under its aegis, as presently drafted. Finally, when an ordinance failed to allow construction of enough units to bring the municipality into compliance with the doctrine, the judge could declare the municipality exclusionary. After successfully challenging an exclusionary land-use regulation, the complainant was entitled to the builder's remedy.

With real estate developers and public interest groups as plaintiffs, the Mount Laurel cases feature an unusual combination of energies. The rare coincidence of private- and public-sector interests testifies to the ingenuity of Mount Laurel II in harnessing the expertise and profit drive of the private sector—the developer—in order to achieve a public end. However, to the three judges that Chief Justice Wilentz appointed it became clearer, as lawsuits accumulated, that the builders were in there for their own profit, and that this was not an unalloyed good. Adam Smith (or perhaps Hobbes) was proven right again. Most builders were ready to make any kind of agreement with a municipality—even where the outcome fed the exclusionary quality of the zoning ordinance—as long as they obtained the zoning changes that would enhance their own profit. Developers and municipalities could easily share common interests that would not further the Mount Laurel objectives. The concern for hands-on supervision was thus amplified in the private-party litigation cases before the trial judges. "I had less uneasiness about the whole litigation process when a public interest group was the plaintiff, rather than a builder. Therefore I felt less of a need for the court appointed master in the public interest cases," explained one of the Mount Laurel judges.[30]

This judge's assessment ignores some of the benefits attached to having private developers for plaintiffs, however. Although public interest groups were surely focused on whether zoning ordinances created the opportunity for affordable housing, they were not always equipped to monitor the development process. In several cases with public interest plaintiffs, courts were called on to monitor the development process for as long as six years. Special master George Raymond, for example, was appointed in March 1980 by a superior court judge in a case litigated under Mount Laurel I; as of 1995, he was still reviewing and advising the court regarding various municipal proposals for completing a 698-unit obligation.

The trial judges fashioned their own interpretations of Chief Justice Wilentz's original proposal that the builder's remedy be awarded at the outset, with municipalities being given ninety days to revise their regulations. Both Judge Skillman and Judge Serpentelli strayed from this recommendation, awarding the remedy after the ninety-day revision period. This approach gave municipalities and builders both the time and the incentive to settle their differences. (Where the plaintiff was a public interest group, on the other hand, a finding of noncompliance immediately triggered the ninety-day revision period.)

In fixing the period for achieving compliance at a mere ninety days, the supreme court in Mount Laurel II set the stage for speedy action. The trial judges picked up on this fiat, reworking judicial customs to fashion and launch compliance measures as fast as possible. They recognized that delay in the application of remedies would shrink capital, increase interest costs, and frustrate builders, let alone delay low-income families' realization of their constitutional rights. The slight breathing space in the process—a door left ajar—encouraged negotiations, compromise, and perhaps even settlement.

In addition, the trial judges introduced their own procedural contribution to induce voluntary compliance. A municipality was likely to hesitate to rezone and take affirmative action unless a court order ratified the settlement in a judgment of compliance binding on third parties. As one court recognized, there "will often be numerous property owners in a municipality with land suitable for lower-income housing as well as various organizations which may pursue Mount Laurel litigation on behalf of lower-income persons." Following this observation, Judge Skillman analogized Mount Laurel litigation to a class action representative of, and binding on, all lower-income persons deprived of the asserted constitutional rights and strove to insulate the community from "litigious interference with the normal planning process."[31] Under his innovative rule, once a municipality demonstrated that its regulations complied with the Mount Laurel Doctrine, it was rewarded with immunity from further suits by nonparty lower-income persons and developers for six years—a so-called period of repose. It meant also that developers with separate Mount Laurel actions pending could not veto a proposed settlement between the municipality and other litigants by insisting on their right to the builder's remedy.

Mount Laurel II called for additional judicial interventions to ensure that municipalities would satisfy their constitutional obligations. The judges, for example, could declare zoning ordinances invalid in whole or in part or order municipalities to make changes in specific sections of their ordinances; in effect, the court could unilaterally rewrite a municipality's land-use regulations. Equally intrusive was the court's option to mandate the approval of development projects. And Mount Laurel judges had a further choice rare in ordinary institutional litigation: the power to order a delay in the construction of a non–Mount Laurel project, presumably one that a municipality was anxious to complete, pending the municipality's rewriting of its exclusionary ordinance and coming into compliance with Mount Laurel I and II.

The New Jersey Supreme Court intended the broad scope of these remedies, and the power they vested in outsiders, to induce mediation and compromise. A municipality that was out of compliance would recognize, Chief Justice Wilentz hoped, that the wiser course of action was to eliminate its exclusionary activities on its own, rather than have a stranger do so. For municipalities living under Mount Laurel II, the reasoning ran, fear of more drastic infringement on home rule in the future would drive "voluntary" compliance.

Naturally, remedy became the continuing focus in Mount Laurel cases. Once a court determined a fair share obligation, the municipality had to revise its land-use regulations so that the construction of low-income housing units sufficient to satisfy the obligation became realistically possible. To ensure that this would happen, the supreme court in Mount Laurel II suggested a three-step arrangement. First, the municipality would have to lift all zoning and land-use restrictions not necessary to protect public health and safety. Then, the municipality could select whatever devices it wished in order to satisfy its obligation. For example, the court suggested, a town could mandate that developers set aside a percentage of their units for low-income families, or it could subsidize lower-income housing or zone for mobile homes. Of course, the municipality was also welcome to suggest additional mechanisms, and if the court agreed, these would discharge the obligation.[32] The final step was approval.

As delimited by the chief justice, these guidelines, far-reaching as they are, revealed the need for continued judicial monitoring. Mount Laurel II suggested possible ways for a municipality to meet its obligation but shed no light on whether a particular device, in a given situation, would create a realistic opportunity for satisfying that obligation. Thus Judge Serpentelli used his powers as special trial judge in *Allan-Deane Corp. v. Township of Bedminster* to clarify the framework for what constituted a "realistic opportunity."[33] A not uncommon trial judge's reaction is found in the opening statement: "Another segment of Bleak House Revisited is before the court. This granddaddy of all Mount Laurel litigation—now a teenager, is here for a review. . . . It is time to write what I hope will be the final chapter in this saga."[34] He suggested three steps: verifying that a municipality's revised ordinances were free from all excessive restrictions not necessary to protect health and safety;[35] examining the sites selected or other mechanisms that the municipality planned to use to achieve compliance; and if the sites selected or mechanisms employed were "realistic," only then approving the compliance package.[36]

The detailed applications of these precepts to the ground were often excruciating. An example from the opinion reveals the complex interwoven analysis that becomes necessary:

> Site G consists of approximately 52 acres. . . . The court appointed master and the experts on behalf of the township and the Public Advocate all agreed that this site is likely to produce 90 lower income units. There is some difference of opinion as to when the units would be built. . . . Access and sewer availability [are] major constraints to the development of this site [as is] the fact that it is heavily wooded. . . . The access road would have to be expanded and utilities brought to the site. However, the principal constraint seems to be sewerage.
>
> Parcel G is not within the franchise area of EDC [the sewer authority] and therefore there would be some delay even if the franchise area is expanded. However, the township and EDC have executed a contract whereby EDC agrees to make application for expansion to include site G in its franchise area if AT & T enters into an agreement with EDC to pay a proportionate share of the expansion of the EDC plant. Testimony supported the proposition that once the Department of Environmental Protection approved the expansion of the EDC plant, the Board of Public Utilities could approve the petition to expand the franchise area within two months. With regard to road access, it is the township's position that because Hills will start constructing homes on site B as it completes site A, it will be necessary to provide access to site B through the very same road which will service site G.

After further discussion of other environmental issues that had to be resolved, the court concluded:

The court finds that site G is an appropriate parcel for inclusion in the compliance package. The agreement to expand the EDC franchise area and the treatment plant's capacity, the likely improvement of Schley Mountain Road in order to provide access to site B and thereby also access to site G, the proximity of the site to parcel B which is the next to be developed by Hills and its location within the area of intense housing demand all justify its incorporation in the package.[37]

Of course, much of the impact of selection of a particular site is not obvious at the outset; implementation involves the court in a detailed and ongoing examination of the municipality's subsequent actions in order to ascertain whether it is carrying out the terms of its compliance plan. Townships could not be allowed to rest on their laurels before bringing affordable housing to reality.

## The Three Mount Laurel Judges

Gibson, Serpentelli, and Skillman stayed in constant communication, especially at the initiation of their effort, in order to set uniform policies that would ensure consistency and continuity in the handling of exclusionary zoning cases throughout the state. Each judge nonetheless felt free to develop his own views of the proper role of a trial court under the mandate of the New Jersey Supreme Court's Mount Laurel II decision.

As a result of *AMG*, the judges were able to agree, with minor variations, on the major issues of quantifying *fair share* and defining terms such as *region*. Despite their consensus on the basic principles and scope, however, the judges revealed substantial variations in their individual approaches to the doctrine's implementation. The differences centered on three major areas: the effect of builder's-remedy-based litigation on municipalities; the pertinent ordinances at the time of rendering decisions; and the scope of the notice requirement.[38]

One aspect of the builder's remedy that Mount Laurel II did not fully discuss concerned whether trial courts should modulate its potentially overwhelming pressure. What often happened in the field was that, once a builder sued, other developers lurking in the wings, realizing that they had better jump onto the train lest it leave the station without them, launched their own lawsuits. Within days, the defendant municipality would find itself trapped in a welter of litigation, overpowered by the onslaught.

Faced with the confusion of multiple suits, Judge Serpentelli came up with one solution. In recognition of the contribution of the first plaintiff, yet in the hope of preserving home rule as far as possible, he ruled that if a municipality quickly settled with the initial plaintiff, it would receive immunity from all further suits. Serpentelli's approach had the double advantage of granting the inaugurating builder a reward while leaving some measure of control with the municipality, though the course of action possibly diluted the municipality's Mount Laurel obligation.[39]

Judge Skillman chose not to use Serpentelli's procedure, which he believed represented too great a judicial intervention. As a result, municipalities in his region did not have the same incentive to make deals with the plaintiffs that first sued them. Rather, they were left with the usual litigation tactic of coming up with plans to eliminate exclusionary regulations as quickly as possible, while hoping that in the interim they could fashion arguments to fend off other plaintiffs who might enter the feeding frenzy.[40]

The trial judges also differed in their interpretations of the standards governing entitlement to the builder's remedy. To obtain the remedy, Mount Laurel II intoned, a builder had to overcome three hurdles: succeed in litigation, promise to build a project that contained a substantial number of low-income housing units, and possess a site suitable from legitimate planning and environmental perspectives.

Regarding the first of these, in what could be termed a quantum-of-energy standard, Judge Skillman held in *Morris County Fair Housing Council v. Township of Boonton* that a builder succeeded in litigation by playing "a substantial part in bringing about the rezoning."[41] Judge Serpentelli, on the other hand, adopted a simpler rule for his courtroom; a builder was considered to have succeeded in litigation as long as the suit was filed prior to the point the court declared the municipality's ordinance to be exclusionary. Sound policy, he claimed, dictated that the remedy not be recognized for a builder who came in after such a declaration, when the rezoning process had begun, even if the builder later played a substantial role. After all, the primary reason for the remedy was the incentive it provided to institute suit against an exclusionary regulation, and this was achieved by the first shot. For Judge Serpentelli, there was a limit to the number of plaintiffs needed to vindicate the constitutional obligation, and he was happy to invoke a straightforward standard that enabled the builder (and the attorney) to gauge with relative certainty the chances of being awarded a remedy.[42] Nevertheless, he recognized that there "is a fine balance to be struck between this court's desire to preserve municipal planning flexibility and at the same time to encourage more than one plaintiff to bring suit so that compliance will be attained and housing will be built."[43]

A related issue on which the three trial judges disagreed was determining the ordinance at the time of decision. Judge Serpentelli, seeking to bolster incentives in the private sector, held that a builder was entitled to the remedy merely by bringing about a decision invalidating an exclusionary ordinance; in other words, he looked to the ordinance in effect at the time the builder filed its complaint. In *Van Dalen v. Township of Washington*, however, Judge Skillman looked further down the line and singled out as determinative the ordinance existing at the time of decision.[44] According to him, by coming up with a plan to provide low- and moderate-income housing prior to the judge's decision, a municipality could defeat a builder by precluding a demonstration that the suit was responsible for the invalidation; this result would follow since the ordinance approved would be the one in effect at the time of decision.

Essentially, Judge Skillman was arguing, compliance was the bottom line the court sought, so it did not matter if a particular builder lost in the process. Judge Serpentelli, on the other hand, argued that the court had a duty to preserve incentives for plaintiffs to bring actions. Before Judge Serpentelli, a plaintiff builder would know that a defendant municipality's repentance would not prevent receiving its just reward. Judge Skillman, however, left potential plaintiffs in a more ambiguous position and went from case to case granting the remedy appropriate to the facts of the particular situation; on the whole, his judgments turned out to be more favorable toward the defendant-municipality.

A final issue on which the Mount Laurel judges differed had to do with the notice requirement, whether in a compliance hearing or a settlement. Following regular procedural requirements to the letter, Judge Skillman required notification of the public advocate (a special position under New Jersey law intended to promote the public interest) and every other imaginable party in the proceeding. Judge Serpentelli, meanwhile, expressed more confidence in the process itself, arguing that in view of the time and attention expended by the court (with the help of the special master), there was no need to bring in other parties to tell the court their version of the facts or conclusions of law.

Judgments differ as to the correct approach toward notice. Courts must strike a delicate balance between the danger of too many parties clogging the proceedings and the need to have enough of them present to ensure accuracy of results and that all interests are represented. Judge Skillman may have been prompted by more than the traditional judicial doctrine of notice to the world. Perhaps in his view, extra notice would provide a safeguard to the public interest because, in Mount Laurel–type situations, while builders purported to represent the interests of the poor, their own financial ends naturally were dominant.

Other planning and political considerations also came into play. For example, when is a site suitable for low- or moderate-income housing?[45] In answering this question, the trial judges addressed two crucial yet contradictory concerns of the New Jersey Supreme Court in Mount Laurel II: the need to eliminate regulations, over and above those protecting health and safety, that generate unnecessary housing costs, and the desire to keep environmental and comprehensive planning goals intact. Through the continued efforts of the three judges, standard criteria emerged that provided starting points for reasoning, left room for divergences of opinion, and promoted negotiations on matters about which, in the end, parties could only agree to disagree. (*Township of Franklin*, for instance, developed a suitability guideline that focused on regional accessibility, proximity to goods and services, availability of water and sewer utilities, environmental suitability, and land-use compatibility.)[46] The human element entered here with a vengeance: while a site might be physically and locationally suitable, an unwilling seller who said, as one Mount Laurel trial judge transmitted it, "I'm not going to sell it for the life of me, just no amount of money is going to do it," would push that parcel over into the unsatisfactory category.

Commentators were alarmed that the Mount Laurel Doctrine would cast the courts adrift in a purgatory of statistical warfare. And the litigation experience that immediately followed Mount Laurel I bore out this fear: questions that had plagued the planning profession for decades (such as how to define a region), together with the quantitative puzzles of macroeconomic forecasting (such as how to establish the present and prospective regional housing need) produced an avalanche of experts, trends, and syntactical formulas that threatened to overwhelm the trial judges. Authors of law review articles were right to argue that statistical warfare and semantic battles over the remedies for exclusionary zoning could go on forever.

But contrary to all these dire predictions, the combination of designated specialized judges, expert testimony, and the application of traditional legal disciplines—plus the overall will to achieve affirmative, workable results—in fact resulted in generally accepted solutions, although occasional ripples broke through the surface of unanimity. If the three judges that Chief Justice Wilentz chose did not discharge the massive judicial task of definition to the full satisfaction of every theoretician, their work was more than sufficient for settling disputes and providing guidelines for municipalities and developers. In any serious effort to achieve a fair distribution of housing needs over a metropolitan area, intellectual puzzles arise and demand solutions; professional expertise, a broad philosophical outlook, and experience on the ground are necessary yet never sufficient for the task. Like many social predicaments, the problem of housing remains incapable of total resolution, involving, as it does, a choice among competing values. Still, in the main, and in a remarkably short period of time, the judges' definitional work matured the law providing land for affordable housing.

In furnishing workable answers to the technical questions that arose in the wake of the Mount Laurel opinions, the three judges prevented the doctrine from remaining an incorporeal dream that historians of a later generation would criticize as the product of an overzealous supreme court insufficiently versed in the realities of real estate and local government or as an instance where the trial system had been burdened with an essentially legislative-administrative task that it could not discharge. From the *AMG* opinion forward, that court's consensus, never appealed, was the guide adopted by the parties in the various Mount Laurel suits throughout the state. That the consensus originated from so diverse a group of planners and experts, representing contending interest groups, blessed with the trial court's stamp of approval, created a lingua franca for the parties. It put to the proof the state of the art of the planning profession. "It was litigated along the edges a little bit," remembers one of the original three judges, "and I disagreed with it in some details, but it at least set a framework and was accepted in its totality for the most part."

Indeed, when the state legislature later created an agency to handle Mount Laurel cases, it codified much of the trial courts' work in setting its standards to remedy the wrong of local exclusionary zoning laws. Although the legislature introduced modifications—presumably in order to slow the courts' initial pace of reform to a course more agreeable to politically powerful interest groups—the legislative and executive branches essentially adopted and extended what the three trial judges had made of Mount Laurel II.[47]

The trial courts sought both to avoid subjectivity and to eschew excessive mathematical extrapolations. Their accomplishment should be seen in context. Their rough-and-ready approach was not atypical of how judges solve problems dependent on conclusions by experts and scientists in other disciplines. When facing difficult technical issues, whether ascertaining housing fair share, disposing of sludge in a water pollution case, or changing prison administration through decentralization, the legal system is able to accommodate professional information and expert speculations—even when these conflict, as is so often the case. The myriad phantoms conjured up in law professors' fertile minds, and the unanswerable alternatives they are skilled at posing, do not change the fact that, once a course is selected, the system can and does move beyond the scholastic struggle. In institutional reform, the chosen methodology must be a fair, but not necessarily a perfect, exemplar. Credibility, not absolute accuracy, is the target. The work of elaboration and adjustment can proceed pragmatically and sequentially from the selected starting point convention.[48]

# V

## Of Special Masters and the Front Line

IF THE three trial judges introduced by Mount Laurel II were the one-star generals in Chief Justice Wilentz's army, then the special masters were the infantrymen, equal parts judicial officers, facilitators, mediators, and fact finders. One of the novel powers that the New Jersey Supreme Court conferred on the troika of trial judges was broad discretion in the appointment of experts. They could be used to assist in identifying a municipality's fair share obligation, or in determining the adequacy of revised ordinances under the doctrine, or in monitoring remedies, or wherever the trial judge thought they could be useful. Originally conceived as cogs in a procedural machine designed to speed matters along, the special masters ultimately had a significant effect on substantive outcomes, altered the nature of judicial proceedings, and as they pioneered and explored, lent to trial decisions the weight of professional expertise and legitimation.

### A Special Relationship

In many ways, Mount Laurel was unique in the relationship it created between judge and special master.[1] To begin with, the Mount Laurel experience did not parallel that of ordinary institutional restructuring litigations: a more or less centralized affair in which there is one case, one set of lawyers, one judge, and one master. Instead, a Mount Laurel restructuring was a decentralized proposition consisting of a series of cases, hundreds of them, scattered around New Jersey, with different plaintiffs and municipalities and requested remedies varying from a few to thousands of units of moderate- and low-income housing. As a consequence, there surfaced a corps of Mount Laurel masters and experts who could parachute into communities and quickly mobilize information, analysis, and consensus.

A whole series of special masters operated in rotation under the orchestration of the Mount Laurel judges. Slowly, a Mount Laurel bar and group of experts familiar with the issues emerged. In much the same way the New York bankruptcy field collapses into a small circle of specialist insiders familiar with each other's capabilities, individuals working as much for the respect and future recommendations of their peers as for the temporary client, the Mount Laurel arena was blessed with the unifying presence of the same judges, special masters, law firms, and planning experts.

The New Jersey courts' extensive delegation to masters contrasted with the diametrically opposite attitude exemplified by federal district court judges confident that by themselves they can supply any special expertise required in institutional breakdown cases in the same fashion as in ordinary trials involving expert witnesses. On their own, such judges believe, they can sift through the diverging theories of conflicting experts and perceive what is solid, what is questionable, and how to cross-examine the expert in order to arrive at their own determinations. The reasoning goes, "My expertise is the same expertise that I have if I have to rule whether somebody's competent to stand trial. I'm not a psychiatrist either, but my business is the same: to listen to people try to educate an audience as to some unknown issues."

Rather than playing the narrow role of fact-finding time-savers for the judges,[2] the Mount Laurel masters acted as both political consensus builders and as specialists trained in the accepted scientific and professional principles of regional land-use planning. Indeed, the special masters assumed roles almost equal in prominence to those of the trial judges. Planning expertise was necessary for making many factual determinations surrounding the evaluation of whether a municipality had met its fair share requirements, as well as for properly applying the law to the facts.

As the court-appointed expert hired by and responsible to the judge, the master was a rod on which the court could lean when it came to arcane matters beyond the usual legal ken. Perhaps more subtly, the practical application of the builder's remedy—the process of spelling out what a builder was allowed to construct—made the master indispensable. Professional astuteness went into determining whether a proposed project and site were suitable from planning and environmental perspectives and then, in the light of these findings, whether a builder's remedy should result. Such decisions obviously called for a level of expertise that judges, trained as lawyers, do not possess.

The role of the master remained crucial after a trial court awarded the builder's remedy. The postdecree activity that Chief Justice Wilentz prescribed for Mount Laurel cases was unprecedented, calling for—indeed, demanding—professional skills of the subtlest sort. Moreover, as the doctrine evolved, Mount Laurel cases increasingly involved alternative dispute resolution rather than direct confrontation and adjudication. The trial courts assigned to special masters the task of threading together settlement efforts, providing a forum in which the parties could argue, negotiate, and reach conclusions. Throughout the proceedings, the special master worked closely with the local legislative body, the planning board, and the complaining parties in order to clear away obstructions in the path to agreement. For bringing about settlements, the master proved indispensable.

As it turned out, one of the more delicate jobs assigned to masters in Mount Laurel cases was assisting municipalities in amending their land-use regulations during the ninety-day revision period. This task required both professional and political skills. It also drew on the expertise to suggest better ways to accommodate fair share that were perhaps new to the town's professionals. In one case, for example, the developer and township came up with a proposal under which their obligation of two hundred low- and moderate-income units would be constructed not on the disputed site but on another parcel owned by the municipality—one in the middle of the neighborhood that was both the poorest and possessed the highest minority population. The master was able to restructure the proposal: the established neighborhood accepted the units in return for a guarantee of water and sewer utilities (it had been operating off individual wells and septic tanks) and was encouraged to create a redevelopment area of one hundred acres, in which it would intersperse affordable housing units with market-priced units. This was an option that had not been considered by the town. "There's nothing in COAH [the Council on Affordable Housing]'s regulations or in any court decision that says, 'Thou shalt not put 200 units of affordable housing in one place or adjacent to a poor neighborhood,' but it seems to me," the master explained, "that when court masters are serving well, they're bringing some of their own judgment about what public policy decisions are consistent with the whole Mount Laurel Doctrine."

After facilitating negotiations and working on revisions, masters were called on to testify that, in their opinion, the revised regulations complied with the requirements of the Mount Laurel Doctrine. At this phase, the supreme court prescribed that all parties in a case be given the opportunity to cross-examine the master. After the master delivered the findings and endured cross-examination, the judge would hand down the decision. Because the master's authority runs in a direct fiduciary line to the judge, the commonly accepted notion was that the court would pay full attention to its staff expert and ratify all recommendations as its own. The trial court was free to disagree with positions that its master took, but in the ordinary course of events, the master's conclusions carried a great deal of weight.[3] Even so, though the professional masters proved themselves indispensable during the different phases of the typical exclusionary zoning case, the court always retained the fundamental responsibility (and power) for ensuring that constitutionally required standards were observed. This was the basis of the relationship: while the masters deployed negotiation—that newcomer to the legal system—to arrive at consensus, they were especially effective against the backdrop of hovering judicial presence and the impending force of equitable decrees should an agreement not be forged.

The parties' awareness of the judge's reliance on the master greatly enhanced the master's power, especially during the ninety-day revision period. One planner recalled his pleasant surprise the first time he acted as a Mount Laurel master. "To my astonishment," he reminisced, "all the lawyers and officials stood up and most politely waited for me to begin." Given the master's access to the judge, lawyers and local planners were well advised to get along as best they could with the judge's designee, whether by casting their arguments in a persuasive manner or by accommodating their claims to the master's sense of what was appropriate in the case. As one master put it, "I don't have the final say, obviously. But the municipalities know what I will recommend to the court, and if they are really serious about the problem, then they will stand by it. But if they know they are making life difficult for the developer because of political pressures, then they know I will recommend what I said was the right thing, and they back off." The dominant role of the master both diminished and enhanced the role of the judges in the course of litigation, waxing and waning in proportion to the judge's expertise and readiness to assert dominion.[4]

As one special master acknowledged, "There are things the man in the black robe can accomplish that I can't; I've seen parties change positions in front of a judge where I've been trying everything to coax them and beat them into changing—it just doesn't happen until they're in front of a judge." In Mount Laurel trials, the interaction became symbiotic, the judge's reliance lending authority to the master and the master's expertise enabling the judge to rule on the merits. "From the start," stated another special master, "all the judges were very supportive of the people they appointed," which, adds yet another special master, "of course made us all that much more effective."

Exogenous—and, on the surface, irrelevant—factors tempered this arrangement. Distance, for example, worked to the masters' advantage. While the judges were sitting in the courtroom, in some instances over a hundred miles from the involved municipalities, the masters were present among the parties. There evolved an acceptance of them as people willing to be on call, ready to come and sit down with the zoning boards or the governing bodies, available to talk on the phone to the local planners, engineers, and concerned citizens. They were there every day to deal with the issues, to smooth ruffled feathers, to pursue negotiations for settlement. Localities grew accustomed to their presence. Such visibility, carrying with it so many chances to demonstrate their abilities, earned masters a substantial role in the final outcome.

Because special masters frequently dealt with the parties independently of the judges, their roles needed to be clearly delineated. Masters could be humble facilitators of a revised zoning ordinance or lofty reformulators of the parties' goals and values. The direction the Mount Laurel trial judges gave the masters, as one of them described it, "was to come up with the fairest, the best, the most intellectually sound decision you could come up with"—a mandate not exactly ringing with precision.

## Neutrality in Approach

Because the judicial cards were stacked against overturning the special master's findings and conclusions, this relatively new role raised a slew of concerns over issues ranging from the masters' often highly informal methods to their sometimes improper usurpation of judicial authority by crusading activist-minded masters.[5] Especially amorphous was the boundary between the jobs of the judge and of the master. The influence of the master derived almost solely and totally from the special relationship to the judge, and the judges moved to discourage the belief among lawyers that the master had become a surrogate judge. This could prove ticklish. As Judge Serpentelli put it, he "was fearful about the notion of using just one person," so he rotated the masters he used in his cases in order to avoid being locked in by any single approach. All three original Mount Laurel judges put the masters under clear instructions that they should never offer an opinion or make a comment that would convey the impression that it was attributable to a judge.

Of course, the master's outlook and stance could be deliberately molded by the judge—in the selection process, in the original charge, and in the response to events during the master's tenure. In this sense, at least, the judge had the final say. Yet after the early trials set initial standards and boundaries, nearly all Mount Laurel cases were resolved through negotiation and mediation. And whereas the judges, on the whole, preferred to stay aloof from the detailed give-and-take until the settlement was ready for signing, the masters took to the alternative dispute resolution process with gusto. "The masters were attending the public sessions," one judge reported; "they had a feel for what the public was screaming about, they had a feel for which lawyers were able to control which clients, all the kinds of things that I wouldn't know."

Most judges agree that, were masters not allowed to exercise informal powers, the unfortunate result would have been a paucity of innovative solutions. Yet there was a grave danger of a master coercing a party to agree to a remedy that the party felt was unwarranted. Moreover, because the process was informal it was almost impossible to prove bias or improper conduct. In this new game, parties tended to be more fearful of a master than of a judge.[6] The legal profession is predisposed to be more comfortable with the system it knows, an arrangement with a judge always at the head of the table. Procedural safeguards of judicial decision making provide a number of opportunities for lawyers to have direct input and to control the way the process works; with a master in charge, the enterprise was more amorphous and paradoxically more closed. In the end, close oversight of the master's activities by the judge, parties, and lawyers, on a case-by-case basis, was deemed the best way to prevent abuses of discretion without at the same time tying the master's hands too tightly.

At times the masters walked a thin line between shepherding a municipality along and persuading it to do what was necessary for compliance. "I thought as a group they handled this reasonably well," reported one acute observer, and a local official noted of one master that "he comes on as a voice of reason." A trial judge summed up: "The feedback I've gotten from lawyers on both sides is that the process was conducted fairly and no one felt they were being unfairly pressured." He went on: "Lawyers are not shy about sharing their views with a judge. They're not timid about disagreeing if they think disagreement is in order, and my experience tells me that the process must have been working reasonably well, or I would have had a lot more grief communicated to me than I did."

By and large, the masters were adept at avoiding traps that might otherwise limit their effectiveness. On the one hand, each acted informally as mediator, adviser, facilitator, and politician—usually requiring the acquiescence of the parties.[7] On the other hand, each acted in a formal capacity as fact finder, arbitrator, and enforcer of remedies—in this capacity imposing judgments on the parties regardless of consent. It was important for the court that its master know how to shift back and forth between the judicial and nonjudicial roles. Recognizing the predicament inherent in achieving and maintaining such ambiguity, the Mount Laurel masters sought to set outside bounds to their exercise of discretion.[8] They organized informally into the Society of Court Appointed Masters (SCAM), which set standards for their operations. Individual masters, however, still displayed considerable independent thought and conduct.

Since the master's task was to facilitate the production of affordable housing as quickly and efficiently as possible, it should hardly be a surprise that, almost always, the master appeared to side with the developer—the purveyor of low- and moderate-income housing—claiming that a zoning ordinance unreasonably impeded a project. The perception of failure to be evenhanded persisted. One master described the situation: "I have had one or two occasions to side with the municipality when the developer departed from the approved plans without permissions. Given its sovereign powers, however, it should be clear that the municipality needs no help in defending itself against a developer."

Yet another concern about the impartiality of Mount Laurel masters is that they are all drawn from the same tight circle of planning experts. In interviews, several lawyers, conceding possible professional bias, suggested that the Mount Laurel masters were not so much strong-minded individuals "calling it like it is" as professionals who, knowing the judges' objectives, provided them with the appropriate evidence. Like lawyers, city planners are mouthpieces for clients; like expert witnesses, they are available for hire outside, as well as inside, the courtroom. A master appointed by the court in one exclusionary zoning trial can, in another case—on the very next day—be hired to advise a plaintiff builder or a defendant municipality.[9] (For a time, only one of the seven professional planners commonly appointed as Mount Laurel masters voluntarily chose to confine his job to representing the court alone, withdrawing from work on behalf of other clients.) Given that the same individual might represent a municipality in one case and a builder in the next, the background of masters raised a significant query: did these experts gain continuous employment as Mount Laurel masters because they were truly proficient in the planning area, or because they were able to deal on an individual and political level with the numerous contending parties and interests at stake in the various suits, or because they held views on suburban affordable housing sympathetic to the New Jersey Supreme Court's?

In the end, success with the Mount Laurel special masters is attributable to the care taken in their selection. The original three trial judges sifted painstakingly through the roster of planning professionals because they knew how much would depend on the quality of their work. Although parties are normally given the opportunity to have input in the selection of a master in institutional restructuring cases, courts frequently reject the nominees put forward; this illustrates the paramount importance they place on trust between judge and master in these delicate and publicity-driven cases.[10] Judges are, after all, delegating a portion of the sovereignty that inheres in the dignity of their office, with all the powers it draws from statute, history, and tradition.

"The planner-master facilitated the negotiation process," one trial judge concluded, "by being an objective third person, simply trying to do the right thing without any axe to grind and that was of great assistance to me." And it may be that professional city planners are well cast in this quasi-judicial role. In their normal practice in the land-use area, they discharge functions that approach what is normally regarded as the practice of law: planners are known routinely to draft zoning laws, seeing the work through all stages, from the surveys in the field to the writing of legal text. They advise municipalities on the latest zoning technologies—and on their reception in respective state courts. The courts' extensive use of masters was in many ways the functional equivalent of the political order's customary use of the professional city planner.

The specialist masters of Mount Laurel II proved to be a breed different from the masters so disfavored by the bar. Prior to 1947, New Jersey practice had featured an extensive use of masters—who were at the same time highly unpopular. Masters were generally perceived as political appointees, as deadwood. Eventually, the New Jersey Constitution of 1947 abolished their use. Revival of the use of experts as high-minded professionals who negotiate, mediate, and report to the court—and on whose extensive supervision the trial judges rely—provides a model for effective management of future institutional restructurings involving complex interdisciplinary understandings.

Rule 53 of the Federal Rules of Civil Procedure approves of the appointment of special masters only in exceptional cases.[11] Presumably, this restriction is meant to preserve the tradition of an impartial judiciary that carries full responsibility for its actions. It may also reflect an underlying fear that the sudden ascent to the stratosphere of judicial power may go to a master's head, or a concern that the master may be less aware than the judge of the need for neutrality and evenhandedness. Perhaps inadvertently, a novice may act unfairly by abusing the broad and flexible equitable powers attached to the position. It remains a constant that the desire for workable solutions must be balanced against the need to uphold procedural fairness. Ironically, suspicion is especially pronounced when the master is a specialist, for experts do not live long in their subjects without forming conclusions that are hard to dislodge.

## Selection of the Master: Generalist or Specialist?

Beyond question, the typical Mount Laurel case did not feature the standard adjudication model of a trial judge alone before parties' counsel. In a sense, the three original Mount Laurel judges found themselves with a staff, albeit a temporary one and hardly the full Weberian bureaucracy: the master appointed in each given case. The importance of the special masters raises several questions. In the larger environment of institutional litigation, what type of person is best qualified for discharging the task? Should the master be a generalist or a specialist? What skills deserve prominence in the selection process?

The appointment of a special master in a complex public lawsuit serves, at a minimum, to free an already overburdened judge from the time-consuming duties of investigation and fact-finding. But the specialized experts can also serve the court in another way: they provide the relevant community with an overseer well suited to manage, monitor, and supervise institutional reform. Consequently, the masters appointed in the Mount Laurel suits had a diverse set of roles to play—roles more intense than those of the ordinary court appointee. In the Mount Laurel cases, the selected master almost always was a professional specializing in land-use planning cases and was appointed primarily for expert knowledge. Taking into consideration the master's broad range of duties (which often culminated in project supervision), the slightly incestuous nature of those duties (which made it possible to serve clients on opposing sides on different occasions), and the complex and evolving political realities of the master's task, job specifications could not be too rigid. Mount Laurel II provided not just a legal framework for the three original trial judges but the equivalent of a master's order of reference. Having received their general mandate from the supreme court opinion, the trial judges could lay down more detailed terms of reference and then appoint specialized experts as masters to handle specific tasks related to their planning expertise.

On the surface, the task of masters in New Jersey, looked at cumulatively, was overwhelming. Masters first had to provide the court with an informed perspective on the exclusionary challenge to the ordinance, identify the needed improvements to the local zoning ordinance, approve the suitability of the plaintiff's site, and set forth an appropriate remedy.

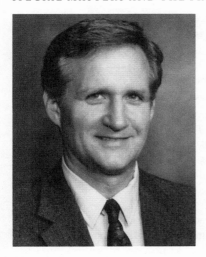

Next, they had to semiswitch positions and assist the municipality, guiding and evaluating ordinance revisions. Then they had to move over to testify that the revised regulation complied with the Mount Laurel Doctrine. Finally, more often than not, they wound up monitoring projects through construction. Many court-approved compliance plans required periodic progress reports. Special masters reviewed them to advise the court if additional enforcement action was required. In addition, amendments to fair share plans triggered review by the master to ensure maintenance of the realistic opportunity created by the original plan. Masters might also be called on to mediate postjudgment disputes arising in the implementation of housing elements and fair share plans.[12] Work continued long after trials ended.

Nor did the job stop with formalities. Once a development was under way, one master reported, "I received frequent calls, not to arbitrate, but to see if the locality's objection was a legitimate one." This meant applying the lens of professional judgment. It also meant informal (and primarily unreviewable) fact-finding, as well as negotiations and political compromises. "I have acted as monitor in such cases over years involving a change of plans," recounted another special master, "sometimes because approved projects were sold to new developers who felt the need to modify the plan to accommodate their preferred product." At other times, he maintained, the intermittent supervision was occasioned "by the performance of the municipality with regard to its commitments—such as filing and pursuing an application to the state for approval of a sewage treatment plant without which the Mount Laurel project could not be built [or] resolving a dispute as to whether the developer should accommodate a state highway realignment through the development site which was proposed by the local planning board in its master plan in the absence of any state or local commitment to the acquisition of the land and construction of the road." Each such difference of opinion, fueled by political pressures from all sides, could be used by an unfriendly municipality to prolong the processing of an application or the progress of a project already under way. As another special master observed, "As for the developer who sued and is thus responsible for having upset the ordinance in the first place, almost by definition it can be assumed that he will not be treated with kid gloves, especially since *he* chose the site rather than the municipality and is likely to be surrounded by irate residents who may have wasted a lot of money in legal fees in pursuing the case against him."

Whatever the background, whether generalist or specialist, a master above all had to be a finely tuned political animal. Dangers abound in pushing an agenda too far ahead of public opinion. Institutional litigation affects the vital nerve center of communities. In many instances, conflict between a New Jersey municipality and a developer was steady before, during, and after a purportedly final judicial decision. Masters who could gain the support of the body politic in acknowledging and implementing the Mount Laurel Doctrine were indispensable; political savvy—"a practical flexibility in shaping its remedies and . . . a facility for adjusting and reconciling public and private needs," in the more formal description of the U.S. Supreme Court—is essential to manage the various interests that make up a community and to ensure that each group is heard, involved, and, to some degree, pacified.[13]

Following this pattern, part of the ordinance revision process concentrated on soliciting initiatives from the locality. "I always make sure to tell them that I am not here to do the plan for their town. Or tell them what to do. I just want them to . . . tell me," one special master elaborated, "how they're going to do it." The master provided the disgruntled with an ear and an outlet for concerns, especially important with so intensely emotional an issue as land-use regulatory ordinances affecting the character of the community. Astuteness and political antennas were in order in dealing with the many parties involved directly in the litigation, as well as with the outside pressure groups.

Interestingly, several of the masters regarded themselves strictly as technicians charged with a demanding professional job: revising an exclusionary ordinance to conform to the chief's opinion. In particular, these masters did not see themselves as engaged in a campaign to win over public opinion. Other masters, however, took a different view. "While I did not seek them out," one explained, "I held myself in readiness to respond to the media and to questions by the public." Still others regarded themselves as settlers of disputes—with whatever consequences that brought along.[14]

Between the Scylla of the law and the Charybdis of municipal acceptance, the master must determine how to coexist with local groups. After all, part of Mount Laurel's ambitious agenda was to change attitudes and generate social learning about values. Neighborhood associations could be vital sources of information and, later, of support for the outcome of litigation. Yet most masters tended to keep a professional distance from public interest groups. One described himself as "completely aloof." This stance of isolation extended to interviews with local newspapers, which were used more extensively by the forces opposed to the Mount Laurel Doctrine than by the judges, masters, and others charged with its implementation.

The role of the trial courts shifted over time as they gained experience in dealing with exclusionary stratagems. Making a choice between the specialist and the generalist master depended on personalities and circumstances. By definition and by profession, trial judges in institutional litigations start out as generalists, for that is the role assigned to them in the political order. In the cases that followed Mount Laurel II, however, the three designated judges took on what can best be described as roles not too different from those of special masters. The supreme court opinion sought to control case management in considerable detail. Accordingly, the judges adopted a hands-on approach, working through conferences in chambers, staying in close touch with the parties via telephone and through the shuttle diplomacy of their appointed masters, moving constantly toward settlements. As case administrators, they were effective in an area that required detailed and specific knowledge; as judges, they were able to call on prominent experts and oversee or force agreement on plans and formulas. These became binding legal-planning first principles. Also, by dint of handling streams of exclusionary zoning cases, they developed their own considerable skills in the area of land use. Familiarity bred expertise, and they learned not only to ask the right questions of contending experts but also to gauge the usefulness and limitations of professional testimony. And the necessarily generalist outlook of a judge, no matter how sophisticated, could always be supplemented by the professional perspective of a specialist master.

## Ex Parte or Not?

As judge and master cut through institutional structures to the heart of experience, the personal bond between them assumes undeniable significance. Both find themselves dealing with unpopular causes, likely to

become embroiled in legal and political controversy. How can the judge
and the master achieve a firm understanding that survives as time goes by
and as modern and unforeseen pressures erupt?

In certain institutional litigation cases, there is a continuous stream of
communication—almost on a daily basis—with the master informing the
judge of events and the court making clear its receptivity to proffered
compromises and solutions. Yet footnote 40 of the Mount Laurel II opinion expressly ruled out ex parte communications between masters and
judges.[15] Some of the trial judges adhered strictly to this admonition—
although they now concede that there may have been occasional conversations with masters about their general impressions of a case. Many
judges, however, were ready to talk frequently with their appointees.
"One judge," a master recalled, "didn't expect me to call up after every
meeting," but that was precisely what another judge requested. "That
the court could have no contact with the master without involving the
parties," one trial judge asserts, "was absolutely impossible and absurd,
and frequently when talking about the potential for settlement and bringing the parties together I had to be able to go to the master and in fact did,
as I've told the chief justice."

The Mount Laurel model bears a greater resemblance to conflict resolution than to traditional adjudication. The mediation necessary to resolve the issues in most Mount Laurel cases could not work in open court;
it depended on confidential exchanges of views, the ability to reveal aces
in the hole in private. "You have to allow people to advance notions and
give them the opportunity to withdraw them without prejudice later on,"
remarked an experienced special master, adding, "In all the cases that I've
dealt with, the parties have agreed that the master has leave to contact any
one of them independently to discuss anything that the master thinks is
appropriate." The reformulation of local municipal plans to erase the
stigma of exclusionary zoning required extensive bargaining between
localities and developers or public interest groups: private probing to
discover what each side was willing to concede, no matter the public
protestations, was essential. Moreover, as in the typical labor negotiation, the carving out of decrees in institutional litigation should not always occur in the open lest each party assume postures and take positions
that become uncompromisable. If ex parte communication is disallowed,
all the parties are more vulnerable to disconcerting surprises at the end
of the road. A judge's last-minute rejection of a carefully hammered-out
deal could sharply discount the master's power of persuasiveness in the
parties' eyes.

Throughout negotiations, the master needed to be in close touch with
the judge. Informal methods (in conjunction with formal evidence-
gathering techniques) enabled masters to aid the judges carry out their

fact-finding, mediating, and monitoring functions.[16] Information had to travel back to the judge. One Mount Laurel judge insisted, "I never felt that discussions with the master gave me any knowledge which if I didn't share it with the lawyers would be unfair." While this statement is obviously redolent of self-interest, it nonetheless reveals the kind of confidence that was felt to exist between judge and master.

Negotiation as a means to settlement calls for ex parte involvement not only with masters but with the lawyers. One Mount Laurel judge was well known to run far beyond scheduled time because he held separate and lengthy meetings with each party in isolation. In his courtroom, individual, one-sided discussions became so common that he rarely requested the parties' consent; in any case, what lawyer would be so assertive as to refuse such a call from the presiding judge?

Over a three-year period, the novel administrative structure that Chief Justice Wilentz had designed gradually matured. It grew through the initial experimentation, the breaking in of the three trial judges, and the dissemination of the rules of the process among municipalities, developers, and the bar. Overall, given the extraordinary sensitivity of the issue, the danger was that Mount Laurel II would prove too complex to provide the much hoped for final word in land-use reform. For the ordinary judge receiving the package, the machine could be too difficult to assemble, with an instruction manual far too diffuse to follow. Apart from the intricacies of its definitions and its remedies, Mount Laurel II, rife with ambiguities, confronted trial courts with perilous involvement in sensitive local decision making. That the three Mount Laurel judges had the grit to follow the map sketched out by the opinion and to iron out the difficulties of unanticipated consequences is a tribute to their ingenuity and determination.

Chief Justice Wilentz could not have fully foreseen the extent of the trial court commitment required to fulfill the Mount Laurel Doctrine. For it was in the context of cases and controversies that the general principles of Mount Laurel II came to life. Only then did the parameters of possible action by both sides to a dispute over affordable housing become understandable to all. Permutations of local exclusionary devices were ascertained, as was the range of effective compliance mechanisms. The roles of the masters—with varying shadings depending on the type of litigation and the form of the regulatory restriction—became clarified; judges and special masters discovered how to work with each other and to tap and coordinate the expertise of different professions. Lawyers also participated in the learning process.

Over and above any particular methodology or technique, the three original Mount Laurel judges were devoted and committed to the social issue at stake. They were prepared to learn. They worked hard to grasp the primary concepts—legal, planning, political, and social—because they were advancing goals in which they believed, goals set forth in the two monumental New Jersey Supreme Court opinions. And they could look to the professional masters for guidance. As the judges presided over the cases brought before them, read the reports of the masters, listened to examinations and cross-examinations, they became more adept at understanding and appraising city planning principles and real estate marketing demands, as well as the objectives of comprehensive land-use planning.

The intertwined roles of trial judge and special master became crucial after the New Jersey Supreme Court made firm its position and fashioned the necessary administrative mechanism for implementing its legal ideal of equal access to housing. Putting this proposition—which slices so close to the nerve center of society—into the world of real estate and land development made for complex interactions (among judges, masters, lawyers, planners, officials, politicians, media). All in all, the pathbreaking system for dealing with institutional breakdown was working—too well, as far as some of the constituencies were concerned. Deep emotional shocks and reactions, culminating in the Fair Housing Act of 1985, were to sweep through the judicial efforts to end the constitutional violations committed by municipalities in their building of regulatory barriers around exclusionary bastions.

# Part II

## AN UNEASY TRIUMPH

# VI

## The Legislature Strikes Back . . .

THE DETERMINED behavior of the New Jersey judiciary—the high court rulings, the three specialized judges presiding over their respective geographic jurisdictions and becoming zoning and administrative experts by virtue of continuous involvement—coupled with the active participation of the court-appointed special masters, further advanced by stratagems of judicial prodding, mediation, and negotiation, and capped by an implementation campaign devised to assure compliance, began to inspire genuine movement toward the realistic availability of low-income housing in the suburbs. New Jersey municipalities could no longer hide from their constitutional obligation to provide access for affordable housing. Hundreds of zoning ordinances were revised. By January 1986 (when the New Jersey Supreme Court entertained oral argument in *Hills Development Co. v. Township of Bernards*, which could be called Mount Laurel III) twenty-two Mount Laurel suits had reached settlement, with over fourteen thousand units prescribed in fair share determinations.[1]

Specific goals had been set to gauge municipalities' progress in meeting regional obligations. Reform had moved far beyond the simple recognition that regulatory barriers created severe economic consequences for inner-city residents. A target for the production of moderate- and low-income housing had been established for the state. And ongoing litigation and negotiation were pushing the parties closer to the statewide goals formulated in Mount Laurel II. More and more suburbs were being brought into the judicially created fold.

But the realization of constitutional rights did not come easily. Consequent upon Mount Laurel, developers and towns engaged in hand-to-hand combat. As one mayor said of a builder, "He thought he was walking into a sleepy little hick town that was a pushover. He's been fighting since 1971 and he's gotten nothing. Before it's through, he's going to get less." Still, such talk was more bravado than reality. With devices like the builder's remedy, developers often got all they bargained for and then some. To another mayor, therefore, the court's backing of developers was "the veil over the mailed fist of dictatorship." From the municipalities' perspective, judges were undoing local regulations that had proven beneficial. Residents firmly believed that restrictive ordinances constituted an undeniable good, keeping land prices up, tax rates down, and undesirables out. The uproar was played out on the front pages of the daily press. Local governments and the judiciary seemed bent on a collision course. For the suburban municipalities, the priority with the greatest urgency was finding some alternative to the judges; they wished to cast off the court's mandate.

On both theoretical and political planes, this sequence of events triggered a crisis in the doctrine of the separation of powers and a new evolution of roles for the different branches of New Jersey government. Municipalities exerted intense pressure on the governor and the legislature to do something—anything—to save them from the clutches of the courts.

## Mount Laurel II½?

Rumblings from the state legislature were heard intermittently during this period. One litigation, in particular, provides an apt illustration of the moves and rejoinders.

*In re Egg Harbor Associates* sought to facilitate the creation of Mount Laurel housing through a capacious interpretation of an environmental statute.[2] A residential community developer in the Atlantic City area had sought permission to build 1,530 residential units, a 500-room hotel, a 300-slip marina, a 22-story office building, and 4,200 parking spaces on a 127.6 acre tract. Addressing the issue of whether New Jersey's Coastal Area Facility Review Act (CAFRA) allowed the State Department of Environmental Protection (DEP) to condition approval of a coastal zone development on the construction of affordable housing, the court sustained a mandatory set-aside of 20 percent low- and middle-income housing units as a condition to approval.[3]

CAFRA had been passed in 1973—two years before Mount Laurel I— and did not, in so many words, grant the DEP plenary zoning powers; moreover, as the title of the authorizing statute suggests, its dominant purpose was to protect the fragile coastal zones of the state. Still, seizing on one clause in the statute that mentions the "general welfare" and another that refers to "residential growth," the court found that the DEP had the right, under CAFRA, to require developers to provide an appropriate amount of affordable housing for low- and moderate-income households. The court's basic theory was that the legislature had conferred broad powers on the DEP to regulate all land use in coastal areas and that enabling statutes should be given "an expansive interpretation"[4] so that the DEP could use its power to control land use for the health, safety, and general welfare of the public to create housing opportunities for the poor and to meet the full range of the regional housing need.[5] This was a big step. The *Egg Harbor* opinion did acknowledge that its generous interpretation might give rise to conflicts between municipalities and the DEP over affordable housing plans; so be it, the court nonetheless concluded, as long as the goals of regulatory reform were furthered.

The decision's potential went far beyond the immediate litigation, affecting development not only in coastal areas but also in other major environmental areas overseen by the state, such as the Hackensack Meadowlands and the Pinelands, which together contain over 4.7 million acres—fully 37 percent of New Jersey's land area. "Protection of the environment," the court maintained, "and the provision of low and moderate income housing are not only compatible, but essential."[6] In clarifying the DEP's role, it reinforced a commitment to housing with a mix and balance of income levels.

In dissent, Justice Schreiber characterized the majority opinion as an effort to "share responsibility or credit with the Legislature, as well as an agency of the executive branch, for [the] Court's *Mount Laurel* initiatives."[7] Schreiber's cautious reading of the statute, which included a contextual examination of each of the phrases on which the majority relied, placed him at odds with his expansionist colleagues. Failing to find a grant of fair share housing authority in CAFRA, which he perceived as a purely environmental statute, he concluded that the legislature had not intended to endow the DEP with the zoning authority for fair share housing that the majority had accorded to CAFRA: "To grant the DEP such authority involves an important policy question—to be decided by the Legislature."[8]

The story does not end there. Agreeing with the dissent as to the proper lodging place of this policy question, a majority of the legislature cut down the court's construction of CAFRA by passing a statute expressly preventing the DEP from demanding "the provision of low and moderate income housing as a condition" for a permit.[9] More than one-third of the state once again became exempt from meeting any obligation to the poor. Although border disputes among the branches of government raise few eyebrows today, the mind reels at the speed with which the legislature repudiated the supreme court ruling in *Egg Harbor*.

## Enter the Legislature

The *Egg Harbor* drama was but the opening volley. It showed a legislature ready and willing to intervene in land-use litigations when it disagreed with the judicial result. Of course, *Egg Harbor* is of lesser moment with regard to the relationship of the two branches than were the Mount Laurel decisions, since legislative intent, and not the constitution, was the basis of that holding. Unlike constitutional issues, on questions of intent the legislature is obviously master—certainly on clarifying what it meant in the first instance—and given the level of judicial commitment to Mount Laurel, the legislature had to struggle to see its will carried out, though always subject to a final interpretation lodged in the courts. The affordable housing doctrine advanced by the courts loomed as the major target. Jarred by the court's continued advocacy of the Mount Laurel Doctrine and the succession of implementary devices crafted by the troika of trial judges, the state legislature at last took steps that were to transform the state's political landscape. The antiactivist campaign of municipalities culminated in the 1985 Fair Housing Act (FHA), which the legislature enacted on behalf of a bewildered but not silent majority in order to narrow the reach of the judges.

After Mount Laurel II, smoldering resentment of judicial interference with local decision making flared into a political firestorm. The prevailing talk in the legislative halls decried the violation of the separation of powers and the inappropriateness of the supreme court's undertaking of executive and legislative missions. As a legislative sponsor of the Fair Housing Act later reflected, "The dominating element in the air [during the act's passage was] an atmosphere of paranoia, confrontation and demagoguery."[10] Bills reflecting varying sentiments about Mount Laurel II were introduced in both houses. Committees held meeting after meeting. Floor speeches were bitter: a Republican lawmaker attacked the doctrine as "absolute communism," and a Democrat responded that his opponent was more concerned about "bluebloods and polo ponies" than helping low-income families.[11] Debate led to action, but the bill that emerged from the turmoil—passed by the assembly, 42 to 34, and approved by the senate in a 22-to-16 vote—ended in a conditional veto by the governor on April 22, 1985, with both houses sustaining the veto.[12] Finally, after various amendments, the Fair Housing Act was signed into law on July 2, 1985. The general mood is revealed in the observation of one sponsor of the law that "the bill we sent to the governor was a better bill than the bill I rise to move today." But, he added, "I urge concurrence because this bill is better than no bill."[13]

Although the rallying point for suburban political support for the legislation was an interim moratorium on the builder's remedy, its motivating drive was removal of the close supervision by the judiciary of local zoning. In the FHA, the New Jersey legislature seemed determined not just to supplant the courts as program administrators but to alter, in significant aspects, the nature of the regional fair share housing obligations that could be imposed on communities. The act directed that the preferred means of addressing fair share controversies henceforth would be through an administrative agency, the Council on Affordable Housing (COAH), composed of nine members selected by the governor, subject to confirmation by the Senate, and imbued with the authority to issue rules, regulations, and orders.[14] Added was the imperative that more weight be given to local concerns in the balancing process.

Home rule adherents sighed with relief. The judicial machinery would be dismantled. What was seen as a more flexible and accommodating administrative instrumentality would now discharge the constitutional responsibility. Yet the legislative intent to displace the courts was not uniform. Several of the original sponsors of the FHA thought they were simply codifying the Mount Laurel Doctrine and, aside from putting an administrative agency at the fore, not changing the course the courts had set. Some understanding of and sympathy with the court's approach was evident even in the heated floor debates. Serious legislative outcry was reserved for a particularly drastic application of the doctrine—the builder's remedy—rather than being aimed at the general principle that the court had enunciated. In fact, the FHA does not in so many words undo the judicial precedent. Quite the contrary: on its face, the preamble codifies the Mount Laurel Doctrine, declaring that "the New Jersey Supreme Court, through its rulings in [Mount Laurel I and II], has determined that every municipality in a growth area has a constitutional obligation to provide through its land use regulation a realistic opportunity for a fair share of its region's present and prospective needs for housing for low and moderate income families."[15]

That being said, the act nonetheless established a host of procedures that diluted the doctrine. To replace Chief Justice Wilentz's marching orders, the new law authorized COAH to define housing regions within the state, to calculate state and regional present and prospective need for low- and moderate-income housing, and to promulgate guidelines and criteria for determining municipal fair share.[16] It further empowered COAH to decide whether proposed local ordinances and related measures would, if enacted, satisfy the Mount Laurel obligation. The legislation also declared its preference for the resolution of disputes involving exclusionary zoning by way of a mediation and review process rather than litigation.

Lines of authority were further changed in that municipalities could elect to petition the council for substantive certification of their fair share housing ordinances and "housing element" plans.[17] COAH can certify municipalities whose housing plans and zoning and other relevant ordinances meet its standards of a realistic opportunity for providing the fair share of low- and moderate-income housing.[18] Once certified, a municipality is shielded from the builder's remedy for six years, with the council providing what is essentially an insurance policy against suit; certification can be set aside in court only by "clear and convincing evidence" of its inappropriateness.[19] A successful lawsuit attacking an ordinance that has received substantive certification as not satisfying the Mount Laurel constitutional obligation would prove to be a rarity.[20]

## The "Mount Laurel III" Decision

In response to what seemed a sweeping away of painfully achieved successes, a number of public interest and builder plaintiffs challenged the Fair Housing Act. Several New Jersey municipalities, all with litigation pending before one of the three Mount Laurel trial judges, requested transfer of their cases to the council's administrative forum. Of the twelve appeals, transfer was denied in all but one. The ensuing *Hills* case of 1986, Mount Laurel III, forced the New Jersey Supreme Court to confront the question of the act's constitutionality, revealing the judiciary's qualms yet its continued determination to support the affordable housing requirement.[21]

After a painstaking review of the FHA's provisions and an acknowledgment of the outspoken objections that the act was a sham aimed to dismantle, not buttress, the Mount Laurel Doctrine, Chief Justice Wilentz nevertheless ended with the resounding conclusion that the FHA was both a constitutional and appropriate legislative response, despite its numerous infringements on previously articulated and exercised judicial power:[22] "The constitutional obligation has not changed; the judiciary's ultimate duty to enforce it has not changed; our determination to perform that duty has not changed. What *has* changed is that we are no longer alone in this field. The other branches of government have fashioned a comprehensive statewide response to the *Mount Laurel* obligation. This kind of response, one that would permit us to withdraw from this field, is what this Court has always wanted and sought. It is potentially far better for the State and for its lower income citizens."[23]

Most objections to the FHA, Wilentz argued, attributed to it and the council a mission of sabotaging the Mount Laurel Doctrine. On the contrary, he responded, there is no "constitutional timetable implicit in [the] obligation . . . , some deadline after which legislation would not be acceptable."[24] Nor did the lack of an assured builder's remedy nullify the act, since that was not part of the constitutional obligation. "We must assume," the court pronounced, "that the Council will pursue the vindication of the *Mount Laurel* obligation with determination and skill,"[25] even though the court recognized that the act's legislative history did not obscure the legislature's intent to nullify future judicial participation "first, to bring an administrative agency into the field of lower income housing to satisfy the *Mount Laurel* obligation; second, to get the courts out of that field."[26] All in all, the presumption of constitutionality had to prevail, and the court acquiesced, however reluctantly, indicating that it was ready to defer, accommodate, and cooperate with a legislative solution—and graciously step aside.

The supreme court's reversal of the denials of transfer to COAH by the lower courts yields a number of contradictory interpretations.[27] One gloss is highly affirmative of the Mount Laurel Doctrine. Legislative involvement in the form of the FHA's enactment reduces the possibility that the location and extent of lower-income housing would hinge on chance—that is, the random event of a builder or public interest group suing; instead, comprehensive statewide planning under the aegis of the council aided by the newly strengthened State Planning Commission would carry the day. By this reasoning, the legislatively created council could be called a positive improvement over the three-judge system, substituting uniformity for the varying and potentially inconsistent definitions of housing need, housing shares, regions, and so forth. Taken as a whole, the argument runs, the FHA commissioned an overall affordable housing plan for the entire state.

This was the opinion's tack. Chief Justice Wilentz's decision argued that the FHA represented a substantial effort by the other branches of government to vindicate the goals advanced by the Mount Laurel Doctrine.[28] The FHA, he further predicted, would lead to municipalities' voluntary compliance through conformance with the standards the council adopted, "as compared to their open hostility to court-ordered rezoning."[29] The *Hills* decision chose to highlight the shared purpose that animated court and legislature alike, seeking to camouflage truly substantial differences with a legalistic blanket. In fact, however, by the very creation of a new administrative agency, by specifying formulas that would allow exceptions from the fair share allocation developed by the trial courts, by ordering a moratorium on the builder's remedy, and by adding the regional contribution agreements as an acceptable compliance mechanism, the FHA can be read as a direct blow to the courts. Indeed, the FHA hovered perilously close to unconstitutionality by altering the scope of the courts' decree powers, interfering with the state supreme court's exclusive power over prerogative writ actions, and impinging on the way the courts were to construe the constitutionality of local land-use controls.[30]

What is the best way to construe *Hills* and its apparent embrace of the legislature's takeover of Mount Laurel terrain? One view suggests that the legislature's recastings constituted a forthright challenge to the court's construction of the New Jersey Constitution and that, faced with direct conflict with the other branches of government, the judges flinched and backed down. In reversing the trial courts' refusal to allow removal of the cases to COAH, Chief Justice Wilentz seemed ready to give up or at least implicitly to agree with the legislature that the court had moved too far ahead of public opinion. The phrasing is muted, dominated by a flattening of nuance; everything takes place in a midrange of tone and color.

Under this interpretation of the outcome, the judiciary had underestimated the depth of local resentment and worry, placing itself on the thin ice of administering minutiae in order to realize reform. The details of implementation—spot calls affecting specific structures and immediate lot lines, even sizes and types of buildings—had become overwhelming. With the new act, the legislature intended to scale back the Mount Laurel Doctrine; the court might uphold the constitution by its lights, but it was bypassed by events. *Hills* accepted the legislature's discipline, echoing the strong desire to keep land-use regulations local in initiation and outlook. The claims of popular sovereignty were too strong for the court to gainsay.

Other schools of historians will offer alternative explanations. Enactment of the FHA, some may argue, was far from a defeat for the judiciary; they may present the legislative result embodied in the act as precisely what the court had always desired. And it is true that, beginning in 1975, and reinforcing its message in 1983, in addition to pointing out the intense public need for low-income housing in the suburbs and for the integration of communities, the New Jersey Supreme Court had sounded another theme of comparable weight, albeit subtler than the discrimination concerns: the hope that, in matters of institutional reform, solutions be legislative and executive. "Legislative action was the 'relief' we asked for," the court announced in *Hills*, "and today we have it."

Only by default of the other branches of government had the exclusionary zoning problem devolved into a job for the courts saddled with the constitutional mandate to guarantee due process and equal protection. Mount Laurel I started from the constitutional root, but in order to make the right to affordable housing in the suburbs more than a hollow trunk, the court set forth the necessary branches for implementation. Then, still looking in vain to the legislature, the court in Mount Laurel II felt compelled to fashion an elaborate administrative machinery in order to convert generalized constitutional theory into concrete legal mechanisms. Within the flexible envelope of the Mount Laurel Doctrine, the three trial judges had received, shaped, and carried out their marching orders. Now, at last, after thirteen years, after exclusionary zoning had come to public attention in an inescapable form through the remedies imposed by the three trial courts, and after constitutional obligations could no longer be avoided, the legislature and the governor had chosen to step in. Having performed the job of herald, sounding the need for change, the court could retire with honor, leaving the field to the legislature's FHA, the result it had always sought. After all, the act established an agency (with a jurisdiction that ran statewide), furnished appropriations, and even incorporated portions of the Mount Laurel language in its preamble. The remedial course the court had launched would continue.

This is the connotation Chief Justice Wilentz obviously preferred, as he repeatedly insisted in *Hills*:

> Most objections raised against the Act assume that it will not work, or construe its provisions so that it cannot work, and attribute both to the legislation and to the Council a mission, nowhere expressed in the Act, of sabotaging the *Mount Laurel* doctrine. On the contrary, we must assume that the council will pursue the vindication of the *Mount Laurel* obligation with determination and skill. If it does, that vindication should be far preferable to vindication by the courts, and may be far more effective.... The Fair Housing Act has many things that the judicial remedy did not have: it requires, in every municipality's master plan, as a condition to the power to zone, a housing element that provides a realistic opportunity for the fair share; it has funding; it has the kind of legitimacy that may generate popular support, the legitimacy that comes from enactment by the people's elected representatives; it may result in voluntary compliance, largely unachieved in a decade by the rule of law fashioned by the courts.[31]

Over and above its role as catalyst for legislative action, the court could continue to act as a reminder of obligations, even if from the shadows. Ever mindful of constitutional imperatives, the court advised in *Hills* (and subsequently amplified in *Holmdel Builder's Association v. Town-*

*ship of Holmdel* and *In re Petition for Substantive Certification Filed by Warren Township*) that it might step back into the fray should efforts lag or inappropriate actions be taken. As the court warned, "[If] the Act . . . achieves nothing but delay, the judiciary will be forced to resume its appropriate role."[32] For the present, however, the court would politely retreat as the legislature moved into the limelight.

A third possible interpretation of *Hills* finds an uneasy alliance between the legislature and judiciary, each acting as a counterweight that cancels the other's excesses. Under this view, COAH is a political orphan, pressured by appeals and amendments, a compromise between the two branches, shunned by both for fear of being damned by association. Yet paradoxically everyone wants control over it, to make sure it does as little damage as possible to constituencies and principles already appropriated by courts or legislature.

While the rosy scenario of Chief Justice Wilentz is unlikely to survive a dip into Oliver Wendell Holmes's cynical acid, it must be said that, at a minimum, Mount Laurel moved the New Jersey legislature to take overdue action to repress the suburban abuse of land regulatory powers that fragment metropolitan areas. Had there been more visible support from public interest groups, the court might have struggled harder to make the actions of the three trial judges more broadly applicable and to elaborate still further the principles of its doctrine. But a weary court chose instead to avoid this more determined stand, although it claimed to remain in a persistent state of readiness to reinforce the Mount Laurel Doctrine when necessary.

At first hurried reading, the statutory scheme and the supreme court acquiescence in *Hills* appear to undo precedents that the three trial judges so painstakingly established in their interpretations. Nonetheless, as the New Jersey situation has evolved (and as could fairly have been predicted from portions of the *Hills* decision), Mount Laurel II and its progeny continue to play a substantial role in the battle against regulatory barriers to affordable housing. For one thing, courts linger as a forum that plaintiffs often prefer outright. There were still ninety-four municipalities under the courts' jurisdiction as of 1991, and seventeen new Mount Laurel judges were operating at the time of the council's birth. Furthermore, appeal from administrative determinations to the court always remains an option. "No one should assume," the court emphasized, "that our exercise of comity today signals a weakening of our resolve to enforce the constitutional rights of New Jersey's lower income citizens."[33] On a more abstract level, the principles announced by the three original Mount Laurel trial judges and their successors continue, by way of a responsive dialectic, to influence the standards and regulations the council issues and to retain an impact on its day-to-day practice.

## Jurisdiction: Choice of Forum, Post-*Hills*

A Mount Laurel dispute can be heard in two forums: the traditional judicial setting, before one of the now expanded twenty-plus trial judges of the Mount Laurel breed, or an administrative hearing, with its own apparatus and appellate procedures before administrative judges. Despite the New Jersey Supreme Court's strong desire to defer to the council ("As a matter of comity, we would yield to the Legislature in this field even if theoretically its exercise of power was in an area reserved to the judiciary"),[34] there now exist two founts of authority for litigation procedures and two sets of precedents—in the council's rules and regulations and in the opinions the courts continue to write. These two sources at times conflict, at times coincide, at times borrow from each other. As the dust settles in the wake of the FHA's enactment, a comparison between the administration of the act by COAH and the work of the Mount Laurel trial judges provides a rare study in the interaction of legislative, judicial, and executive branches.

Detached as it was from the fray, the court nevertheless recognized in *Hills* that the enactment of the FHA created the potential for forum shopping—an opportunity plaintiffs' lawyers certainly would not fail to notice. In an attempt to ensure some degree of consistency between the administrative and judicial forums, *Hills* went beyond the usual dose of deference to state administrative law: banking on the FHA's statutory framework to meet the demands of reform, it ordered the trial judiciary to conform decisions "to the Council's determinations."[35] Although it made no similar public declaration, the council walked its mile, moving toward fitting its principles and criteria to those formulated by the Mount Laurel courts.

The FHA's provisions on jurisdiction allow a trial court to process any litigation that comes before it under the rules established by Mount Laurel II and follow-up decisions. But it also contained a critical provision aimed at pushing the courts out of the picture: any party can file a motion requesting transfer of its case to the council, and the court must grant that request unless the move would give rise to a "manifest injustice."[36] In the cases on appeal in *Hills*, two Mount Laurel trial judges maintained that a balancing of all relevant factors was necessary before such removal to COAH could occur. The supreme court reversed this position. Now, only the injustice caused by the actual transfer may be put on the scales, and moreover, that detrimental impact has to be one that was unforeseen: only unanticipated and exceptional unfairness would warrant denial of a transfer.

To be more precise, problems such as delays in the production of low-income housing, potential loss of suitable sites, or significantly increased infrastructure costs for developers in themselves would not be sufficient to support a claim of manifest injustice. Nor would the loss to a public interest plaintiff—who, for instance, had fought for many years and was just about to attain a settlement replete with affordable housing—amount to an injustice within the statutory meaning. Even if a plaintiff could demonstrate that the defendant municipality had acted in bad faith, the court in *Hills* went on to say, such proofs would not block the municipality's ability to remove to the council.[37] In essence, the claim of manifest injustice would be confined to the narrowest, most extreme situation.

Above all, costs and time for compliance are generally less under the COAH process than in litigation within the judicial forum. Once a municipality files a "resolution of participation" with the council, it is free to pursue the benefits the FHA affords. To begin with, it may petition the council for "substantive certification" of its housing element and ordinances,[38] which in turn carries a number of advantages, among them, access to certain grants-in-aid for housing that ensure local control over land use. If no objection is filed to the municipality's petition and if COAH finds that the proposed fair share plan is consistent with its criteria, then the council grants certification. If objections are presented, the FHA mandates a "mediation and review" process; should this process not resolve the particular dispute, the council may refer the issue to an administrative law judge, with final determination to be made by the council after receipt of the judge's initial recommendation.

Overall, substantive certification becomes an important goal for municipalities within the growth areas outlined in the state plan because it relieves them of the uncertainties and potential burdens of Mount Laurel litigation. Speed remains a desideratum within the process, much as it was in the courts. The locality is required to adopt its fair share housing ordinance within forty-five days of the grant of certification. If it fails to file—and here the legislature makes clear its desire that nonparticipation no longer be an option, before either the council or the court—the municipality loses the benefits of the FHA unless it adopts a resolution of participation and files it with the council, together with a housing element plan and fair share housing ordinance, prior to the initiation of any litigation. Any municipality that chooses to stand still may face a race if there is a plaintiff looming on the horizon; should it fall behind, it will be subject to suit and to all the remedies that Mount Laurel II provides.

Subsequent events have not ratified the hope of *Hills* that, as the FHA unfolded, "practically all" localities would follow the substantive certification process.[39] By August 1991 only 154 towns—27 percent of the state's 567 municipalities—had filed resolutions seeking certification at COAH, a figure only slightly improved by March 1993, when 182 towns—

31 percent—had filed and another 48 had filed housing elements but not yet petitioned for certification.[40] On February 1, 1995, the total number of municipalities that had received substantive certification was 147. Thus nearly two-thirds of municipalities shunned participation and are still subject to trial court litigation and the much feared builder's remedy. Indeed, 75 localities find themselves stranded in the never-never land of failure to choose; having presumably elected nonparticipation, they cling, ostrichlike, to the hope of somehow eluding the storm altogether.[41]

## Procedure

Enactment of the FHA has meant far fewer cases for judges, because municipalities may choose the initial jurisdiction, and not surprisingly, many select the council. For those cases that do go to court—perhaps because of a trial judge's reputation for delaying the inevitable by stretching the process to its limits or for imposing lighter requirements than the council might—the same procedures for quick resolution that the original three trial judges had developed before 1985 continue to govern the exclusionary zoning cases.

As to actual compliance by municipalities, the FHA not only stamps with legislative approval the varied mechanisms that had sprung up within the judicial framework but goes on to authorize additional compliance devices, thus increasing the municipalities' repertoire of remedies.[42] The troubling element—as is often the situation in institutional litigation—is the shadow that falls between idea and reality. Compliance devices are only as good as their administration or the market that drives them. Within the Mount Laurel Doctrine's original judicial framework, individual judges varied as to how forcefully they probed municipal plans, how diligently they pursued ordinance revision, and how forcefully they tested how "realistic" an opportunity a municipality was providing for lower-income housing. Where COAH will fall on this spectrum is as yet unclear; its specific techniques for bringing proposals to reality are hazy, and there is no consensus yet on how vigorously it will enforce the various compliance mechanisms that the act contemplates.[43]

### The Fair Share Formula

Fair share analysis played a major role in determining how much of a Mount Laurel obligation is to be borne by a given community. That the legislature intended revisions in that mechanism is clear; at the least, under the belief that the courts' fair share numbers were simply too large for the suburbs to digest, the act prescribed that the methodology for determining fair share housing allocations be formulated anew by the council. This posed a significant legislative challenge to the formulation that Judge Serpentelli so painstakingly fashioned in *AMG*. That early case had yielded the *AMG* formula, a working consensus as to the definition of fair share from assorted population projections and theoretical analyses of job opportunities, achieved after Judge Serpentelli had insisted that city planning experts keep working until they reached an agreement satisfying the constitutional and statutory mandates of Mount Laurel II.[44] Drastic though it was, this course of action had seemed the best way out of the maze, and one of Judge Serpentelli's colleagues, while doubting that he himself would have taken such a rash step, now expresses admiration for the audacity of the move and the resulting beneficial consequences.

The *AMG* formula, with slight modifications, survived as the rule of the state throughout three years of litigation only to face revision by COAH. And whether the changes imposed by the council are the sort the legislature intended or are in any measure as extensive as they appear on the surface, they shed an ironic light on the legislature's resumption of authority. The act, in placing ultimate responsibility for number crunching with COAH instead of the courts, wanted to diminish the burden on localities, and on the face of it, COAH's statewide need methodology meets that desire; for example, COAH's initial need figure for affordable housing units (145,000) is considerably less than the number the Mount Laurel judges prescribed (243,000). The council's program, however, is scheduled for implementation over a six-year period, rather than the ten-year period that the courts assumed, so that while the totals diverge sharply, the per annum figures are much the same—roughly 24,300 units per year.[45] On the other hand, the council does appear to have obliged in part by lowering the allocations for suburban areas.[46] For the period 1993–99 (the FHA requires COAH to determine the unmet need for affordable housing every six years), it has lowered its estimate to 118,000, primarily because of earlier overoptimistic calculations of projected growth. But, again, the technology employed is primarily that of the courts: in COAH's own words, "The methodology developed by the Council is very similar to the one developed in Superior Court prior to the formation of the Council."[47]

However, although a special creature of the legislature, the council quickly developed its own agenda along with its special turf. Its desire to generate a singular product, one of which it could be proud, assured that it would establish a fair share doctrine with some bite. "Signals are being sent," said the executive director as early as October 1988. "We've been telling towns all along: keep up the initiative, come forward." Indeed, the council's vigorous interpretation of its mandate sometimes went beyond what the legislature must have envisioned. A few of its regulations lent such broad scope to the Mount Laurel obligation that disputes flared once more within the legislature.

One prominent example of independence is the COAH position that a densely developed suburb cannot be excused from its fair share obligation simply because it has no vacant land. COAH issued a regulation permitting the razing of existing single-family homes to make room for high-density projects for low-income families. Under this rule, Fanwood, a 1.2-square-mile borough of eight thousand people twenty miles west of Manhattan, was forced to consider a proposal by three local developers to tear down six single-family houses and replace them with seventy-five condominium town houses (fifteen of them Mount Laurel units). At the time Fanwood filed its plan with COAH, the town claimed that its fair share number of eighty-seven should be reduced to zero because it did not have appropriate vacant land for affordable housing construction; the objecting developers argued that an adjustment was not warranted because they owned sites capable of development with affordable housing. COAH determined that, while it would not require a municipality itself to demolish structures to make room for Mount Laurel housing, it would consider a site containing residential structures if a property owner expressed a willingness to use it for that purpose. To some this came as a bombshell. "It's akin to declaring open season for developers to come in and destroy neighborhoods," exclaimed a borough council member.[48]

Charging that the rule gave any builder capable of assembling a site sufficient leverage to change a neighborhood's character and that it would drag into extensive litigation developed suburbs otherwise devoid of land suitable for Mount Laurel housing, the legislature (proving, without knowing it, the truth of a comment in a *New York Times* editorial that "even supporters of the decision acknowledge it has enormous potential for fostering negative public attitudes toward the Mount Laurel process") took a drastic step back into the fight.[49] The so-called Fanwood Amendment ("an Act concerning the demolition of certain habitable residential structures"), enacted on August 3, 1989, prohibited the council from requiring localities to consider land parcels already improved with sound residential structures as potential sites for Mount Laurel housing.

The sweep of the amendment was quickly tested in the *Paramus Substantive Certification No. 47* case.[50] In its fair share plan, the village of Paramus—presumably with an eye open to potential conflict with the Fanwood Amendment—sought to avoid a builder's remedy on the ground that the community was intensively developed and already in the throes of severe traffic congestion. Instead, Paramus sought to satisfy its fair share obligation by extracting developer subsidies of land and $2.5 million in exchange for zoning concessions that permitted more intensive commercial development of a shopping center; under this arrangement, six structures would be demolished in order to build a proposed 274-unit Mount Laurel project. Over a competitor's objection, the council approved the subsidies-for-concessions plan. So did the lower courts. On appeal, the supreme court permitted the demolition of the already developed property in order to construct the new housing. The reasoning was that the amended state legislation was directed only at situations in which the council *required* towns to consider developed sites, whereas the Paramus decision was voluntary.

The *Paramus* case is the clearest example thus far of COAH's expansive view of its own role and of how the agency, at times, has raised legislative hackles. Indeed, the Fanwood contretemps demonstrated the council's readiness to push the affordable housing remedy, even in straitened circumstances, to the point where the legislature feels the need to curb the council publicly. While the Fanwood Amendment, as the council and the court now construe it, is not as broad a rebuttal as the FHA itself was to the Mount Laurel Doctrine, it serves as a warning to the wise: the agency and courts are now both on notice that the legislature is on the lookout for specific rulings it deems excessive. In an ironic twist, the *Paramus* holding shows how the court gives encouragement to a more activist council, even though the council itself is a creature of legislative rebuff to the judiciary.

COAH's aggressive posture in pursuing the Mount Laurel Doctrine is largely attributable to increased knowledge and experience, as well as a growing sense of mission. The more studies it commissioned, the more figures it accumulated, the more it became convinced of the need for low-income housing throughout the state. Furthermore, council members and staff alike grew impatient with towns that continued to fight or ignore the Mount Laurel decisions or make believe that they never existed. Basing its actions on those portions of the FHA preamble that afford substantial latitude to the "do good" aspects of the program and partially influenced by pressure from public interest groups, the council generated a vigorous methodology that belied the fears openly expressed at the time of the *Hills* case that the operations of COAH would emasculate the Mount Laurel rulings.

### Regional Fair Share: A Further Alliance of Court and Council

Once a municipality provides land for housing its own poor, how much more room must it make for the region's poor? The first step is deciding how to carve the state into regions. After Justice Hall's enunciation of the original Mount Laurel Doctrine in 1975, various trial courts struggled with the issue of demarcation until Mount Laurel II, when the New Jersey Supreme Court invoked the State Development Guide Plan. The plan established six classifications for the state—growth, limited growth, agricultural, conservation, environmental, and coastal zones—and the three Mount Laurel trial judges relied on them to develop their own regional formulas.[51]

Although the FHA asked the council to consider pertinent research studies, government reports, decisions of other branches of government, and public comments, it chose not to restrict the agency to any one approach; indeed, the act expressly exempted COAH from having to espouse any particular school of thought in determining its policy for designating regions within the broad mandate of the doctrine.[52] COAH has run with this baton. Instead of foraging through the myriad judicial definitional criteria for coming up with individualized demarcations, COAH cut the Gordian knot: by administrative fiat, it simply designated six regions for the entire state. That was that.[53]

The council also ruled that all municipalities must provide for some portion of their own need ("indigenous needs"), and municipalities containing land designated in the state plan as part of a growth area must also provide for their fair share of the regional need ("prospective" and "reallocated present needs").[54] This accords with the FHA's direction to maintain consistency with the overall master plan of the state (now renamed the State Development Regional Guide Plan, or SDRP), which indicates, in broad strokes, where development and redevelopment are to be encouraged and where they are to be limited.[55] Thus, despite the legislature's express rejection of the courts' allocation methodology—certainly their overall totals of housing need—the council confirmed, in large part, the approach the trial judges evolved in carrying out Mount Laurel II.[56]

COAH also copied to a large degree the courts' persistent deference to state-generated plans. Indeed, in many ways, both COAH and the State Planning Commission can be said to owe their continued existence to the good housekeeping seal Mount Laurel II and its progeny affixed to the SDRP. State-designated "growth areas," used by the trial judges, were also relied on by the council in fair share allocation. A corollary policy, adopted from a formulation by the judges, states that a lack of "centers" designated to receive growth will not absolve a locality of its fair share obligation. This limitation was of benefit to the planners at the State Planning Commission: for one example, they issued an interim plan linked with COAH's affordable housing estimates. More specifically, one policy incorporated COAH's estimates of fair share housing needs and went on to propose future collaboration on projected housing allocations.

# THE SIX HOUSING REGIONS OF NEW JERSEY

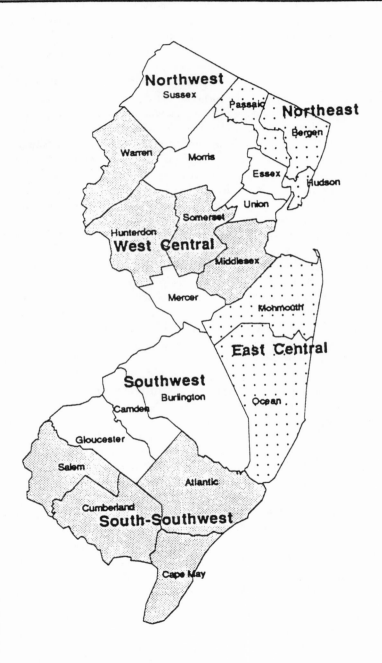

In addition, COAH adapted its count of substandard units—with only slight modifications—from the courts' earlier interpretation. By direct reference, the council based its count on the definition that Judge Serpentelli used in his *AMG* opinion, where a unit qualified as substandard if the 1980 Census reported it as overcrowded or lacking in adequate heating or plumbing. The council expanded these criteria, adding age, lack of complete kitchen facilities, lack of private access, and lack of an elevator for structures over four stories. COAH claims that these new benchmarks minimize the possibility of classifying good housing as bad while enhancing the ability to flag deficient housing units. Interestingly, the council method yields about eight thousand more unsound existing units overall than the *AMG* method did, yet about twelve thousand fewer in the inner cities.

Moving from the definition of region to the determination of actual fair share obligations, the FHA called for the council, during the first seven months after its formation, to determine for each region the present and prospective needs for low- and moderate-income housing. Once it established need figures, the agency was to adopt criteria to further guide localities in determining their fair share of regional housing need.

In formulating fair share figures, COAH again moved along the methodological line first laid out in the courts. Under council regulations, a municipality is required to provide its fair share of the regional needs if it finds itself in what the state plan identifies as a growth area. Determination of fair share thus repeats the familiar three steps: In what region is the municipality located? What are the present and prospective needs for lower-income housing within that region? What is the municipality's immediate obligation with respect to the present and prospective regional needs?

*Present regional need* is defined for a locality within a growth area as consisting of at least some portion of the locality's indigenous need plus its fair share of the region's surplus present need. For *prospective regional need*, the council resorted to a new formula. To arrive at a figure for the cutoff year of 1993, for example, COAH's approach would require predicting the population increase in the region between 1987 and 1993, forecasting the number of households that will exist in the region in 1993, determining how many more households will exist in the region in 1993 as compared with 1987, and identifying the extent to which this increase in households will consist of lower-income households. *Total need* between 1987 and 1993 would be composed of indigenous need, reallocated present need, and prospective need. Before adjusting the figure for demolitions, conversions, filtration, and spontaneous rehabilitation, the council placed the number at 199,966 units for the entire state.[57]

The issue of what factors might suffice to mitigate local fair share obligations shows an additional interplay between agency operations and the prior work of the court. The FHA required the council to adopt "criteria and guidelines" to enable a locality to reduce its Mount Laurel obligation in certain circumstances. In addition to considering historic preservation and environmental concerns, the council was instructed to take into account possible drastic alterations in the established pattern of community development and insufficiency of vacant and developable land.[58] A further mitigating factor mandated by the act is the absence of public facilities and infrastructure, if their construction would result in prohibitive costs to the public. In one illustration of mitigation in practice, COAH determined that only ninety-four acres of developable land existed in Roseland and accordingly granted it a downward adjustment of its Mount Laurel obligation from 260 to 165 units.[59]

Dispute swirls around COAH's discretionary flexibility on fair share. The public advocate (the position was abolished in 1994) contended that, whenever COAH adjusts one locality's obligation downward, there should be a compensating increase in the number of lower-income housing units required elsewhere in the region. COAH opposed this measure, arguing in *Calton Homes, Inc. v. COAH* that "such reassignment would be difficult to do fairly, and impossible if some of the regional municipalities were already certified."[60] The court upheld the agency's contentions in *In re Borough of Roseland.*[61]

Would this possibility of lowered obligations have evolved had jurisdiction remained with the courts? Part of the basis for questioning the legitimacy of the courts' involvement in the fair share formulation is their inability to make discretionary choices in a fast-moving process that requires flexibility. But the adaptability shown by courts of equity— certainly by the three trial judges—is remarkable. Mitigation of fair share is not unknown in the courts, and they usually recognize the need for step-by-step pacing in the formulation of judicial remedies and the phasing of fair share requirements. In fact, the courts did countenance loosening through dicta or holdings in specific cases and over time might have provided further dispensations. For example, they adopted a policy of cushioning impact where the imposition of the Mount Laurel obligation would cause sudden and radical transformations, although such policies were used sparingly "and with special care."[62]

Like COAH, the courts identified preservation of historical or important architectural sites or of environmentally sensitive lands as mitigators to the affordable housing requirement. As Judge Serpentelli pointed out in *Allan-Deane,* "It has, in fact, been the policy of this court to permit adjustments of the fair share number produced by the *AMG* methodology in those cases in which a municipality has voluntarily stipulated noncompliance and fair share at an early stage of the litigation and has agreed to become compliant within a specified period." He added, "Similar adjustments have been permitted in other cases where equity dictated that approach."[63]

Whether the courts would have gone further, as experience grew, is a matter of speculation. They might have, carefully plotting out relaxations shaped to the individual situations appearing before them, but the alternative route—over and above a readier responsiveness to public pressures—is quicker: given the agency's power to prescribe across a broad range of future activities, the exceptions available to localities are found in formally promulgated regulations that are generally applicable. The administrative flexibility that the FHA confers on the council to make further adjustments in the fair share formula and to cap the development within any municipality might be both more realistic and responsive to the needs of home rule communities than doctrines the court could have developed over time in individual cases.

This is not to say, however, that the judiciary could not have addressed the relaxation of fair share obligations. The court has the power to vary orders if a proposed project is deemed more likely to result in actual construction or is clearly more suitable from a planning perspective. Courts are sensitive to public reactions on volatile issues and are fully capable of taking a perspective extending beyond the case at hand. Indeed, several of the newer Mount Laurel trial judges, possibly out of an urge to settle cases and reduce the burden on the docket, have acquired the reputation (deserved or not) of meeting the pleas of localities by reducing even further the number of units that the council has prescribed.

Not all fair share innovations are equally accessible to the legislature and the courts. The FHA specifies filtering, residential conversions, and spontaneous rehabilitation—three turns of phrase for the trickling down of higher-end housing to lower-income residents—as techniques for satisfying the Mount Laurel Doctrine. The council quantified the effects of these techniques by prescribing what it called precredited formulas, which produced the following numbers statewide: 51,004 for filtering housing supply, 12,102 for residential conversion housing supply, and 4,530 for spontaneous rehabilitation housing supply.[64] It can be assumed that, over time, judges would have seen that housing need is reduced to the extent that higher-end units become available at lower prices through the operation of the real estate market; however, lacking the immediate power of legislative fiat, the judiciary's adoption of these modifications probably would have been at a more leisurely pace. Nor presumably would the judges' precredited numbers have been as generous as the council's.

Other provisions of the FHA are aimed, in omnibus fashion, at specific bottlenecks or blatant examples of unfairness that asserted themselves in the course of Mount Laurel litigations and in debates on the legislative floor. For example, the act deems the rehabilitated substandard units to be usable credits against the local obligation. It also extends credit for past production of affordable housing. And again, a final escape valve enables a municipality to adjust the amount of time it has to satisfy its obligation, though not the magnitude of the obligation itself.[65] These provisions are typical tempering devices that courts could have learned to apply in their exercise of equitable discretion.[66] Courts also would have been able, as experience unfolded, to limit the number of units any one town had to assimilate, a means of addressing the density issue that emerged as the most troubling by-product of the Mount Laurel Doctrine.

On still other divisive issues one can only speculate about what the judicial interpretations might have been, absent legislative intervention. In the more limited role of reviewing the council's actions, the courts proved extremely deferential; as the supreme court recognized, because "the FHA legislative scheme is novel, the implementation of its goals is necessarily an evolving process."[67] Consequently, the overall jurisprudential question remains: had the courts continued to exercise jurisdiction unfettered by the FHA, would they have developed significant methods of mollifying local hardships? If so, would the means of adjustment have been molded to the peculiar circumstances of each case, or would the relaxations have coalesced into a set of comprehensive rules? Perhaps in being rubbed into reality's mud and forced to confront individual circumstances, the courts would have developed an adjustment methodology better tailored than the FHA's to the realities of specific local situations. Yet legislative fiat is undoubtedly a speedier, if rougher, way of responding to the hardships that inevitably arise in the application of a uniform rule such as the Mount Laurel Doctrine. The legislature's resolution through the FHA represents a balancing of interest groups that in the end tipped the scales toward municipalities. Courts, bound to uphold lofty constitutional principles even at the expense of disruptive local changes, would probably have reached a different point along the spectrum of accommodation to political pressure.

### Compliance Mechanisms: The Builder's Remedy

New restrictions on the much castigated builder's remedy constitute the major change that the legislature brought about when it resized the world created by the Mount Laurel judges. In putting forth the remedy, Mount Laurel II had suggested that a proportion of 20 percent low-income to 80 percent market-rate units would be a "reasonable minimum" that satisfied the criterion that a "substantial proportion" of housing be devoted to low- and moderate-income units. As a matter of practice, however, the 20 percent figure became a functional maximum: almost invariably 80 percent of a project's units were middle-income or higher.

This ratio raised the problem of excessive growth at the community level. Mount Laurel II made the remedy readily available—in one attorney's famous phrase, "like clubbing baby seals." Not only did a locality have to accept the fair share units to satisfy the constitutional requirement, but it also was called on to absorb the complement of higher-end units the market-driven remedy required. Complaints of excessive density and congestion, of the spoiling of suburban atmosphere, of the destruction of small-town character were the charges most frequently leveled against the Mount Laurel Doctrine in the legislature. The Hills Township development was trotted out as a particularly nasty example. Newspapers throughout the state carried photographs showing the wave of building in that locality overwhelming the bucolic countryside, blotting out sun and sky. And Hills was far from unique. A total of fully 2,800 units rose on 1,600 acres in Bedminster and Bernards townships. Most sell at prices ranging from $115,000 to $650,000, but 560 are Mount Laurel units selling at $35,000 to $90,000. Piscataway Township received a fair share assignment of 4,192 units, which, with the builder's remedy, could have yielded over 20,000 housing units. Cranbury Township, a farming community of fewer than 800 households, had to provide 816 units under the *AMG* formula, which translated, under the 20 percent set-asides, to over 4,000 units.

Given all these dire consequences, it is hardly surprising that the FHA pounced on the builder's remedy. First, the act imposed a moratorium on the remedy until five months after the council adopted its own criteria and guidelines.[68] Then it charged the council with formulating standards to prevent municipalities from being "drastically altered" as a result of Mount Laurel compliance. With such authority, the council subsequently ruled that drastic alteration would be presumed if a municipality's fair share exceeded 20 percent of its estimated 1987 occupied housing stock. Undoubtedly this provision reflects the sense of outrage that citizens— and many city planners as well—felt when a community, after losing a legal struggle, found itself compelled to double in size almost overnight.[69]

The council also capped at 1,000 the number of dwelling units any one municipality could be required to construct to come into compliance with Mount Laurel. In its judgment, a fair share ceiling couched in absolute terms was necessary to prevent dramatic changes in communities' established patterns of development.[70] In *Calton Homes*, however, the court overturned the cap on local fair share as "arbitrary and unreasonable"[71] and as "exacerbat[ing] disparity in the obligation imposed on various municipalities in the same region."[72] What particularly caught the court's attention was that an absolute top could accommodate neither the circumstances surrounding the municipality's obligation nor its relation to other municipalities within the region.[73] The court's response was to increase the obligation in that case from 1,000 to 1,850 units.[74] This is yet another instance of absolute standards collapsing as the common law courts build doctrine case by case, leaving encompassing directives to emerge only from a series of unique fact patterns.

Currently, a builder contemplating a Mount Laurel challenge before the council must recognize that the right to a builder's remedy is no longer automatically available, no matter how exclusionary the municipality or how appropriate the site. To be sure, the council is said to look favorably on developer initiative and to place the burden of proof on a town if it has been slow to seek certification under the FHA. But that is a slender reed on which to rely.

The potential level of disagreement among the different branches of New Jersey government raises concerns. Their continuing cooperation is essential to avoid the evils of exclusionary zoning. To effect the sweeping social change that the Mount Laurel decisions envision, all available troops must be mustered. Even after the legislative branch is mobilized, the judiciary cannot simply fold its tent and slink away (as it did in part in Mount Laurel III). The interplay needs to continue; the court's presence is essential to the resolution of the constitutional dilemma that it has pushed to the front of the state's policy agenda.

The builder's remedy remains the most powerful mechanism available to enforce compliance with the Mount Laurel Doctrine, and its continued use by the judiciary is crucial even under the new administrative scheme. The intimidating stick for municipalities considering whether to enter into voluntary settlements is that failure to do so will lead to the builder's remedy. "The remedy is the carrot," as the court tersely states.[75] Should the judiciary fail to afford builders this remedy, then the process of voluntary compliance and mediation inevitably will slacken, because there will be little incentive for the municipality to bend.[76]

It seems safe to assume, however, that the New Jersey courts, remaining active partners with COAH, will continue to rely on the builder's remedy. In doing so, they reaffirm the role they have played since the inception of Mount Laurel. In inventing and declaring that courts would employ the builder's remedy, Chief Justice Wilentz took the step that propelled the judicial branch to the forefront of political activism in precisely the manner that those advocating a more cautious exercise of judicial power abhor. The builder's remedy put the courts at dead center of the ongoing debate between state and local power over whether adherence to home rule would weaken the resolve to eliminate discrimination and inequality in local land-use controls. It became the weapon of choice for countering the intermunicipal quarantine of affordable housing, and its continued availability in court is as crucial as ever.

## Compliance Mechanisms: The Regional Contribution Agreement

In addition to the fairly standard compliance techniques that the three Mount Laurel trial judges developed, including mandatory set-asides, use of municipally owned land, fund-raising from state resources, and more aggressive pursuit of state or federal grants, the New Jersey legislation introduced a noteworthy—and deeply controversial—compliance mechanism, the "regional contribution agreement" (RCA). Under this arrangement, a locality, by entering into a contractual agreement, can transfer up to half its Mount Laurel obligations to another locality within its region. The only condition precedent is that COAH must approve the RCA before it can go into effect, such approval being contingent on a finding that the agreement establishes a realistic opportunity for low-income housing with convenient access to employment and that it "is consistent with sound, comprehensive regional planning."[77] Aside from this condition, sending and receiving municipalities are left on their own to negotiate a transfer price and other major terms.

The RCA first had to survive the charge of perpetrating racial stratification in metropolitan areas.[78] In the 1991 case of *In re Township of Warren*, for example, Judge Skillman rejected the public advocate's challenge to an RCA on the ground that it would shift Mount Laurel housing to a municipality already burdened with a disproportionate share of the region's lower-income households. The decision rested on legislative intent. The legislature, he emphasized, "must be presumed to have been aware that such agreements ordinarily would be entered into between suburban municipalities with small minority populations and urban municipalities with substantial minority populations." Warren's Mount Laurel obligation had been originally calculated at 946 units. Under COAH's formula, its responsibility was reduced to 367 affordable units; of these, half were sent under the RCA to New Brunswick, with Warren agreeing to pay out $4.3 million for the privilege.[79]

Although the RCA provision undermined the suburban remedy aspect of the affordable housing requirement, in its favor it may be said that many regard the provision as the political glue that holds the FHA together. After all, at the time of the statute's enactment, there was a legislative stampede to undercut the Mount Laurel Doctrine. In the same Panglossian vein, without a mechanism like the RCA, one has to wonder whether the legislature would have enacted any statute that supported the production of low- and moderate-income housing in suburban areas. So perceived, RCAS appear as a safety valve to a doctrine of integration so potentially disruptive of perceived local prerogatives that the entire ship of low-income housing production could sink without such a concession. RCAS allow a move in the right direction after all, just at a slower, more politically realistic pace. Indeed, although arguments can be advanced to the contrary, the RCA ended up as the jewel in the crown of the legislative counterreformation.

On July 17, 1992, as if to put a total end to the prolix policy criticisms of RCA and to reiterate that it did intend the mechanism to be an alternative to suburban location for affordable housing, the New Jersey legislature ordered that "the Public Advocate shall have no authority to become involved in, or take any position with regard to, any action challenging [RCAS] . . . approved by [COAH]."[80] Legislative intent, the amendment states unabashedly, should not be frustrated by delays caused by the public advocate or any other challenger.

Exemplary of a key divergence between legislative and judicial aspirations for Mount Laurel reform, the RCA shifted the rationale of the Mount Laurel doctrine away from the broad goal of ending geographic segregation surrounding inner-city minorities and toward the raw provision of low-income housing.[81] RCAS evoke a disheartening picture of the haves continuing to distance themselves from the have-nots. Suburbanites who would fight to the death to exclude people of low income from within their towns' borders and to maintain the value of their houses—their major (often sole) capital asset—are amenable, it turns out, to paying a form of ransom, through taxes, that preserves local control of new entrants while allowing lower-income housing to be built elsewhere.[82] An early evaluation study showed that, of forty-five municipal plans certified by the council, the eleven towns using RCAS had a higher average per-capita income, higher average residential values, and lower average equalized property tax rates than did the thirty-four other communities. By dint of the legislation, the option of buying out of the affordable housing obligation displaced the goal of integration and population redistribution.

RCAS, then, are likely to contribute to the most troublesome inadequacy of the Mount Laurel Doctrine, the problem that has dogged reform from the start: too few of the intended beneficiaries—African-Americans and other minorities from the inner city—enjoy the benefits of the new housing. Putting an end to the exclusion of racial minorities from suburbia through the revision of local exclusionary regulatory power is the implicit theme of Mount Laurel I and II. Yet by and large the homes built so far have not gone to the inner-city poor; with their weak credit ratings and meager incomes, they can rarely qualify as purchasers or even as tenants. Instead, many of the new homes built to satisfy long-debated fair share obligations, bargain priced at $40,000 to $70,000, are snapped up by people who qualify as low- and moderate-income buyers only because they happen to be at a low point in their lifetime earning potential—professional families just starting out ("junior yuppies"), divorced persons, graduate students, and the retired.

In a further subversion of the spirit of Mount Laurel, the option of contracting out fair share obligations generates competition among the receivers, not the senders, of new low-income construction dollars, leading to abuses of a reform process whose framers presumably never anticipated extensive bargaining. Since it is the poor communities that bid against one another for much-needed housing money from richer localities, the sending municipalities wield the power and do not always use it responsibly. Recently, the suburb of Parsippany–Troy Hills backed out of a nearly finalized $6.6 million arrangement with the city of Newark for 294 new and rehabilitated units because it was able to negotiate a $5.1 million deal with Elizabeth for the same number of houses.[83] Certainly this type of free-for-all represents the operation of a free market, but the idea that laboriously determined local obligations can be reshuffled in a bargaining process driven by human want sits uncomfortably with the broad social agenda articulated by the Mount Laurel Doctrine.[84]

Regarded as remedies for housing scarcity aimed at providing shelter for people in need, in one sense RCAs help carry out the reform goals of Mount Laurel.[85] By February 15, 1995, 39 RCAs had been completed, involving a transfer of 4,172 units and $80,982,795 to inner cities. But the option frustrates what may be viewed as the more significant underpinning of Mount Laurel: the aim of unlocking New Jersey's inner cities. Regional bargains do not merely undercut the objective of affirmative geographic integration; they raise the walls of regulatory barriers still higher around the suburbs. To those who regard the court's intervention as a deus ex machina for redistributing lower-income populations more widely over the state territory, the FHA's intermunicipal balance-of-payment provision is a counterproductive form of bribery, a hollow and hypocritical device that embodies the true cynicism of the New Jersey legislature acting on behalf of suburban constituents. In the usual run of affairs, judges dig into legislative intent in interpreting statutes; here, the legislature probed the constitutional impetus underlying a court opinion and interpreted that motivation in a direction that displaced a large chunk of the judicial mandate.

The New Jersey Supreme Court found it necessary to exercise extraordinary constitutional powers in order to transform a large segment of social reality deemed offensive to legal norms. Although the *Hills* decision contained an eloquent statement about the powers of the judiciary, the upshot, to the surprise of many observers, was that the court withdrew from the battlefield. In the aftermath of the court's approval of the New Jersey legislature's resumption of authority over affordable housing requirements, an uneasy balance persists among the branches. Emboldened by its successful confrontation with the courts, the legislature (as the embodiment of the popular will) may be more inclined to be assertive in the future when it disagrees with actions taken by either the courts or COAH.

# VII

## . . . And the Judiciary Responds:
## *Holmdel* and *Warren*

ENACTMENT OF THE FHA extended the interdepartmental dance. Now that the legislature had introduced COAH into the situation, the court's participation, if any, in enforcing the Mount Laurel Doctrine remained up in the air. In two ensuing opinions, *Holmdel* and *Warren*, the New Jersey Supreme Court resolved any doubts about its role, spelling out continued and rigorous protection of its previously articulated stand. COAH or not, determinations by the supreme court would continue to affect the operation of fair share determinations. Indeed, *Holmdel* and *Warren* well deserve their popular labels of Mount Laurel IV and Mount Laurel V.

### COAH Vindicated

*Holmdel* involves a review of developer fees as a new and potentially significant method for obtaining money to pay for affordable housing. Local governments in New Jersey, like their counterparts throughout the nation, increasingly rely on the practice of exacting from developers off-site improvements—facilities essential to support an influx of new residents—as the price of admission into the community.[1] With the virtual withdrawal of federal and state funding for infrastructure such as roads, sewer and water systems, and parks, municipalities have little other choice in their efforts to provide the public support systems indispensable to growth.

The legal status of developer fees and exactions is still being worked out in a series of litigations throughout the country. State courts now hold at least three different views concerning the intensity of the relation that must exist between an exaction and the needs generated by a development.[2] And recent U.S. Supreme Court opinions in *Nollan v. California Coastal Commission* and *Dolan v. City of Tigard* have set federal constitutional minimal levels on the essential nexus between the impact of the proposed development and the locally imposed exaction.[3] In New Jersey, builder associations initiated suits claiming that fee ordinances are beyond the authority granted by the FHA or the state zoning enabling act and, moreover, that they fall totally outside the police power of the state. As such, they argued, the obligations were disguised invalid taxes and confiscatory takings.

The contentions came to a head in the 1990 *Holmdel* decision, where a builder's association challenged a wide range of local ordinances imposing mandatory fees on new development as a precondition for receiving a permit.[4] The ordinances varied in their terms. Some of them offered a density bonus as a quid pro quo for the fee, while others did not; several gave developers a choice between constructing low-income housing and paying an in-lieu fee (the amount varying among the ordinances) to an affordable housing trust fund.[5] Each of the challenged municipalities had received substantive certification of its housing element from COAH.

In a decision reminiscent of the two landmark Mount Laurel opinions, the New Jersey Supreme Court upheld the validity of fee ordinances. In essence, the *Holmdel* opinion showed two branches of government—the courts and the council—united in pushing for a common interpretation of the legislature's intent. The court not only gave an expansive construction to the powers conferred on the council but lent the agency its own mantle of power. Reversing the appellate division's conclusion that the ordinances at issue were facially unconstitutional in that mandatory provisions for in-lieu development fees were unauthorized revenue-raising devices, the court found that the collection of fees for the purpose of low- and moderate-income housing as a condition for receiving permission to build or in order to obtain a density bonus was constitutional as well as statutorily authorized; furthermore, it was consistent with the FHA, as long as—and here was the catch—the council promulgated in advance a system of rules governing fee collection.

The court turned first to statutory purpose. The lower court had held flatly that "the Legislature would have specifically authorized such fees if it so intended."[6] Writing for the supreme court, Justice Alan B. Handler reversed this view of statutory construction. After a general analysis of the state's zoning enabling law and the traditional scope of police powers, he interpreted the FHA in a way that conferred independent powers of a broad-ranging nature on COAH. Although the FHA did not expressly authorize development fees, he wrote, it did confer extensive powers on localities to provide a realistic opportunity for affordable housing, and these powers necessarily carried along with them the means of levying fees.

How did Justice Handler arrive at this interpretation? Drawing on a pattern of administrative practice—the council's custom of approving voluntary fees in other circumstances—he was able to construct the scaffolding, indeed the foundation, for upholding the fees in the absence of specific statutory wording.[7] Under the COAH regulations to which he referred, developers could pay a voluntary fee in exchange for an offsetting incentive—for example, a density bonus. Drawing comfort from the premise that the "understanding of legislation by the administrative agency responsible for its implementation can be most instructive in ascertaining legislative intent and statutory meaning," the court offered the council's regulations as evidence that mandatory fees "are not inconsistent with the FHA."[8]

It is important to recognize that the court's conclusion vis-à-vis COAH was hardly preordained. In granting certification and approving the housing plans of municipalities whose development fees were challenged, COAH had avoided ruling on their validity, concluding only that such fees were "not required to implement the fair share plan."[9] But the court insisted, "As we view the matter, each ordinance has a direct and material bearing on the municipality's effort to meet its fair-share affordable-housing obligation"; given this, it found the development fee ordinances to be a constituent part of the locality's housing plan. Justice Handler elaborated that COAH's approach "suggest[s] an understanding that [fee ordinances] are not invalid or *ultra vires*."[10] A contrary reading would be equally availing, however: COAH's refusal to rule on the ordinances could suggest doubts about, rather than an endorsement of, development fees.[11]

Justice Handler then moved to a review of Mount Laurel I and II and their applicability to the litigation before him. Throughout his recounting of the history of the court's attempts at reform, he shone a spotlight on the persistent paucity of affordable housing in New Jersey and explored how existing patterns of development could be understood as contributing to the shortage.[12] In prose resonant of the original rationale in

Mount Laurel II, he determined that it "is fair and reasonable [for a locality] to impose such fee requirements on private developers when they possess, enjoy, and consume land, which constitutes the primary resource for housing."[13] Scarce resources (vacant developable land, sewer capacity, road access, and the like) are irrevocably absorbed for uses other than affordable housing at the same time those uses generate a need for that very housing, exacerbating demand without contributing toward its fulfillment.

The court admitted that its conclusion flew in the face of the previous New Jersey rule for off-site improvements that required "a strong, almost but-for, causal nexus" between the public activity to be funded by the development fee and the development made subject to the fee.[14] Steeped in the Mount Laurel tradition, however, Justice Handler concluded that the application of such a rational-nexus test was not apposite. Put simply, development fees—as the functional equivalent of mandatory set-asides—should be accorded a similar validity where they are devoted to the grand purpose of affordable housing.[15]

A countervailing by-product should be noted. As a result of increasing reliance on developer exactions, those who produce or depend on low-income housing must absorb fees that add a substantial percentage to the sales prices of homes. Thus, ironically, development fees may evolve at the margin into yet another regulatory barrier to the entry of low-income housing.[16]

What is so striking about the consequences of *Holmdel* is that the dynamic between the court on one hand and the executive and legislature on the other remained but slightly modified even after the FHA's passage and its judicial confirmation in *Hills*. The supreme court's claim that the existence of administrative procedures allowed it to determine whether the challenged ordinances were "in conformity with the legislative intent of the Fair Housing Act" masks a more straightforward fulfillment of judicial desires.[17] It was in Mount Laurel II, after all, that the court first proposed inclusionary zoning devices such as mandatory set-asides, a proposal ratified by the legislature in the FHA. In *Holmdel*, the court seemed to be taking the logical next step of sanctioning development fees as a means of paying for the affordable housing programs mandated by the state, first by the judiciary, then through the FHA. The decision effectively expanded COAH's powers and charged it with requiring the implementation of fee ordinances as a monetized version of mandatory set-asides.

In one of *Holmdel's* bolder elucidations, Justice Handler found that the council's regulation authorizing voluntary fees balanced by compensating benefits implied the permissibility of mandatory fees—even without compensating benefits. On this issue of reciprocity, the court sent COAH a mixed message. First, the court made arguments as to why the FHA does not require such benefits. Later on, it described the COAH regulation on voluntary developer fees as permitting the granting of such benefits, whereas the regulation in fact *requires* their award.[18] Then, the court stated that COAH "might well choose" to follow in the commercial and office developer context the approach that the council had taken in the residential developer situation.

Was the court suggesting that COAH grant optional compensating benefits or that it require compensating benefits outright? If the court was not recommending an approach for COAH, then why did it say anything at all, particularly since it had already insisted that it was COAH's responsibility to decide "whether a system of development fees should include counterbalancing density bonuses"?[19] Whatever the answers, although the court had implied in Mount Laurel II and expressly affirmed in *Hills* that nothing was closer to its heart than having the legislature occupy the field and the council receive extreme deference ("an administrative agency's exercise of statutorily-delegated responsibility is accorded a strong presumption of validity and reasonableness," it averred on yet another occasion),[20] it still could not refrain from launching initiatives of its own and giving a parental push when its Mount Laurel Doctrine came into play.

The *Holmdel* opinion retained a built-in elasticity that allowed for stronger judicial measures if the threat of administrative inaction turned real. While it invalidated the fees at issue because the council had not set standards for their enactment, the court sanctioned the use of development fees in general, and it did so in the broadest policy-oriented terms. Justice Handler's language justified developer fees not only as an option for municipalities but as a policy initiative from the judiciary. The fees were "conducive to the creation of a realistic opportunity for the development of affordable housing . . . [and] it is fair and reasonable to impose such fee requirements on private developers."[21] (Not surprisingly, quite a different note is sounded in the rueful conclusion of one developer's lawyer that *Holmdel* simply "lays out an elaborate means of opening the pocketbook of the building industry to finance the court's Mount Laurel opinions.")

The unavoidable message was that if COAH and the legislature did not respond actively to changes in the area of affordable housing, the court was ready to reinvigorate its policy objectives.[22] It is thus no stretch to read *Holmdel* as an indication that the court would adopt a most benevolent attitude toward the exercise of municipal power (and the rulemaking authority of COAH) when it came to the provision of affordable housing. As Mount Laurel III foreshadowed, the development of low-and moderate-income units in the suburbs had become the motive driving the court's definition of statutory and regulatory power.[23]

## COAH Rebuffed

In April 1993 the New Jersey Supreme Court flexed its muscles once again in a unanimous opinion that frequently referred to and quoted Mount Laurel I and II. *Warren* involved the validity of a COAH regulation authorizing a municipality to provide an occupancy preference to households residing or working in the municipality for up to 50 percent of its Mount Laurel fair share housing.[24] COAH had granted certification to housing element and fair share plans containing a local preference that had been filed by the townships of Denville, Hillsborough, Holmdel, and Warren and the boroughs of Bloomingdale and Roseland. This time, the COAH action failed to receive the court's approval. Emphasizing that the percentage of minority residents in a municipality was substantially smaller than their percentage in the related housing region, the supreme court (reversing the appellate division) invalidated the local preference as perpetuating exclusionary zoning in violation of the Mount Laurel Doctrine.

The townships claimed that the preference addressed the needs of households with an existing connection to the community. At the very least, ran an intuitive argument, it would surely increase local support for the doctrine. The lower courts had gone to the point of holding that the preference was not constitutionally infirm even if it had a disparate racial impact. Notwithstanding, focusing on COAH's methodology, which derived a municipality's fair share from regional, not local, data, Justice Gary S. Stein held that occupancy preferences did result in impermissible discrimination. The minority population in five of the townships was less than 2 percent, but when COAH made the calculation on a regional basis, the minority population ranged from 8.6 to 52 percent. Because of the disproportionately low population of minority residents and workers in the six municipalities, therefore, the regulation ended up favoring white rather than minority households as the occupants of newly constructed affordable housing.

Bowing politely to COAH's right to adopt regulations to implement the goals of the FHA, the court nevertheless chose to emphasize the "fundamental inconsistencies" between the result of occupancy preferences and the detailed methodology employed for calculating and allocating the regional fair share of low-income housing.[25] "The occupancy preference," the court ruled, "does not further the statutory goals of the FHA."[26] Justice Stein concluded that "the weight COAH has assigned to housing demand by eligible local residents and eligible local workers in calculating and allocating prospective regional need and reallocated present need does not justify a fifty-percent occupancy preference for eligible residents and workers."[27] "We cannot discern," he elaborated, how the formula "is consistent with and advances the purpose of the regional obligation."[28] The final ruling was that local occupancy preferences—absent a regional analysis to support the standard—do not comport with the Mount Laurel Doctrine.[29]

A strong, assertive judiciary was clearly resurrected in *Warren*. And it came by way of a unanimous opinion in a highly delicate political area.[30]

## Where Does Power Lie after Mount Laurel IV and V?

The court's continuing—albeit intermittent—supervision of the council brings back memories of the days when the courts were riding high in the Mount Laurel saddle and the legislature was about to rope in their freedom. Although COAH is more a replacement than a successor to the courts in deciding the fate of New Jersey suburban land-use regulations, it has not avoided the baleful criticisms, culminating in legislative rebukes, previously reserved for the judiciary. And sadly, the outside world draws little distinction between court and council; the average citizen lumps both together. The chief counsel of the New Jersey League of Municipalities even went to the point of advising its members not to deal with COAH, just as he might have warned them about the courts.

To its bewilderment, the council finds itself in the same narrow corner the three trial judges formerly occupied, driven there by institutional mandate. In the aftermath of the FHA and *Hills*, then, the courts and COAH appear to have more in common than may have been anticipated initially. In their handling of the Mount Laurel Doctrine, courts and council share an awareness of the awkwardness of their position; they know full well that a groundswell of public sympathy for municipalities would eliminate the legislature's willingness to confront the blatant concerns of racial segregation and inadequate housing in the suburbs. Courts and council, thrown together by the common opposition, end up relying on analogous tests for satisfying the regional fair share obligation, and the reaction of one to novel pleadings or defenses has considerable influence over the other.

In dealings and appeals since the enactment of the FHA, the New Jersey Supreme Court continues to defer to COAH as it struggles with the administrative tasks of Mount Laurel that had earlier beleaguered the judiciary. Such judicial deference is evident in *Holmdel*/Mount Laurel IV. Throughout his opinion, Justice Handler emphasized the critical role played by the council "in the adoption of ordinances that address municipal affordable-housing needs."[31] He acknowledged the broad legislative mandate granted to COAH, citing, among other matters, the agency's power to determine a municipality's fair share obligation, its ability to establish affordable housing programs, and its authority to approve "the methods of implementing municipalities' housing elements and fair-share plans, . . . including approval of any regional contribution agreements."[32] In addition, he cited the council's educational responsibility, exercising its authority in part "to inform the public and guide the agency in discharging its authorized function."[33] COAH, in short, has broad powers and responsibilities as part of its oversight of the fair share housing system.[34]

Yet despite the court's expressed intent to defer to the council and despite its willingness at times to ally itself with the agency against the legislature, one senses in the *Holmdel* and *Warren* rulings a continuing desire, almost a need, to assert judge-made policy within the administrative framework. *Holmdel* finds the rule making on fee ordinances incomplete because the agency failed to address the very issue raised before the court: the availability of mandatory development fees in the same sense as mandatory set-aside measures. In remanding the issue to the agency for the necessary further elaboration, the *Holmdel* court expected a wideranging response, one that would "address the types of developments that will be subject to fees, the amount and nature of the fees imposed, the relationship of the fees to other inclusionary-zoning measures such as mandatory set-asides and density bonuses, the conditions for the creation and administration of affordable-housing trust funds, the requirements for the use and application of such funds, and whether a system of development fees should include counterbalancing density bonuses."[35]

By any reading, the opinion directs the agency to do far more than it had originally intended. And there is another unintended consequence: by placing COAH at the center of a new funding source for New Jersey localities, *Holmdel* granted the agency crucial chips in the territorial game of competing branches of government. In stressing the need for developer fee schemes rather than their appropriateness, the court inserted its own policy vision. The council absorbed that vision, subsequently issuing feeordinance regulations that relied intensely on the *Holmdel* opinion, its guidelines, and its specific requirements, all in an apparent effort to fulfill the court's wishes.[36]

For the court did not relax its hold. As *Warren* puts it, "Acknowledging the complexity that surrounds implementation of the FHA, this Court has accorded COAH wide leeway in fashioning regulatory approaches to meet fair housing goals, and, at the same time, insisted that COAH exercise that regulatory responsibility and do so in a reasonable and accountable way."[37] Behind the scenes the court may be, but it is ready to play its part in formulating metropolitan land policies. By temperament and by the terms of the disputes arising before it—even, to some degree, by the nature of appellate opinion writing—the New Jersey Supreme Court finds it difficult not to involve itself in the administration of the Mount Laurel Doctrine under the FHA. It will continue to make its voice heard.[38]

The hoped-for outcome of equality of access to suburban land, from the initial court formulation through the legislative reaction and the judicial counterresponse, depends on the court's continued exercise of equitable discretion in applying the Mount Laurel Doctrine. Much hinges on the courts' expansive interpretation of the council's powers. The years of Mount Laurel litigation and subsequent enactment of the FHA have not transformed the hearts of the people. Of the state's 567 municipalities, only some 200 have submitted applications for certification. And complying units have not as yet been built on a sufficient scale. The judiciary—whatever setbacks it encounters—cannot gracefully withdraw. Nor should it. Without its oversight and impetus, the Mount Laurel administrative structure cannot function effectively, nor can the legislative budgetary process be trusted to achieve the initial goals.

Judicial obituaries are premature. *Holmdel*/Mount Laurel IV stands as a declaration of judicial vigor. And the even bolder position taken in the 1993 *Warren*/Mount Laurel V opinion must extinguish any lingering doubts. Both on appeal and on remedy, there is still only one superpower in the world of land-use planning: the state court system. More than any other branch, the judiciary has interests, exposure, and reach that are statewide. Even when the legislature moves in with its enactments, seeking to preempt the field, it cannot relegate the judiciary to a backwater. After all, as the court astutely and self-referentially construed it, "The central goal of the Fair Housing Act is to implement the Mount Laurel doctrine."[39]

There is, of course, a potential cost to the court's maintaining its hovering presence. It endures a drumbeat of criticism for its attitude toward local police power regulations, and the possibility of constitutional amendment or the outright loss of judicial position (because the state senate must approve a judge's reappointment after an initial seven-year term), or simply the sad recognition by weary judges that the firepower of the municipalities is too concentrated, is an oppressive threat. However, *Holmdel* and *Warren* together demonstrate the court's reluctant readiness to pay the price for upholding the mobility rights of minorities.

Years of diplomacy and negotiations have not fully achieved Justice Hall's and Chief Justice Wilentz's goals of unlocking the ghetto and undoing the spatial mismatch between residences and jobs. If the judiciary is pushed into quiescence, the life opportunities of the politically and economically disadvantaged locked up in the inner city will be diminished.

And there is a danger that this may be the inevitable course of events. There are inescapable limits on what even a superpower can accomplish. If the Mount Laurel litigations become an instance of the court's having overreached and failed, only doubt and irresolution will follow in the exercise of land-use controls. Reform will be locked in tugs-of-war over particular regulations and in more stratospheric battles over the separation of powers.

The harsh realities of public sentiment exist. When mayors proclaim eagerness to stand at the city gates and bodily prevent entry by developers or when bumper stickers call for the impeachment of judges, they constitute simplistic responses to complex social problems, signs of the bigotry that diminishes the intellectual and political life of the nation. Like other states, New Jersey has allowed metropolitan areas to become deeply segregated to the point where there is a precarious imbalance in the living conditions, jobs, and transportation of individuals on the basis of class, race, ethnicity.[40] The court's show of force in launching the Mount Laurel Doctrine is instructive precisely because so many New Jerseyites—including academics, public interest groups, legislators, and governors—under pressure from interest groups, have begun to doubt whether constitutional principles of fairness and equity and community are worth the disruption of neighborhoods, the decline of housing values, and the outrage of the middle-class citizenry. The Mount Laurel decisions are a contemporary reminder of Justice Cardozo's vision that the judiciary's "chief worth" lies in its "making vocal and audible the ideals that might otherwise be silenced, in giving them continuity of life and of expression."[41]

# Part III

## INSTITUTIONAL REFORM THROUGH THE COURTS

# VIII

## The New World of Judicial Remedies

THE MOUNT LAUREL Doctrine's checkered twenty-year history provides a social science laboratory that tests whether courts, through wide-ranging, often intrusive remedies, can effectively reorder ongoing institutional practices that systematically breach constitutional or statutory norms. How do the benefits of such judicial implementation measure up against the costs of achieving its objectives? "The measure of any desegregation [or other] plan is its effectiveness."[1] Without resultant housing in suburbia, the sound and the fury signify little.

Several key questions order this inquiry. Is the judiciary capable of effecting lasting change in society, given the inherent limitations that shape and bind it as the branch of government that wields the power of neither the purse nor the sword?[2] Does the successful reconstruction of failed social institutions hinge on the structural character and procedural apparatus of the way judges operate? Or is it hampered by them? Can the courts' ability to bring about change be reduced, as Thomas Carlyle's view of history would have it, to the personalities of individual judges and their ingenuity at implementing successful remedial mechanisms? Do the ends justify the means, even if methods chosen violate the contours of an ideal adjudicative model? Finally, is the delicate balance of functions among the different branches of government—and the ultimate legitimacy of courts—threatened by too free an exercise of judicial discretion and power? Understanding the Mount Laurel experience, and drawing conclusions as to the utility of institutional restructuring in furthering social justice, requires exploration of all these inquiries as they merge, blend, and interplay.

## Effectiveness of Courts: The Power to Move Mountains

Did the courts succeed in producing discernible changes in the zoning practices of New Jersey municipalities? Did the Mount Laurel judicial intervention alter metropolitan demographics, disperse inner-city concentrations of minorities, and make realistically possible—as Justice Hall would phrase it—an appropriate variety and choice of housing in suburban areas? One view, currently dominant in the world of the academy, denies the very legitimacy of the inquiry itself. Put simply, this argument runs, courts are inappropriate venues for restructuring social institutions, no matter how grave the illegality of the disputed actions or how dramatic the judicial intervention. In combating majoritarian wishes, the courts can at best produce hollow victories—and at enormous cost.[3] This futility thesis—a prime weapon in the reactionary arsenal[4]—argues that judicial attempts at social change are doomed to remain cosmetic and illusory.

A contention is also advanced—startlingly often by proponents of reform—that if another avenue is available for restructuring a failing institution, that path should be followed rather than the judicial route. The reasoning is that the courts are a diversionary grail; judicial rhetoric leads only to a false sense of accomplishment as repugnant reality persists. In the end, clinging to the courts as the saviors of society, lawyers encourage a naive vision of change without pain. To support this thesis, its exponents cite examples of institutional litigation deflecting the battle from the substantive political forum, where true revision is possible, to the domain of harmless litigation, from which only paper decrees can issue. Constrained by the traditional adversarial system and by the inability to acquire pertinent knowledge about complicated social issues, to assess alternatives, or to monitor implementation, courts cannot bring about social transformation; as institutions, they lack the resources, staff, and flexibility of administrative agencies. Further, by its quintessential nature, adjudicatory decision making is piecemeal and reactive. Hence the warning: those content to celebrate superficial palliatives as progress are a persisting danger to their own causes of reform.

The Mount Laurel history flatly contradicts this critique. The professional observers closest to the operation—planners, lawyers, appraisers, builders, lenders, municipal officials, and judges—hold an unshakable belief that the decisions exerted enormous influence on the land-use world outside the courtroom. And indeed the briefest survey of the sharp reactions from mayors, neighborhoods, and state legislators reveals the overwhelming impact of the Mount Laurel decisions. To those who bore the brunt of the decrees, it is beyond cavil that the courts proved powerful, vigorous, and effective proponents of land-use reform; they would not echo Stalin's question about the pope: "And how many troops does he command?" In fact, opponents of the Mount Laurel Doctrine see the past eighteen years as an era during which the court ran roughshod over the ideal of democratic majority rule. The very strength of the public outcry points up the intensity of the intervention. After all, this is the commonsense understanding that should settle the effectiveness debate in short order.

Tangible consequences also bear out Mount Laurel's impact. One readily cited result is the 15,400 affordable housing units in the New Jersey suburbs that had no prospect of being built without the Mount Laurel decisions. A second outcome is the number of units available for building as a result of remedies requiring rezoning of ordinances held to be exclusionary. Between 1987 and 1992 zoning revisions allowed for the construction or rehabilitation of 54,000 additional low- and moderate-income housing units in the suburbs; of these, 75 percent were formulated under the aegis of the courts, the balance occurring under COAH's jurisdiction. In approximately five years, New Jersey either built, rehabilitated, or voted for one-third as many low-income units as it had produced in the previous six decades. This record is all the more remarkable in that between 1987 and 1992 only 153,000 building permits were issued throughout the state.[5] And these numbers do not take into account the quantity of affordable housing built in communities acting to forestall Mount Laurel litigation or as a result of cases settled outside the court's jurisdiction.[6] By anecdotal account, these units come to large numbers. Behavior has changed in suburban localities.

Indirectly, but no less significantly, the courts' activity also brought about the institutionalization of reform (slow-paced though it may seem to many) in the shape of the legislature's partial, reluctant, but nevertheless actual ratification of the Mount Laurel rulings in the FHA.[7] Finally, the Mount Laurel Doctrine has had an effect—not readily susceptible to measurement but no less real—on individuals, whether inspiring them to act idealistically or persuading them to reexamine their attitudes toward integration in housing and land use.

Striving for a realistic outcome was always the judges' goal. From Mount Laurel I through *Warren*, they contoured their formulations with care and precision, lest the risky operation prove fatal. Attention to the production of housing was paramount. Indeed, the courts' reliance on private real estate developers through the builder's remedy can be interpreted as an effort to co-opt the working land market in order to finalize the public policy they had worked so hard to carve out.

But if the Mount Laurel Doctrine is of such power, how can that be reconciled with Alexander Hamilton's denomination of the courts as the "least dangerous" branch? As Hamilton pointed out, in terms reemphasized ever since, courts lack power outside the moral sphere. For him, "the judiciary . . . may truly be said to have neither FORCE nor WILL, but merely judgment" and is "least in a capacity to annoy or injure."[8] Within the world of constitutional scholarship, this is taken as both description and prescription, a warning to the third branch to be keenly aware of the limited scope of its power to effect social change. "We the people" must ultimately rule according to majoritarian values and without interference from elite officials sitting on the bench. Yet if Hamilton's formulation still has a powerful resonance to many, it hardly applies as empirical truth to the New Jersey experience, as the state's suburban mayors, chastened by the crucible of experience, would surely agree.

For decades, the wall of legal barriers surrounding the suburbs had stood strong, erected brick by brick from over thirty years of court decisions.[9] Process determined this outcome: the New Jersey Supreme Court had long employed a presumption of validity as the major criterion by which it measured challenges to local zoning ordinances. Wherever the legality of a municipal regulation controlling land was in the least debatable, the court gave the benefit of the doubt to the local council. On another intellectual front, the court turned regionalism on its head, allowing localities to exclude any use if there was room for its location elsewhere in the region. Paradoxically, this conception of total local power over zoning not only kept conservatives happy but found support from critics on the left. The extension of local zoning power over developers was hailed as a progressive advance, the triumph of the public interest over the avarice of the individual builder.[10]

Yet after Mount Laurel I, litigation quickly evolved into the weapon of choice for public interest groups seeking land-use reforms. The head-to-head confrontation of the Mount Laurel courts with the most representative bodies of government—the grassroots local townships and villages—dramatizes a key judicial dilemma: how can courts vindicate constitutional rules protecting minorities' rights to equal access to land yet also give proper deference to the authority of local elected officials who choose actions that may infringe on such rights? As the New Jersey courts grappled with balancing the home rule claims of municipalities with the necessity to provide affordable housing on a regional basis, a poignant picture emerges of judges being drawn, however reluctantly, into an elaborate process of weighing, implementing, and micro-managing.

The scathing charge that courts lack the competence, the ability, even the patience to implement social policies over time is not borne out by the New Jersey experience.[11] While the accusation may apply to the first Mount Laurel decision, in which Justice Hall left a bit too much to the remedial discretion of localities, it certainly cannot be leveled against the inventive machinery that Chief Justice Wilentz devised in Mount Laurel II, nor its implementation by the three trial judges. This evolution is un-deniable proof that, over the long haul, courts can implement their vision even when they are not supported by elected or administrative officials. They should not be demoralized by doubts about the potentialities of their efforts.

In shifting the focus from civil rights to institutional reform, the New Jersey courts had to adapt—in function, outlook, and procedures. Ensu-ing tensions demonstrated that persistent judicial vindication of the right to live in the suburbs was inseparable from an uneasy sense that such involvement somehow exceeded the proper bounds of judicial conduct. Caught between a fictional ideal and a constitutional imperative, the New Jersey judges groped for a contemporary definition of their role. Paul Freund once noted optimistically "that the processes of law—the proce-dures and ways of thought of lawyers and judges— . . . may help us to live with uncertainty and ambiguity, may teach us to cope with the great antinomies of our aspirations."[12]

In Mount Laurel, the conflicting demands of community and consti-tution could never be wholly reconciled by judges at once sympathetic to competing visions of society.[13] Still, these same judges not only re-vealed the jagged fault lines between rich and poor, whites and non-whites, but undertook the reordering of land-use regulations in metropol-itan areas. This success should not be minimized: courts, when pressed and when imbued with the will, can develop, organize, and sharpen the tools that produce significant social restructuring.[14] There is no Millsian iron law ruling the social world that poses an insurmountable barrier to judicial engineering. It is a tribute—no less fervent word will do—to judi-cial persistence in a tinderbox atmosphere under the most adverse of circumstances.

## Inadequacy of the Adversarial Process Model in the New Litigation

If the ineffectiveness or futility plea does not bar courts from entering the arena of institutional litigation, ought not the fear of undermining their own legitimacy by departing from the traditional adversarial model keep courts from participating in institutional restructuring cases? When courts' actions take on executive and legislative hues, do the resulting adjustments disturb the delicate relations among the branches of government that collectively are the extraordinary achievement of the Constitution? Does this so dissipate the oracular distinction of disembodied justice that its awesome allegorical majesty is lost?

One answer is that institutional reform litigation inherently introduces a dimension to the analysis of judicial conduct that undermines traditional views of the separation of powers.[15] Inattention to functional demarcation on all sides runs through the Mount Laurel history. The fact is that each branch of government exercises a mixture of powers in carrying out its operations, and when courts undertake institutional restructuring as a result of a constitutional violation, the already muddled boundaries among judicial, executive, legislative, and administrative actions become even harder to draw. Mount Laurel II's creation of a statewide trial-court machinery is a managerial and executive action, while its framing of the four-to-one inclusionary remedy is properly characterized as legislative. The New Jersey legislature, for its part, took on executive functions in designing the Fanwood Amendment. COAH acts in the capacity of what is most accurately described as a quasi-judicial body in hearing and deciding motions, a power neither granted nor assumed by the legislature but bestowed by the judiciary in *Hills*.[16] The lines of power separation are inevitably blurred in the world of action.[17]

Through lawsuits, the Southern Burlington and Camden City NAACPs, acting on behalf of the Lawrences, requested that the court, not the legislature or the executive, address the overwhelming and seemingly intractable problem of exclusionary zoning. Pushed into leading the fight, the New Jersey judiciary became a last but preferred resort for reform. Other avenues, such as a change of heart by the suburbs, action by the state legislature, a move by the federal Department of Housing and Urban Development, or even congressional preemption of local regulations, were seen as unlikely or unavailing. Energetic lawyers and wise decrees were not enough to remake entire sets of community practices, however; the courts cleverly buttressed themselves by enlisting the business sector. Real estate developers desiring to build—not affordable housing, of course, but shopping centers, office buildings, apartment houses, and expensive individual homes—gave the courts their foothold.

New Jersey history's response to the charge that an activist judiciary can lose legitimacy is clear: fear or caution in the exercise of power can undermine legitimacy and dignity just as surely as an excess of activism can. Inaction blurs grandeur and generates contempt. Institutions erode when they allow challenges to pass them by, for power not deployed is soon lost, frequently irretrievably. The failure to rise to a challenge leaves

the social problem untouched and the political stalemate unresolved. A successful remedy, on the other hand, invests legitimacy in the initiating court. Americans take pride in the independence and purposefulness of their judges.

Traditionalists would convert the extant legal structure into a religion in which technology determines the creed. They argue for passivity in policy and direction and the worship of methodology over the ends that might be sought. They are unable to imagine an acceptable procedural mechanism that copes with the substantive issues of institutional breakdown. Their argument denies the view of the law as an instrument of social and political change, a view that, frankly, has inspired generations of lawyers and vitalizes its moral claim to obedience.

The social reconstruction goals of Mount Laurel I and II marched forward under the banner of constitutional rights, about whose discovery and revelation the judiciary, rather than the legislature, is the acknowledged expert. This constitutional framework furnishes the base of the courts' jurisdiction. Although the New Jersey Constitution does not expressly define an entitlement to live in the suburbs, for Mount Laurel purposes the New Jersey Supreme Court read the first paragraph of the first article of the constitution as an equal protection clause. Through this power of actualization, set out by Justice Hall in doctrinal elaborations that daringly opposed prevailing federal interpretations, the court produced the doctrine that Mount Laurel II would transform into the law of the state.[18]

The Mount Laurel I ruling concededly is not the extension of slowly accumulated decisions; it did not refine previously enunciated rulings into a full-flowered constitutional right to live in the suburbs. Indeed, the sharp reversal of doctrine in Mount Laurel I offends the tenets of standard legal culture, which would set limits on novel judicial expansion of rights. But the urgent needs of deprived inner-city households, not to mention the chasm dividing them from suburban jobs, made the court leap over the fence of precedents beyond what Justice Traynor once termed the continuity scripts of the law.[19] In the justices' eyes, the chances of realizing their hopeful vision justified judicial intervention.

New remedial approaches are jarring to the conventional model of adjudication. Ordinarily, the term *litigation* evokes a mental picture of an adversarial process, involving two parties locked in combat before an impartial body with the power of decision. A long history dictates that established procedures be followed in order to assure society at large (not to mention the immediate parties) of the fairness of the proceedings; a collective evolutionary wisdom warns, for instance, that evidence not made part of the record should not be considered and that matters removed from testing by cross-examination should be excluded as potentially improper influences. But the task of correcting a continuous pattern of wrongdoing by government shifts the center of gravity and induces a different perspective.[20] The adversarial process model breaks down when extended to the remedial focus of institutional reform litigation.

Classic trial procedure concentrates on assigning liability—determining who should bear the burden of a court judgment. In institutional restructuring cases, however, the main judicial task is to shape a workable remedy. At the trial level in post–Mount Laurel II cases, liability was conceded right at the outset. Neither Judge Skillman nor Judge Serpentelli can recall a case in which the defendants seriously claimed compliance with the Mount Laurel Doctrine. "There were a couple of cases," one recounted, "in which the municipal attorneys would come to my chambers somewhat sheepishly and say, 'I can't concede liability,' so there were pro forma motions for summary judgment where it was just that there were political obstacles to the defendants conceding anything." Judge Gibson, who relied heavily on mediation in the less intensively contested cases that formed the majority of his caseload, had no occasion to litigate liability.

A court's role changes drastically once a case moves from determining liability to formulating remedies.[21] In fashioning equitable relief, a court operates from different levels of logic, appeals to other kinds of justification, and falls back on strategies aimed at whole constituencies.[22] Above all, the judge typically needs specialized knowledge to grasp a complex technical situation. Without a basis in reality, a remedy cannot hold; highly technical questions to do with science or the complex interactions between economic and political policies—questions that form the core of many institutional decrees—require judicial sifting through alternative plans on the basis of practicality. The conventional trial model, relying on information generated solely by the litigants, cannot provide a sufficient basis for the work of institutional reform. Furthermore, shaping the decree requires not only participation and bargaining by the parties but also the involvement of those who are to live with the change. Effective outcomes will not occur without discussions and negotiations—which often must be held in private, with parties kept unaware of the confidential positions of others.

Ultimately, the actualization of a solution, not some academic model of adversarial norms, must be the touchstone for institutional reform litigation. To claim that constitutional rights must be the prisoners of procedural technology fashioned for other forms of litigation is a form of willful ignorance. The Mount Laurel cases, in their remedial phases, are a fine argument for institutional reform through judicial intervention.

## Techniques for a Successful Institutional Remedy: Do's and Don'ts

Scholars have leveled the astonishing accusation that judges attach little significance to the feasibility of remedies,[23] and moreover are too remote from conditions to fashion corrections where that becomes appropriate.[24] Whatever the merits of this theoretical criticism of other institutional trials, it does not hold for exclusionary zoning cases. By far, the greatest proportion of the energy the Mount Laurel judges and masters expended went into implementing and monitoring remedies.

The sound corrective designs achieved in the Mount Laurel trial courts owe much to the forethought that cut away precedential underbrush. Delays so condemned in the popular mind—the stretched-out tactics of discovery, the myriad interrogatories, the volleying of motions, the slowness of appeals—were pushed aside. Care was taken that motions and depositions not replace the framing and finishing of houses. The snarled procedure that normally renders courts poor institutions for rapid response is thus absent in the Mount Laurel cases. With the traditional procedural mechanisms streamlined, the New Jersey Supreme Court positioned the trial courts to apply the Mount Laurel Doctrine vigorously to end the exclusionary ordinances of local zoning authorities. Analysis of the techniques developed at trial should help judges and lawyers in future situations of institutional wrongdoing where courts find it necessary to exercise extraordinary constitutional powers in order to transform a large segment of social reality deemed offensive to legal norms.


## Professional Expertise

The three Mount Laurel judges managed to navigate a long journey into the unknown, even within the constraints of a conservative legal culture. Their use of experts as high-minded professionals to negotiate, mediate, and report to the court provides a lesson and a model for effective management of future cases of institutional restructuring that involve complex interdisciplinary understandings. By relying on the expertise of the special masters, as Mount Laurel II liberally allowed, the three judges were able to resolve technical issues, probe the reality of compliance, and contour reform decrees to the actualities of the real estate world. Drawing on both the plan formulated by the state planning commission and their own enhanced knowledge, they were able to hammer out changes to zoning ordinances that realized the goals of the Mount Laurel Doctrine, making affordable housing presumptively realistic.[25]

Several of the procedural innovations that grew out of Mount Laurel cluster around improved case management; for example, experience highlighted the need for long-term supervisory capacity, which was best carried out by special masters. Rather than playing the traditional role of time-saver and generalist (with skills differing little from those of the judge), a Mount Laurel special master supplied the perspective of an expert trained in the intricate field of land use and environmental planning—a professional presence that enhanced the parties' receptivity to the courts' proposals.

Despite rules to the contrary, a continuing (and synergistic) ex parte dialogue between trial judge and special master proved indispensable to a successful result in Mount Laurel cases. In view of this appraisal, the state rule (as well as Rule 53 of the Federal Rules of Civil Procedure, which permits the appointment of masters only in exceptional cases) should be liberalized and ex parte communications allowed as a matter of course. Resort to special masters in setting and interpreting professional standards is indispensable where institutional reform depends on technical know-how. For Mount Laurel, as for other complex litigation, one conclusion emerges: it is counterproductive, in an institutional reordering case, to erect a Chinese wall between the two exponents of judicial power. Throughout the course of the lengthy proceedings, the master must have available guidance from the judge who is charged with the ultimate power to decide the restructuring of the institutional arrangement.

## Speed of Response

The most effective intervention will be swift and strong; it is easier to accept intrusive judicial supervision and to avoid alienating public sympathy when the intervention is acknowledged to be temporary and will be terminated as quickly as possible. Thus the succession of small, incremental changes that some advocate in instituting social reform does not work in the world of institutional litigation.[26] The New Jersey Supreme Court placed reform within a limited time frame: municipalities were given but ninety days from the day they were declared exclusionary to reach compliance. It also streamlined procedural rules, granting the trial judges specific powers to expedite litigation. It allowed only limited motions and one appeal—and that directly to the supreme court, bypassing the appellate division justices, who had proven unduly sympathetic to the home rule demands of local municipalities.

Clearly, in addition to demonstrating responsiveness, the court needs to act decisively and with certitude if it is to project the necessary authoritative aura. The time it took the supreme court to decide Mount Laurel II, as well as the tortuous path of the *Madison Township* litigations, left an impression of uncertainty, of a lack of forceful and decisive action, which sparked unwarranted hopes in the localities that the exclusionary zoning issue would somehow go away. Hesitation merely creates an opportunity for the opposition to marshal forces and spread defiance.

## Affirmative Remedies

All the modifications in case management techniques are subsidiary to the one ultimate goal: an effective outcome. And a forceful product depends on a forceful compliance decree. To this end, the Mount Laurel courts broadened traditional scope to encompass explicit affirmative measures rather than the customary prohibitory injunctions couched in the negative. Hairsplitting over the jurisprudential difference between negative injunctions and affirmative requirements is of little value to a court ordering structural change.[27] Outright specification of the desired actions, including details of the affirmative reordering that defendants must take, is the wiser course. Low-income housing production stalled in the decade after Mount Laurel I, with its decree phrased in the less intrusive negative, and accelerated after Mount Laurel II, when the court pushed forward the builder's remedy and did not hesitate to establish affirmative requirements for local measures as well as the granting of incentives and subsidies.

### Clear-cut Targets

Incorporating definitive markers in the decree—setting targets, arranging timetables, specifying compliance mechanisms, quantifying numbers, formulating flow charts—is essential. Vague prescriptions will not do the job. The reversal of the *Madison Township* opinion clearly illustrates the need for clarity in directives. Local fair share calls out for quantification: an effective remedy must specify the timing and type of the tasks the defendant agrees to undertake.

### Alertness to Details

The overall advantage of using judges to correct breakdowns in societal institutions is the painstaking care they take in formulating the details of remedies and shaping them to the individual contours of the particular cases before them. A judge can hold what are in effect joint drafting sessions with parties' lawyers. Consider the example of one federal district judge presiding over a mental retardation reform case: "We didn't come up with any damn fool remedy. I worked four years with all the parties and as many experts as I could surround myself with, and we took the five institutions that were under my control, and we went over them building by building, room by room, position by position, and literally patient by patient, client by client."

Even though the institutional defendant has conceded liability at the outset, a judge must be concerned with objectivity. The desire to convey this message accounts for the importance accorded procedural fairness—applying the rules of evidence, retaining the ability to cross-examine, enabling all sides to present their case in open court, and documenting what is said and done at trial as a basis for possible appeals—so that the average citizen can sense the rightness of the proceedings. The need to portray objectivity explains the numerous witnesses and the myriad papers in institutional litigation: the record must be solid. The end result, it is hoped, sets forth the details of the case in a way that educates participants and observers—increasing the possibility for an effective remedy.

The three Mount Laurel judges took ample care to ensure the clarity of remedial decrees in order to avoid later claims by the parties that they had not fully grasped the significance of the undertaking. The judges would routinely communicate with defendant municipalities, refusing to approve a proposed compliance program unless local officials began the course with their eyes open, fully aware of the costs. They tried to make sure that the funding limb on which the municipality was climbing could support the weight; in this fashion, claims down the line of unfair surprise were ruled out. The effort was broad in sweep: the judges sought to ascertain that every remedy made sense from fiscal, planning, and community standpoints. Eventually, it became normal practice for judges to examine each component of newly revised zoning ordinances. As experience evolved, they set standards for evaluating the effectiveness of various methods of compliance.

### Realistic Remedies

Feasibility is a prime consideration. When the Mount Laurel judges grappled with the issue of a parcel's "suitability"—whether a proposed plan for compliance would in fact bring about the mandated low-income housing—results became the paramount issue. "I'm not disposed to approve the plan unless I find that there's a likelihood that if I approve it, it's going to generate the promised number of units within the six-year period. So I'm going to have to figure out what my standard is based on, the type of compliance mechanism being utilized," one Mount Laurel trial judge stated. "If a town's saying it's going to rely on inclusionary zoning to generate $x$ number of units, I have to develop a standard to evaluate whether an inclusionary zoning technique will, in fact, generate the promised number of units. For example, I'll have to work out the suitability of the land; if the land is not suitable, it is not going to get built. This is not all just academics. It is supposed to be real. I've got to look at the economics—are sufficient incentives being given to the developer in terms of enhanced equity so that there's a likelihood that the developer will have economic reason to develop the land in accordance with the new zoning? It's got to make economic sense."

Suitability issues went beyond the realm of real estate finance economics. The aura of bad faith following Mount Laurel I grew so intense that the trial judges had to figure local, even personal, recalcitrance into their calculations. For example, they would carefully scrutinize an owner's willingness to develop a site. One judge described the process: "If the town comes to me with a parcel and says, Judge, here's a possible site for all these reasons—it has the sewage, the water, it has roads, it has access, and it can be economically developed. What happens if the owner's a bigot? What happens if the owner perceives Mount Laurel as a race issue, even as opposed to a rich man–poor man issue, and he is committed to fighting it from now to kingdom come? That surely is not a realistic opportunity if I let the municipality rely on that." Also factored into their decisions were more mundane matters such as clouds on title and other legal or practical issues that could delay development of a parcel. If a judge concluded, for all or any of these reasons, that a locality's rezoning would not provide a realistic opportunity for affordable housing, alternative measures would be imposed.

A scenario frequently encountered by the judges was a town relying on a do-it-yourself approach. It might propose, for instance, to use municipally owned land for lower-income housing, and this can be commendable if the value and amount of land offered are adequate to accommodate the necessary housing. From time to time, towns also proposed to issue bonds to provide the necessary capital. Even though the cost of housing was in excess of the potential selling price to lower-income people, such towns claimed the ability to carry the loss through tax-exempt extended interest payments. In each of these cases, the judge needed assurances that the local proposal was feasible, that the financial commitment over the years was bearable, that the bonding was within the debt-paying capacity of the municipality—in other words, that the project was financially feasible. In one case, the court made its judgment contingent on the municipality's commitment to bonding on an annual basis; this produced a legally binding obligation to carry out the affordable housing promise, breach of which could lead to a lawsuit.

## No Micromanagement

For all the importance of precisely defined affirmative measures, however, judicial micromanagement can trap the unwary. Aided by the contributions of court-appointed experts and masters (and subject, of course, to judicial supervision of final results), the sharpening of the compliance decree ought to remain within the discretion of the defendants. Correcting systemic wrongful governmental conduct requires the participation—however recalcitrant and forced it may be—of the government officials being prodded.[28] The posture the Mount Laurel trial judges and the masters adopted was, "You tell us what you want to do, and we'll see if it's okay." The standard practice, as one master described it, was to defer to the local planning board, asking, for example, "Where's your survey, your maps, your master plan—and I will respect your policy decisions so far as I can." A similar view is expressed by a Mount Laurel judge: "In a setting, particularly where municipalities feel they are being put upon,

where they are philosophically not in agreement, if you can get them to buy into a result it has a much better chance of success, not just because it saves time, sometimes it takes longer to resolve than it does to litigate, but because the parties themselves incorporate the result."

In other words, cooperation, not command, is the prudent initial course of remedy. Such an approach accommodates the uneasiness of a democratic polity with nonmajoritarian judges making and administering policy choices. Trial judges are better served by stressing institutional self-correction. The initiative, as well as the burden of taking it, is the responsibility of the legislative and administrative machinery of the defendant municipalities. The court should not begin from scratch to construct a revised zoning ordinance or devise a program of affordable housing or embark on a course of zero-based city planning; instead, it should adopt the more traditional judicial position of reviewing actions taken by others.

### Negotiation from Strength

Fashioning a successful remedy calls for formal and informal bargaining among the parties and their lawyers.[29] Negotiation and mediation, supplemented by occasional shuttle diplomacy by the special masters, helped to revise the terms of the offending local land-use regulations in many Mount Laurel cases.[30] The supreme court's innovations created a new form of governance—a combination of administrative and judicial approaches. Emphasis turned away from the outright confrontation of the ordinary trial; instead, in-chambers resolution of issues became the norm in carrying out the mandate of Mount Laurel II.

It is the presence, not the deployment, of the Sword of Damocles that produces the desired result. For a successful outcome depends on the court's formal capacity to coerce, that vital arrow in the judicial quiver. If soliciting remedial plans from the parties themselves was the primary course the Mount Laurel courts followed, the continuing presence of a judge with the power to impose a plan if the parties failed to agree moved the process along.[31] While a last resort, the trial court at sticky intervals may need to play the role of the heavy. A rough-and-ready attitude pervaded the early Mount Laurel courtroom, backed by the implicit threat of the builder's remedy or contempt power. The promise of these and other responses was sufficient to bring the light of "reason" into the proceedings. The trial court could declare a zoning ordinance invalid in whole or in part; it could order a municipality to make specific changes in its ordinance, listing detailed revisions in particular wording. The judge could even mandate local approval of affordable housing construction. Indeed, when pressed, the court came close to taking over the legislative functions of the municipality. Yet another remedial tool that aroused extreme local anxiety was the judges' ability to order a delay in the construction of projects, even those having nothing to do with the Mount Laurel Doctrine. To the extent that the municipality and developer dreaded having projects held hostage, this technique pushed fulfillment of the Mount Laurel obligation. In general, one official remarked, "The message has to be, Let's do it now ourselves before it's forced upon us by the courts."

Without the iron fist within the velvet glove, intransigence leads to procedural delay and cases being settled at the expense of setting realistic fair shares. Although the New Jersey Supreme Court put the best face possible on its repertoire of remedies, playing up the hoped-for voluntary response, the potentially drastic infringement of home rule was all too clear: targeted municipalities had little choice but to cooperate, looking forward, as consolation, to future freedom from litigation.

In an interview, Judge Gibson recalled that he and the other Mount Laurel judges used conferences and discussions in chambers more extensively in Mount Laurel cases than in other types of litigation. Judge Serpentelli told of one striking example. An exclusionary ordinance passed by a town whose residents were mostly retired senior citizens was under attack. After considerable maneuvering by all sides, the judge directed that the entire township committee appear before him. "I gave them a lecture about what the Mount Laurel case stood for, and I was also very specifically trying to make them understand that I was not there as enforcing my personal whims and desires, but that this is what the supreme court said had to be done, and that they had agreed to do it, and failure to do it would mean contempt. And that if they wanted to do something else that was okay too, but they had to do it." Within sixty days, the town voted to pass the zoning changes, overruling the local mayor's strident opposition.

## Use of the Media

Convincing the public of the rightness of the court's actions is an essential element of any remedy. Coalitions are of the essence; organized groups are best qualified to foster support for judicial action, and in institutional litigation, the organized bar is especially crucial to defending the pinnacle of the profession or, at the least, to setting the bounds for civil debate.[32] In the end, media support can be the key to community acceptance of judicial teachings. But this proved to be the weakest aspect of the Mount Laurel prescription, though it was accorded some lip service. As one Mount Laurel judge put it, "I think that every judge has a responsibility to try to convince the listener, the public, of the rightness of what's going on, because we want the public to continue to believe in the system, and that doesn't happen if judges make decisions that people don't understand. Because we are educated in the field we can't simply say, 'Oh, well, we understand what the judge's role is,' and be complacent about that." Implementation nonetheless remains shaky.

Given the inevitable controversies accompanying institutional restructuring, courts need to recognize that the race runs a long course—and that it is a race. Winning demands a more accepting attitude toward the media, such as judges are beginning to demonstrate (albeit with considerable reluctance) in permitting the television cameras into their courtrooms. Judges must descend from the mountain to participate in the world of opinion. This should not prove embarrassing; they need not discuss the details of particular cases—it is the principle of banning exclusionary zoning, for example, that needs explanation and justification, not the identity of specific parties or particular factual scenarios—but they should feel free to comment publicly on a general jurisprudential level.

## The Archimedes Principle

Finally, one overarching consideration must be kept in mind: in framing an effective remedy for reordering an ongoing practice, a court must recognize that a political or economic lever is crucial for achieving proposed goals. Identifying this fulcrum requires political antennas sensitive to forces outside the courtroom—not just the media but also the various interest groups whose participation is necessary for establishing a modus vivendi. Decisions are far from self-implementing; their potential impact hinges on mobilizing a broad range of human motivations. The judicial search for a lever in the Boston Harbor case, for instance, led to a threatened court moratorium on all hotel and office development in the city; this pushed the real estate industry to pressure the legislature, which responded finally by founding a new financial and administrative agency, the Massachusetts Water Resources Authority.[33]

Mount Laurel found its key in the builder's remedy, which harnessed the personal profit seeking and affirmative commitment of the private market to meet the affordable housing target. What the courts were actually doing by offering site-specific relief to developers (although nowhere stated in so many words) was co-opting the support of the private sector in the judicial work of remedying institutional failure: marry the profit motive with a public interest, and the couple becomes irresistible. This was the grand strategy for achieving social reform without dependence on the political actors within the executive and administrative branches who might have resisted the Mount Laurel Doctrine or implemented it in a hostile spirit.

Of course, this is easier required than done. The history of the Mount Laurel Doctrine underscores the difficulties of remedies that rely on catching business cycles at the proper moment. Ripeness is all. Had the New Jersey courts come to an enforceable decision by the early 1980s, they would have harnessed fully the developers' search for profits and thus used the building boom to burst the barriers of exclusionary local regulations. Unfortunately, the phases did not coincide. Just after the period of judicial reconsideration from 1975 to 1982 and the long wait for positive responses from recalcitrant communities, just after the first cases were tried and initial standards set from 1982 to 1985, the land development market responded to its own economic cycle—and fizzled. The fickle New Jersey building boom subsided into recession. The wisdom of co-opting private actions to fuel remedies must wait for the next swing of the business pendulum to be tested fully.

The existence of a constitutional flaw in the structure of municipalities' ways of regulating their uses of land is an inescapable reality. Only a change in habits of mind can modify such a large slice of social reality; only a revamping of the traditional judicial format can handle the overall undertaking to restructure large-scale ongoing activities of local government. To redress deep wrongdoing, the courts must act simultaneously as instruments of criticism and reconstruction, couching their remedies so as to bring the legislative practices of municipalities into line with the legal ideal of equality of access. If one grants that the New Jersey judges have a transformative vision of law, the appropriate remedy calls for freeing the legal imagination from habits of passive, private law adjudication, an unadventurous model that assumes the world is flat. The Mount Laurel process is just as valid as the traditional form of adjudication so deeply etched in lawyers' psyches.

The constraints—of efficiency, competence, resources, limited discretion, and impartiality—that thoughtful scholars point out and involved judges themselves note are not insurmountable in pressing institutional restructuring by the courts. Through the intelligent formulation and supervision of remedies, the judiciary turns out to be the most accessible (and realistic) instrument for bringing about changes in metropolitan zoning and housing patterns. The New Jersey courts, at first tentatively and then with greater certitude, tempered their concepts through practical tests. Their ordeal by fire did not subvert the legitimacy of the judiciary as an institution. To the contrary, it is a refusal to uphold the moral values proclaimed in the basic documents of our society that could lead to this outcome.

What the New Jersey experience brings home is that constitutional rights call for vindication by effective remedy or they, and their interpreters, compromise their principal claim to moral authority. The court recognized that the decision in Mount Laurel II placed judicial legitimacy at risk, "but it may be even more at risk through failure to take such action if that is the only way to enforce the Constitution."[34] Without affirmative judicial intervention, the wrongful conduct of municipalities inflicts injuries not adequately redressed elsewhere. Inaction at the start, or a subsequent passivity in the face of a municipality's flouting or ignoring a decree, only sows deeper cynicism about courts—indeed about politics and government—and undermines judicial authority far more surely than forthright action in pursuit of an ideal ever could.

# IX

## Discretion and Its Discontents: Checking Abuses

IN AESCHYLUS'S *Prometheus*, Zeus is described as a tyrant because he exercises power "according to no fixed known law." Pronounces Prometheus, "I know that he is a savage and his justice is a thing he keeps by his own standard." The rallying cry of some critics of judicial land-use reform is similar: will not the wide discretion that necessarily accompanies the setting of institutional remedies result in the unprincipled application of power by the courts?[1]

Remedies aimed at providing affordable housing in suburbs within a metropolitan area, involving so many land configurations, variables, and conflicting values as they do, cannot be realized without the exercise of substantial judicial discretion.[2] Yet while arguments may rage over the wisdom of the policies formulated in the two major New Jersey Supreme Court opinions, following articulation of the Mount Laurel Doctrine as the lodestar, trial judges did not stray from the domain of the rule of law. Over a short period, the judges produced a series of decisions consistent with reason and precedent and marked by predictability. Individual formulations of remedies tended over time to converge into doctrines aligned with precedent and ultimately became routinized into a system of rules and maxims. Through application of evolved standards to new fact patterns, discretion was confined, and arbitrariness and capriciousness checked.

That many of the Mount Laurel remedies fell into an accustomed arena for judicial action also reduced the potential for standardless conduct. Mandatory set-asides, inclusionary zoning, overlays, and other techniques for curbing exclusionary zoning differ only slightly from land-use technologies that had cropped up from time to time in earlier judicial proceedings. Judges had accepted the validity of such novel city planning techniques as floating zones and transfers of development rights.[3] Probing into exclusionary zoning mechanisms—and the next step of ordering affirmative remedies—was thus not too far afield from the ordinary New Jersey land trials. Familiarity lent ease. The judges could draw from a base of doctrinal experience (and limits on choice), and they were comfortable doing the job.

Furthermore, checks on judicial discretion are more powerful in state than in federal courts. State judges may be subject to periodic reappointment or reelection and thus lack the tenure, salary assurance, and insulation from politics that federal judges enjoy. This constraint operated visibly at least twice in the course of the Mount Laurel cases. Under the New Jersey Constitution, the governor has the power to reappoint judges who have served for seven years, such reappointment requiring approval by the state senate. Both Justice Stewart Pollock and Chief Justice Wilentz experienced perils worthy of Pauline in obtaining reconfirmation because of their Mount Laurel opinions, and the latter's reconfirmation battle spurred a full-scale constitutional crisis. Wilentz barely squeaked by the senate with a vote of twenty-one to eighteen and then only after strenuous arm twisting by the Republican governor, Thomas Kean. So vehemently did a senator from the chief justice's home county feel about the Mount Laurel opinion that he was prepared to veto the appointment despite the chief's conspicuous qualifications on other scores.

Such political brawls hardly dignify the appointment process. Worse, they hold dark portents for the future—most notably, the danger that judges may decide cases not on their merits but on the basis of improving their chances of reappointment. Thus far the court has remained afloat despite the chop of the political majority, but such a threat can only limit the independence of a judiciary that must on occasion render antimajoritarian conclusions. Perhaps it would make more sense—at least in state judicial systems—to carve out an important role in the judicial selection for a recognized consortium of minority organizations. Certainly, leaving confirmations to majoritarian whims undermines the special minority protection that an independent judiciary must provide. Despite its awareness of the sharp political reaction to its decisions and of its own ultimate vulnerability, the New Jersey Supreme Court remained firm in the Mount Laurel cases, biting the constitutional bullet, holding tight to the reform ideal. At the same time, however, the majoritarian threat may account for the court's ultimate, if somewhat hesitant, acceptance in *Hills* of the FHA and COAH. Unquestionably, judges are now on notice that moving too far from the mainstream risks retribution. No matter the outer bravado, the surrounding political climate acts as a restraint.

Of all the potential checks on judicial arbitrariness, the most blunt, certainly the most immediate, is the media. The extensive news coverage accompanying such wide-ranging institutional litigation as the Mount Laurel decisions curbs the overextension of judicial power. Investigative reporters, increasingly influential because of the freedom-of-information laws, deserve acknowledgment as potential restraints on abuse of discretion.

The remedial framework that the Mount Laurel Doctrine envisions— decentralization wherever possible—also harnesses discretion. Recognizing the grassroots nature of all land-use controls, the trial courts leave to the offending municipalities, with minimum supervision by special masters, the task of devising acceptable solutions to the polycentric problems of exclusionary zoning.

## The Conscience of the King

A final check that theorists of the judicial role often overlook is the character of the judges themselves and their individual understanding of the scope of institutional litigation and the court's role as an agent of change. Whether it is the ideals of a judiciary molded in the Holmesian tradition—that of a minority combating majoritarian prejudice in a search for truth—or Brandeis's pursuit of social justice, or Cardozo's urgency to reinvigorate the common law with modern thinking, a special joy arises from fulfilling a mission that goes beyond law books and legal briefs. It falls to each judge to balance opportunity with restraint.

Experienced judges become all too familiar with the standard elements of the run-of-the-mill cases that ordinarily come before them. By contrast, institutional litigation challenges them to the core. Judges' personal beliefs and styles were highly relevant considerations in Mount Laurel. In large part, the power driving the reform proceeded from the commitment of individual judges (especially those on the New Jersey Supreme Court) to a chosen philosophy of law broader than any hidebound legal text. While such personal involvement created uneasiness among commentators, the particular evolution of the Mount Laurel Doctrine served to limit abuse of discretion.

Because the New Jersey court system is strongly hierarchical, with the chief justice playing the pivotal role in the appointments, assignments, and promotions of judges, the development of the policy at the top has special advantages. Springing fully formed from the brow of the supreme court, the Mount Laurel Doctrine did not require a soup-to-nuts realization in the lower courts. The standards for conduct were laid down at the outset, prior to the appointment of the three trial judges. Instead of having to anticipate the intricacies of appellate review, they knew where their parameters lay after the massive detailing of Mount Laurel II, and such prior understanding reduced the need for the check on trial court discretion that appellate review would have provided.[4] Thus the relationship between the appellate and the trial courts in Mount Laurel cases resembled a consultative process more than the conventional review from on high of the ordinary trial court decision.[5]

The New Jersey Supreme Court launched the doctrine's *social policy* component—traditionally the most difficult task for a court to perform—when it disallowed the use of local sovereign power to lock moderate- and low-income housing out of the suburbs. In handing off the doctrine's implementation to the lower courts, it left trial judges with the less strenuous task of enforcing *legal policy*, familiar terrain to any court. This delegation should be appraised as the novel twist of Mount Laurel II: that decision (transforming and basing public policy on constitutional doctrine) assigned the trial judges, in the role of foot soldiers, the job not of questioning why but of carrying out the orders their superiors had enunciated.

"It is the Bible," agreed the different trial judges, referring to Mount Laurel II. "That doesn't mean," one went on, "that every question that arose was necessarily answered by that opinion, but a great many were, or at least there was enough guidance there that I felt that I could extrapolate from that opinion what the result would be." The comprehensiveness of the Mount Laurel II opinion guided, within each judge's mind, the interplay of personal convictions, beliefs, and values in ensuing litigations. And in carrying out the administration of the doctrine, the trial judges, whatever their levels of personal commitment to reform, had little freedom to consider alternative visions of appropriate land use in metropolitan areas.

In addition, judges recognized that their credibility and effectiveness rested in major part on a widespread perception of their disinterested objectivity. To maintain that status, they strove to base each decision squarely on the merits, struggling to adhere to the traditional judicial role, sensitive to accepted constraints on their authority—especially the duty of impartiality—while grappling with novel and complex remedies. One judge observed, "I think that once a judge starts to conceive of him-

self as functioning as an administrative agency, you're losing the judicial role to some extent. I think some of the litigants had that image of us, that we were appointed by the chief justice to promote open housing, which would be the kind of way you would describe the mission of an administrative agency. I had trouble with that conception of what our role was. It didn't sound sufficiently impartial or judicial or whatever. Some attorneys thought that being appointed one of these Mount Laurel judges might be an indication that we were really committed, and that we were put in that role to get as many judgments entered against municipalities as quickly as possible and to get as much low-income housing constructed as fast as possible." He concluded, "I at least never envisioned the role that way."

The judges' internal control over excessive discretion remained strong. None of them, in turning attention to a particular Mount Laurel case, rejected the accepted conception of judicial office. All felt limited by precedent, by the dictates of Mount Laurel I and II, by the passive role bred into them, and by the plain reading of Rule 4:41-1 of the New Jersey Court Rules, which tilts toward limited uses of masters. None of the trial judges saw himself as writing on a procedurally blank slate.

But institutional reform cases do present a major intrinsic difficulty. Often the procedural framework makes the judge appear to be pleading the case of the plaintiffs directly from the bench. In the traditional adjudication model, the judge preserves the mien of impartiality by giving equal time and attention to all the parties. In institutional reform cases, however, there is in a profound and disquieting sense no true defendant in the classic understanding of the term. The question before the court is not whether a statutory or constitutional function has been properly discharged. Quite the contrary—by the time litigation begins and the parties are before the court, there is general agreement that the administrative branch of government has botched the handling of a social need or, in the Mount Laurel situation, that the locality is engaged in exclusionary zoning practices that violate constitutional demands. Liability is not the issue.

After the lawsuit is brought in traditional cases, there follow defenses, counterclaims, motions, discoveries, depositions—the apparatus by which the defendant attempts to avoid the charge and the plaintiff searches for evidence of liability. That protracted pursuit is not what counts in institutional breakdown cases. By and large, the term *defendant* is a sobriquet for purposes of identification only, since the accused is rarely in a position to contest the alleged violation. "One thing I found out very early in these cases," commented one Mount Laurel judge, "is that in most of our trials there was no dispute—the municipalities were in violation of Mount Laurel, and they had no desire to litigate that question. In some cases, there were stipulations to that effect early on. In other cases, at the conferences, the attorneys for the municipalities would say politically they could not concede a lack of compliance, but if the developers' attorney or the public interest attorney filed a motion for summary judgment, it would be unopposed, a pro forma opposition at most."

The impecunious plaintiff is as much a feature of institutional reform cases as the confessedly liable defendant. In such cases, the judge has little choice but to step in on the plaintiff's side to assure movement. Plaintiffs rarely command the resources or staff adequate for the large-scale litigation that institutional reform entails. In its need to promote the real interests underlying the litigation, rather than just those of the nominal plaintiff, the court ends up playing part of the plaintiff's traditional role. Though such assistance is primarily procedural, it can easily be perceived as reflecting a bias on the part of the bench.

Hierarchical obedience to the supreme court's express marching orders and a sense of judicial decorum are not the only measures of objectivity. The trial judges cannot be relieved of personal and professional responsibility. Willingness to perform the arduous role assigned to them—especially against the roiling tides of public opinion—requires a commitment that goes beyond traditional factors. Several of the shortcuts of the newly prescribed Mount Laurel trial procedures distressed the more process-oriented judges, but their personal accounts suggest that, for some at least, the tradeoff was acceptable because they were working for a worthy cause. Clearly the fate of minorities locked into inner-city neighborhoods remains a galvanizing force in the Mount Laurel struggle for enforcement, crystallizing personal beliefs and experiences (introducing at times an element of self-righteousness) and pushing the trial judges beyond rote execution to creative reform within the interstices of the formulations by the supreme court. Intuition, empathy, and personal visions of the ideal community—in effect, internalized notions of social justice rather than explicit text or precedent—played a paramount role. The New Jersey judges were sufficiently self-confident not to require the world's approval, though none would have minded receiving it.

The achievement of Justice Thurgood Marshall, as extolled by his former colleagues on the U.S. Supreme Court, was an ability to impose the demands of life's experience—too often the tragedies of the human condition—on abstract legal rules. A source of inspiration, the morality tale can sensitize the normally indifferent to a miscarriage of justice. And the opportunity to exercise that sense of justice is beneficial to the system as a whole, bringing individual belief systems to bear on the realization of technical doctrine. Through the office they hold, judges are able to remind us—and themselves—of society's highest aspirations. This image of the judge as teacher, leader, prodder of the social conscience is what leads law school graduates to regard judicial appointment as the happy capstone of a successful legal career. The blending of constitutional duty, conscientious application of legal norms, and individual fulfillment is a background theme of the Mount Laurel judiciary's transformation of land use in the metropolitan areas of New Jersey.

## Courts as Political Institutions

If the courts are understood to have a special duty to right constitutional wrongs, even or especially against the grain of the majority, that understanding is tempered by the expectation that they bring objectivity, as near to absolute as possible, to the resolution of conflicts. This view of detachment is both naive and unrealistic. Still, one source of the tension over the role of the Mount Laurel judiciary is the impossibility of removing exclusionary zoning from the expressly political and subjective. Failure to recognize that controversy can and will coexist alongside a neutral, dispassionate judiciary leads not only to an exaggerated notion of judicial objectivity in ordinary litigation but also to overblown valuations of the abuse of judicial discretion in institutional restructuring cases.

Views that stress the dangers of creeping discretion trace back to the brilliant theory spun out by Lon Fuller in support of the classic adversary

model of adjudication.[6] Fuller defined judicial legitimacy as a function of the court's withdrawal from complex multiparty issues to concentrate on individual disputes. Interdependent or polycentric problems, declared Fuller, are out of bounds for judges. Because such problems involve managerial and discretionary insight, they are beyond a court's ability and, if undertaken, lead to the subversion of judicial legitimacy and the forfeiture of moral force.

Old-time opponents of judicial discretion reflexively shudder at any move in the direction of institutional litigation and reform. The current generation still views the Fuller characterization as axiomatic but draws a different conclusion: that the complex polycentricity of institutional restructuring calls not for withdrawal but for innovative approaches, for adaptation by the courts rather than a throwing up of hands. As federal court judge Jack Weinstein, who has presided over school desegregation, Agent Orange, and other major institutional litigations, argues, "Such many-centered problems call for informal consultations and weighing of complex alternatives using a managerial decision-making process. . . . A skilled master . . . to coordinate the efforts of the parties, is crucial if a just and workable remedy is to be devised."[7] On a more specific issue, Weinstein notes that "Rule 53's requirement that the case referred to a master be 'exceptional' is more than satisfied when a court is faced with a polycentric problem that cannot be resolved through traditional courtroombound adjudicative process."[8]

Abstract models of the judicial role fail to take account of the contemporary judicial forum and process. The outdated ideal of judge as philosopher-king must be reconciled with the reality painted by peers—a tough, savvy lawyer who has scrambled up the greasy pole to reach the pinnacle of the profession.[9] Traditional academics envisioning judges as supremely uncommitted drain the blood, emotions, experiences, and intuitions that are an inescapable and indispensable part of the art of judging. Broad, untested generalizations flow at commencement speeches, their content determined not by reality but by an ideal voided of cultural identity or definite historical inheritance. Swept away are the realities of trial, the partisanship and tactics of lawyers, the dirt and sweat of bringing about social reform, the political and social struggles in which legal concepts are encased.

For one cannot remove courts from the political, social, and economic systems of which, inescapably, they are a part by placing them on a marble pedestal of neutrality or philosophical aloofness. In his debates with Judge Stephen Douglas, Abraham Lincoln was fond of quoting a letter written by Thomas Jefferson in 1820: "Our judges are as honest as other men, and not more so. They have, with others, the same passions for party, for power, and the privilege of their corps."[10] When identification with the political and social milieu of the period intrudes on the workings of judicial life, its recognition is more honest than the superficial pose of Olympian remoteness. And while the prototype of adjudication as a series of intellectual arguments buttressed by tested evidence and bound by clear precedent retains an undeniable appeal, the increasing reality for courts is that, even as they strive to separate personal preferences from judgments, they cannot avoid making choices that are to some degree political as they balance the competing factors in institutional restructuring. What is more, just as in other intense constitutional litigations, values dictate logic. Differences in fundamental outlooks cannot be papered over. Institutional litigation is essentially a matter of politics, involving a broad canvas of deal making, negotiating, consensus building, and persuasion to arrive at a single decision.

Because deeply divisive issues mirroring the dilemmas of society are before them, the courts should adopt approaches that are subject to examination as critical as that focused on the actions of other branches of government. Judges themselves are proper subjects of reform. Heightened scrutiny (and positive response to evaluations) would enable them better to discharge the responsibilities increasingly devolving on them in a changing democracy whose institutional inadequacies periodically result in constitutional or statutory law-breaking by public institutions.[11]

And the political element is unlikely to subside when it comes to the ongoing refinement of remedial plans. Judges are acutely aware that everything they do in institutional litigation is viewed, for better or worse, through an interest-group lens. As worry mounts over the stagnation and inadequacies of certain social institutions, courts, it seems likely, will be increasingly called on to induce social change and to tailor their remedies to fit the nature and degree of the denial of constitutional or statutory rights. Broad arguments that social reform is impossible to achieve through the courts are frequently advanced in order to disguise disagreement with specific judicial outcomes. The inevitable presence of politics—no matter what branch of government undertakes responsibility for change—must be acknowledged, not hidden, so that procedures can be devised to keep abuses to a minimum as the open-ended process of institutional restructuring proceeds.[12]

In the end, courts need considerable flexibility to respond to the bureaucratic roadblocks and chronically uncooperative defendants that typify the intensely debated social issues raised in institutional litigations.[13] Indeed, once the judge enters the fray seeking to redress past constitutional transgressions and prevent future ones, a wide component of judicial discretion becomes essential if the outcome is to be a solution worthy of the proceedings. And as in the New Jersey instance, a frequent resort to special masters inevitably broadens the usual bounds set for the exercise of discretion.

The record of the Mount Laurel trial courts shows that discretion, once granted, does not inherently spin out of control. Instead, it serves a limited purpose within the larger program of reform. Necessity becomes the mother of legitimacy. Although critics of the so-called imperial judiciary in institutional restructuring cases argue that such exercises of discretion erode legitimacy, the New Jersey courts were, if anything, oversensitive to the traditional limits on unbridled exercise of judicial power. The judges paid special heed to precedent and relied extensively on the initiatives of the parties and their attorneys, and in pursuit of compliance mechanisms, on the municipalities themselves. In fact, judicial restraint may have gone too far: the retreat in *Hills* can be attributed in large part to self-imposed crippling by the traditional judicial model of abstention.

# Part IV

## THE LEGACY

# X

## Leadership in Institutional Reform: Rallying Support for a Vision

OVER A long and tedious period, the New Jersey courts engaged in a struggle with the state's localities and legislature that stretched the judiciary to the limits of its power. This battle for reform made New Jersey the cynosure of urban planners and land-use lawyers nationwide. Recently, local planning experts have been tapped to testify in New York, Pennsylvania, Oregon, and other states seeking to adapt the Mount Laurel experiment. The reason? The spirit of America is uneasy: throughout the country, communities are grappling with the ominous spectacle of two separate nations evolving within major metropolitan areas, one locked into the physical decay and environmental deterioration of inner-city slums, the other barricading itself behind physical and psychological suburban walls. Those who espouse the American dream of equality despair over this growing chasm. Others see neighbors of different races, classes, incomes, or outlooks as a threat to their own private dream. The resulting tension and inaction, only slightly disguised by the lip service paid to democratic goals, lead to an unhappy sense that Americans are not following through on their highest and most fully articulated principles of opportunity and fairness.

## Exercising Leadership

Once their jurisdiction was invoked, the New Jersey courts seized on and enunciated basic principles for social life in the Mount Laurel cases. Although it is regarded as the most conservative, insulated branch of government (somewhat unreasonably, given that judges are hardly cloistered in a social vacuum, but to the contrary are successful lawyers, politically astute and sufficiently respected by a president or governor to warrant appointment), the judiciary bears the burden of enforcing federal and state constitutional protection of minorities, while at the same time giving due weight to majority interests. Constitutions, the holiest documents in the secular government of the United States, offer a powerful mandate (and shelter) for the courts.

For this reason, perhaps, a fever hovered over the early phases of the Mount Laurel decisions: a rush of excitement over what they might portend and heavy speculation over the future course of events. As time passed, however, the long haul of institutional reform litigation sapped vigor. Controversies raged on. Municipalities joined together and had their way in the state legislature. The court, making a virtue out of necessity, graciously allowed itself to be upstaged. Political strength was king. Paramount in their own precinct but struggling against powerfully mounted public opinion, it was hard for the courts to exercise the leadership needed to temper the political clout of an arithmocracy. The Mount Laurel crises demonstrated that the judges' power, while far-reaching, was hardly absolute; even the most powerful potentate can take full control only in special places and on selected issues. Although the court was not likely to hold on indefinitely to the central position of leadership that it enjoyed at the outset of the exclusionary zoning battle, its diminished strength may be partly attributable to its own unwillingness to direct the public's imagination in salutary directions.

The moral power of the courts is especially critical where institutionalized prejudice, layered on top of the usual frictions and inefficiencies of large organizations, blocks institutional reform. In the case of Mount Laurel, arguments and excuses grounded in estrangement from the economically disadvantaged and politically inconsequential fostered institutional inaction. If the courts were not fully equipped to build public support for the Mount Laurel Doctrine, that grail also eluded governors, legislators, academics, religious leaders, and the business world. Public interest groups found themselves so perplexed by metropolitan fragmentation that they were barely able to summon up the energies to state a position; after tremendous soul-searching, a few organizations came out with what can charitably be characterized as a moderate, balanced statement, a token gesture in the larger struggle for deconcentrating the inner-city poor.[1]

To succeed in any institutional reform litigation—to effect difficult changes in social reality—the judiciary is forced to deal with perceptions. As the conflict developed in the Mount Laurel cases, the challenge was to curb the groundswells of public sympathy for the residents of affected towns that sapped the state's willingness to confront exclusionary regulatory barriers. Looking back, the outset of dramatic judicial intervention signaled by Mount Laurel II was marked by a war of words rather than efforts at public persuasion. The judges did not mince terms; they made no effort to avoid the epithet *exclusionary*, and neither did they hesitate to voice their frustration in harsh language. As the supreme court phrased it on one occasion, "Mount Laurel remains afflicted with a blatantly exclusionary ordinance. Papered over with studies, ratified by hired experts, the ordinance at its core is true to nothing but Mount Laurel's determination to exclude the poor."[2] "Our trust was ill placed," Chief Justice Wilentz confessed.[3]

The judges did not pretend to harmony where none existed, and this harshness exacerbated local hostility to the courts. Opposition grew more bitter as the reform effort took on recognizable dimensions and towns began to envision themselves transformed in physical appearance by the sheer numbers of units called for by the builder's remedy.[4] As the Mount Laurel judges pressed on, local newspaper descriptions and photographs of mayors decrying the undermining of their chosen way of life became more difficult to ignore; other media portrayals of disruption of the small-town way of life began to chip away at the court's authority.

There is another way to comprehend the courts' difficulties in persuading the citizenry. Mayors, local papers, and suburban officials are not constrained by judicial norms of conduct. Faced with unwanted edicts on local power, they play by their own rules—which, often, are no rules at all. Driven by self-interest, they play to win, negative campaigning and all. All the actors, competing intensely among themselves, are far less predictable (and controllable) in their actions than, say, the opposing counsels in the standard adjudication model. The courts, on the other hand, abide by canons of conduct formulated not only for an earlier era— before McLuhan's global village and the emergence of negative ads and attack politics—but for a different type of litigation, one between individual parties and about issues that are less politically volatile and emotionally explosive than exclusionary zoning. The unpleasant reality of the Mount Laurel litigation was that local governments were prepared to subordinate civil considerations to preserving a way of life. They launched violent counterattacks—reinforcing barriers to entry, inventing unlikely causes for delay, suddenly discovering pollution threats—all to avoid granting building permits. Even when under judicial mandate, they shuffled their feet, placing red tape and bureaucratic hobgoblins in the path of the developer.

Until the chastening blow of Mount Laurel II, municipalities continued to do business as usual despite the stern warnings of Mount Laurel I. Local land-use regulatory process was unaltered. No one in the state rushed forward to set standards, issue regulations, monitor activities, or enforce the law. That job fell to the judiciary. The fair share ideal set forth in Mount Laurel I and II was applied, tested, denied, and reasserted in hundreds of cases that came before the trial courts, but there was simply no local consensus for reform. The New Jersey courts fought on despite this absence, but on shaky ground, adjudicating in a climate of suspicion and widespread opposition. Their experience points up the need to revise the court's traditional role vis-à-vis the public. Through the fight for continued institutional reform, state courts in each generation must come to grips with such revisions. They must reexamine the nature of judicial power, especially its relationship to the public at large, and sculpt a new paradigm of behavior that gives them a political face commensurate with the emerging understanding of the judiciary as a political body.

Its struggle against stacked odds took a toll on the New Jersey judiciary, particularly on the three trial court judges. "It is most certainly true," one Mount Laurel judge observed, "there has been a remarkable diffusion of power in the state. No one is the unchallenged boss everywhere." Trial judges came face to face with intense reactions. Under the pressure of human emotions, it was hard to retain the mien of a dispassionate decision maker concentrating on abstract constitutional principles, even though that is the chosen role of a judiciary dedicated to the rule of reason.

## Fostering Civil Rights Support

Another aspect of the Mount Laurel Doctrine's alienation from community-level concerns is more difficult to understand: the failure of civil rights groups to make it a focus of solidarity.[5] A necessary constituency for the courts' opinions already seemed in place—minority groups excluded by local zoning ordinances—but support was tepid at best. Political reality furnishes an explanatory key for this seeming anomaly: the metropolitan schism fosters a politics of ethnicism; it does not promote a politics of coalition in which leaders bargain and compromise in order to expand their base through gathering support from groups with roots different than their own. In the late 1960s and early 1970s the gripping issue for African-Americans was political control of the inner cities, and in many areas they were slowly but surely gaining a foothold in city halls around the country. Political leaders of the black community were understandably lukewarm in their support of Mount Laurel; from their perspective, it removed voters from the inner city, where minorities, through concentration of numbers, could attain political power.[6] Thus the Congressional Black Caucus, dependent to a considerable degree on the concentration of blacks in predominantly minority districts who vote as a bloc for black representatives, was indifferent to the reforms of Mount Laurel. When Kenneth Gibson, the African-American mayor of Newark, was on the board of COAH, he attended only meetings that included a discussion of regional contribution agreements, whereby funds are transferred to inner cities; he was not interested in bringing affordable housing out into the suburbs.

Many political activists saw efforts to integrate the African-American population more or less proportionally into the suburban portions of metropolitan areas as a political ploy to disperse their voting power throughout autonomous, predominantly white areas.[7] Extremists even attributed base motives to the Mount Laurel proponents, branding metropolitan integration as an outright white conspiracy to retain political dominance.[8] Several made the preposterous claim that the white majority was only yielding the suburbs to minorities because energy shortages were making them less attractive settlements. Such was the reaction that undermined support for Mount Laurel; if pressed, black leaders would favor the doctrine, but never enthusiastically.

This is but the latest variation on a long-standing dispute over urban policy.[9] Subscribers to the neoconservative view maintain that the Mount Laurel remedies only hasten the flight from the cities of upwardly mobile black and white people, leaving the inner city to the leaderless hard-core poor. Others of a more liberal cast argue that the proper course of reform, as in the Model Cities program of the Great Society, should be to redirect resources to improve the quality of life in the inner city, attracting industry and the middle class back to the older neighborhoods. Whatever the merits of these arguments, self-governance for African-Americans— acquiring and consolidating power in the cities—took precedence over opening the suburbs.

Members of racial and ethnic minorities already living in the suburbs had a far different perception of the Mount Laurel litigations. They were able to see a real payoff to themselves. The Burlington NAACP members residing in the suburbs, the plaintiffs in Mount Laurel II, supported the doctrine because they were ready to move to better parts of the suburban region with which they were already familiar. They were eager to leave the old houses of the rural past, sequestered in suburban segregated patterns, and move to more desirable areas. They saw the advantages of Mount Laurel in helping them end vestigial suburban enclaves. It was far more difficult for inner-city residents to recognize the direct benefits of Mount Laurel projects. Lack of resources made them suspicious of the entire undertaking. Furthermore, given the absence of affirmative marketing, many potential beneficiaries of the doctrine were simply unaware of its existence.[10] The "build it and they will come" attitude, as one developer terms it, misses major opportunities.[11] Special outreach efforts, statewide advertising, and counseling seminars and workshops are necessary to inform inner-city minorities of housing availability.

In the end, economic forces were at the root of much minority skepticism. Many inner-city minority residents do not have the ability to borrow the money necessary to buy even low-cost housing; they have little or no credit history or must deal with lenders unfamiliar with or hostile to them as borrowers. Moreover, as the courts pressed forward with the builder's remedy and housing came on the market, dwelling units still remained too expensive for many inner-city residents. For this, some blame must attach to the rigid standard ratio of affordable to market housing laid down in Mount Laurel II. The four-to-one bonus ratio was far too narrow a straitjacket; to be effective, the exact bonus of added market units should be custom-tailored to each case, based on the developer's write-down costs on the Mount Laurel units compared to the potential profit from each bonus market unit. As time passed, it became clear that the court's formula had not squeezed the developers hard enough: society had paid an unrealistically high cost to protect builders' profits. The income of the very plaintiffs in Mount Laurel II could not cover the debt service that the new housing units required.

Here, the courts and their remedies may be faulted for failing to stress rental housing. Out of deference to the suburban ethic, the zoning revisions and other compliance mechanisms included in the courts' remedies were drafted with individual home ownership in mind. Special masters, for example, spent considerable time assuring social and aesthetic compatibility by making the outer appearance of the affordable units architecturally similar to the detached or row house styles of the more expensive units in each subdivision; they did not regard garden apartment rental units as a suitable alternative. The result of the courts' and masters' misjudgment was that, for many, the so-called affordable housing remained tantalizingly beyond reach: the down payment required to purchase a home became an insuperable obstacle to residence in the suburbs. It all seemed a hoax. The court could set out the constitutional entitlement and put in place a system for its recognition, but it could not script the movement of minorities out of the central city and into the suburbs.[12]

## Convincing the Public

Confronted with parties coming to court in bad faith, having long ignored legal requirements, the Mount Laurel judiciary needed to muster broad support for its position. Admittedly, a court is not supposed to act according to what the political barometer shows as prevailing sentiment. "Enforcement of constitutional rights cannot await a supporting political consensus," as Chief Justice Wilentz put it.[13] Nevertheless, in its sensitive position as guardian of the rights and interests of minority groups, the court must try to make its workings understandable to the public for which it exercises judicial power. The task is exacerbated in Mount Laurel, for the obligation imposed on municipalities—undoing the mismatch between ghetto residence and job availability—is a difficult sell. Only by clearly stating (and giving reasons for rejecting) the alternatives, furnishing weighty reasons for conclusions, and showing an appreciation for the difficulties of the other side, can a consensus be reached.

In the face of local outcry, often laced with outrageous charges, the courts' cupboard of traditional reactions seems rather bare. Instead of rebuffing attacks in the media, a court can choose not to dignify them with a straight-on response and hope that eventual success will justify its interpretations. But a timid approach to judicial participation in the political debate, one that hews closely to the conventional practice of restraint, can leave the court with less, not more, ability to obtain public support for its position. The courts should not avoid dispensing information even if the chances of persuading the majority in an atmosphere of crisis are minimal. The task is too acute to be left to time. There is a whole wall of social indifference that will not be budged by a judicial opinion. Crystallized habits and entrenched institutions lead to a failure to communicate and a lack of support for court action.

A poignant illustration of the difficulties facing courts in the area of spatial integration comes from a federal judge's recent attempt to introduce low-income housing into a suburb. Under the subheading "Yonkers Neighbors Wait to Hear a White 'Hello,'" the *New York Times* reported:

> On one side of Clark Street, black families were raking leaves, playing catch, decorating their identical new homes for Halloween. On the other side of the narrow street, their white neighbors sat outside on the stoops, in the fading

sunlight of a recent afternoon, and stared openly at the newcomers across the way.

It has been four months since 24 low-income families moved here, on the former site of a parking lot near the Yonkers Raceway, and began planting flowers outside the colonial-style town houses that a Federal judge ordered the city to build after decades of intentional segregation. But residents on both sides of the block, who knew virtually everyone on their own side of the street, said they had yet to exchange a single word with any of their new neighbors.

The sad conclusion to the story: "On both sides of Clark Street, people blamed those living across the racial divide for the lack of communication. And residents on each side, who see each other every day, asked a reporter what those on the other side thought about them."[14]

Mount Laurel shows that implementing decisions, no matter how strongly based on constitutional imperatives, requires sophisticated, imaginative, and subtle judicial strategizing. Simply put, the court has to inspire public support. In complex institutional restructuring cases, the court cannot confine itself to opinion writing. Instead, it must recognize that, at that point, it is the branch of government doing the heavy lifting. For judicial policy makers who rely exclusively on the dignified statement from the bench, the risk is that no one will hear their message; here, silence is not golden. Enforcing constitutional and statutory norms against majority wishes, judges become subject to the same tests of the marketplace for contending ideas that govern the actions of other sectors of the government. Mere passivity is unlikely to prevail in the current world of public opinion; wordy, remote decisions that adhere strictly to legal issues and arcana have little hope of mobilizing supporters, let alone of disarming opponents, of social reform. The benefits of desegregation are collective, abstract, and difficult to sell to angry individuals. An economic or emotional lever has to be found to further the judicial ends.

The Mount Laurel courts failed to offer a range of arguments that could have generated greater public support for land-use reform. Take just one striking example: economic growth and productivity—goals widely accepted by suburban homeowners—are shackled by metropolitan fragmentation. Economists have shown the link among jobs, housing for workers, and economic expansion on the one hand and the rising need for a heterogeneous workforce in the suburbs on the other.[15] Indeed, the burden of long commutes—reduced productivity, dwindling labor pools, delays of congestion—is well documented in the record of many of the Mount Laurel litigations. So is the absence of adequate public transportation from the inner city to suburban workplaces.

The overwhelming need is to allay trepidations. Yet the Mount Laurel opinion may have fanned the flames of racial fear by not paying enough

attention to it. Undoubtedly, Chief Justice Wilentz believed in integration per se as a constitutional imperative and a societal goal. But the race issue was muted in his opinion; economic segregation was its dominant theme. Racial isolation, and its relation to class distinctions as the prime evil of exclusionary zoning, needed open discussion, not silent skirting.

In a different strategic vein, judges could shift public attention from one group of beneficiaries to others who would also gain from the banning of exclusionary ordinances. For example, opinions could stress the

demand in the suburbs for low-income housing for the elderly, an increasingly large cross-section of the population. The severe plight of
newlyweds unable to afford the typical suburban housing price is another mustering point for support. The emerging forms of the American
family—the divorced, the single parents, the retired—also all stand to
gain from the Mount Laurel Doctrine; they could both expand the coalition and increase the appeal to the public at large.

Examples of successfully integrated housing developments from other
parts of the country might also be employed to reassure locals that
low-income residents can be good neighbors. That housing for minorities
can coexist in the suburbs elsewhere—and with benign consequences—
comforts the alarmed. Well-planned placement of housing developments
is receiving increasing support from advocates of growth management—
at least those who are not segregationist wolves concealed under the hides
of environmental lambs. Expert planning advice (often tendered at trial)
on blending high-density development into the suburban environment in
a way that preserves swatches of the state's natural resources can make
the Mount Laurel Doctrine more palatable—and supportable.

Traditionally, courts have been reluctant to explicate any published
decision over and above its text. The matter speaks for itself—or so runs
the legal maxim. Indeed, a later commentary by the author of an opinion
may have unanticipated effects on newly arising cases and may distort the
weight given as precedent to the wording of the original passage. But
these qualms about commentary belong to the tradition of judges as
rulers of their private domains crafting their opinions in solitude, without
consultation, without experts. Judges locked in the struggle for institutional reform no longer fit into this paradigm; if they remain aloof and
assume that legal opinion writing alone will somehow succeed in rallying
the necessary support to their interpretation of the law, they are doomed
to disappointment.[16]

Along with concluding a controversy, an opinion in a major case has
to expound a basic philosophy. In terms of persuasiveness, legalese
counts less than the instinct, intuition, and adaptability of the writer. Although carefully organized, logical in its sequence, and demonstrating
professional competence and a fine legal craftsmanship, Mount Laurel II
regrettably failed to persuade and convince in a way required by the tense
New Jersey situation. Statements such as "the State controls the use of
land, *all* of the land," to which Chief Justice Wilentz gave prominence in
his opinion, were anathema to the private property owner.[17] Nor did a
holding flatly advanced, without elaboration or sauce, that helping the
poor migrate to the suburbs was a legal obligation due those who suffer
under the status quo appeal to the typical suburbanite. Where the perceived harms of a judicial decree are as personalized as they are sweeping,

filling up the interstices of everyday life, constitutional justifications need persuasive expositions. Lawyers, as a class, might appreciate the role of an impartial arbiter in expounding basic democratic freedoms in a rule-of-law society, but this understanding may not be shared by society at large—certainly not by those repressed by economic recession or the grind of the two-salary life.

Attention to the media is essential. No supporter of the Mount Laurel Doctrine undertook a wide-ranging public relations campaign that would have helped it survive the avalanche of adverse publicity that accompanied its promulgation. One-on-one explanations to newspaper reporters are well worth judges' time; that way, they can make sure the press understands what they are doing. Newspapers report to the public what is happening, and if a reporter does not fully understand the court's actions, chances are that the article will not present the actions in the best light. Sitting down with editorial boards of newspapers is the way to more balanced interpretations. For belief in the law to be sustained, people must understand how it makes sense, that there is a natural fairness associated with it. Those who must live with a remedy need to understand it. Perhaps it would be incommensurate with the dignity of the judiciary for a judge or master to appear on television for an interview or a call-in show, but what about mustering support from the state or local bar association or making speeches to the chamber of commerce and other organizations of interested citizens? These are all possible avenues of explanation for judges in whose courtrooms constitutional rights are being debated. Dialogue may not win over the hearts and minds of everyone, but it can surely lead to an appreciation of the court's occasional anti-majoritarian positions and the intelligence of its underlying rationale.

The New Jersey Supreme Court's attempt to impose legal reform on unwilling localities is a dramatic innovation. A court order, effective when imposed on parties to private litigation, carries less weight when it seeks to push an entire state to a greater awareness of ethical obligations. Further judicial reasoning and exposition—within and outside the written opinion—is necessary to expedite a reform program. Legal obstacles might be razed in the courtroom, but the social underpinnings of prejudice are more stubborn. Not only is the judicial printing press addressing the litigants or importuning the executive or the legislature, but it is also campaigning for a public constituency. The newsroom is as much the forum as the courtroom.

In the Mount Laurel litigations, the judges chose not to draw on their ability to publicize issues to move the consciences of the public at large. While several of the special masters—who served as intermediaries between the judges and the body politic—held themselves ready to respond to questions raised by the press, none took the initiative of directly engaging the attention of the media or of actively explaining the social purposes behind the litigations. Though less mired in tradition than the judges, the masters still failed to meet with editorial boards of newspapers or television stations to clarify issues. This inaction left the struggle to win over public sentiment to local officials and municipal planners who often presented one-sided accounts of the judicial intercession.

In recollection of things past, the Mount Laurel trial judges—even the more active of the three—still do not think it appropriate to rally public opinion or even to draw on the support of bar associations and other lawyers. They simply do not see selling as their job. Nor are they willing to engage in broad-based education and community relations programs that might ease the transition for all social classes. None of the judges, who had gone to the outer limits of their capacity in overseeing resolutions to individual cases, feels comfortable with the idea of actively campaigning to dispel distortions. "We cannot be seen as salespeople for our products," rejoins one trial judge. For too long the constricted, elitist view of judges' role has been pounded into their consciousness. An occasional commencement address or speech to a bar association, setting forth the broader goals of their Mount Laurel Doctrine, is as far as any will go. And this is the norm: though many judges have pursued careers in politics, as a group they still recoil from the stresses of the illogical, steamy political process.

One Passaic County mayor succinctly summed up his feelings toward the seven unanimous justices of Mount Laurel II: "They're nuts!" Should judges respond in kind? Certainly not, but their refusal to engage in further dialogue meant that the reasoning behind the Mount Laurel opinions was never explained or reinforced for the average citizen outside the courtroom. The rationale for dispersing the concentrated poverty of the inner cities was never communicated in a striking fashion. Nor did the judges dramatize the horrendous housing conditions in New Jersey's inner cities or put forth brutal images such as those judges have employed in other institutional litigations to bring home the degrading conditions of prisons or the ravages of environmental pollution. Yet who but the most fervent aficionados will sit down and read lengthy legal opinions, no matter how literary or well constructed? Who but a few can absorb the detailed discussions judges hammer out so carefully in their efforts to address all the intricacies of complex cases?

It is for this reason that as court master in the Boston Harbor cleanup case—with the dour acknowledgment that one picture is worth a thousand words—I took representatives of the press and the television media on inspection tours of Deer Island so they could witness visual evidence of the immense Dickensian powerhouse, the Hitchcock-like digesters of sewage, the end-of-the-world piles of sludge pouring untreated into the waters of the harbor. Such educational missions inevitably exert a powerful influence on viewers and readers, opening their rational processes to the values and implications of the judicial struggle to remedy institutional breakdown.

The litigation process in Mount Laurel did not serve the function it could have discharged in the broader social milieu—that of a catalyst for mustering support, for educating the public, and for opening up discussions that might heal divisions between the central cities and the suburban municipalities. The New Jersey courts did not go far enough to assuage the fears, legitimate or impeachable, well founded or mythical, of the citizenry. They left community concerns unattended. Declarations of human rights and constitutional legitimacy need specific reinforcement and coalition support in a democracy where public sentiment is the ultimate judge. Above all, the vision of a society based on diversity, plurality, and tolerance, couched in broad, constitutional terms such as *general welfare*, is a message that judges must not merely enunciate but also imbue with life and immediacy.

The canon of judicial ethics, as presently formulated, precludes judges' responses over and above the particular written opinion.[18] This rule ought to be revised for cases of litigation involving institutional reform. "There's such a backlash against Mount Laurel already, and that's due to misinformation," explained the League of Women Voters' housing specialist.[19] "People just don't know," she added, "what the decision really says." In the heat of battle, judges cannot rest on the romantic belief of a Cardozo that somehow, by the legal equivalent of the economists' invisible hand, right will triumph over evil. The strength of the courtroom is its pragmatism, the daily experience that allows the fact finder to analyze people and institutions in a down-to-earth fashion. The problem of exclusionary zoning invites boldness. A court's arguments, keyed to political, rather than judicial audiences, as well as a judicially directed exposure of decision makers to the blighting impact of exclusionary zoning on the lives of ordinary human beings, could make essential differences. Yet so far the courts have offered timidity when it comes to public discussion.

In 1990, in one of those ironic twists that bring a lusty afterlife to events confined to the dry and dusty bin of history, Jack Kemp, then U.S. Secretary of Housing and Urban Development, appointed former New Jersey governor Thomas H. Kean as chairperson of an advisory commission on regulatory barriers to affordable housing. As governor of New Jersey during much of the 1980s, Kean had decried Mount Laurel as a communist doctrine and sought to repeal the State Development Guide Plan. In his new institutional role, however, Kean wholeheartedly adopted the New Jersey Supreme Court's approach. He recommended fundamental changes in existing laws to eliminate suburbia's regulatory barriers, most especially zoning regulations, which impede housing affordability. "Millions of Americans," he wrote with eloquence, "are being priced out of buying or renting the kind of housing they otherwise could afford were it not for a web of government regulations."[20] Had this change of heart come about during his tenure of power in New Jersey, when his opinions carried the weight of office, the history of Mount Laurel could have been much different.

# XI

## The Last Recourse:
## Why Judges Intervene

THE MOUNT LAUREL litigations bring to the fore the residual role of the courts in the checks-and-balances system of a constitutional democracy. Local governments, ordinarily endowed with total discretion in the exercise of zoning power, are found to be seriously and chronically in constitutional default. In such a state of affairs, whatever a court's adherence to the separation of powers as usually enunciated or whatever the loyalty to the conventional division of powers among the levels of government as typically argued, the strict rules of judicial insulation become inapposite.[1]

### Reordering of Governmental Behavior

To modify a phrase from the philosopher David Hume, it is both appropriate and necessary for the court to fashion judicial remedies to remove local exclusionary regulatory ordinances. By *appropriate*, I mean that the court is neither overstepping its authority nor improperly impinging on the prerogatives of the other two branches of government. By *necessary*, I mean that, without judicial intervention, the problem will remain with us for the foreseeable future.

Judicial fashioning of remedies in the Mount Laurel situation is appropriate for four major reasons. First, and foremost, a legal wrong is asserted. The judicial struggle with suburban decision making is not of the court's choosing; rather, the burden of coping with exclusionary local zoning is thrust upon it. Liability on the part of the defendant municipality is conceded; at this point, it is the court's responsibility to rectify past wrongs and to seek an end to the present and future violations of the law. Courts are not roving law enforcers seeking to right wrongs wherever and whenever they arise. The legislature passes a law; it is violated by a government agency; a party petitions for redress; and the court must respond. The constitution enumerates protections; they are transgressed by an institution of government; and the court is called on to declare the right and establish a remedy to undo the violation. One can hardly claim in these instances that judges are indulging in what the ancient common law picturesquely termed champerty and maintenance, stirring up litigation where none would otherwise occur.[2]

Any charge that the Mount Laurel courts are expansionist is fundamentally contrived: the court is performing the function it has been assigned under the constitution or a statute. Courts by law must hear the claims of illegality put forth by plaintiffs and the responses by defendants and then make a determination. Once the claims of a builder or a public interest group regarding a Mount Laurel exclusionary zoning ordinance are proven, failure to provide appropriate relief from defendants' ongoing wrongful conduct and practices would render nugatory the original determination of liability and eventually serve to undermine the role of the judiciary in guaranteeing a lawful society.

Second, the court by its nature is a disinterested and objective referee in cases of major institutional breakdown, answerable to no special interests or narrow loyalties and subservient only to the fair and equitable application of the law as formulated by the framers of the constitution and legislators and as construed by judges. This is not to deny that, pressed by the force of events, even the court may become an advocate for a particular position or side. Indeed, once the predicate finding of liability is established, the court, as the three Mount Laurel judges have conceded, inevitably moves to support the plaintiff in seeking the remedy that will end the defendants' illegal practices and vindicate the public rights. But the curbs, both traditional and adjusted for the new situation, confine too extensive an exercise of discretion.

Third, and most especially in cases involving fundamental interests, the court acts as a trustee for future as well as present generations. As political institutions, the legislative and executive branches of government are buffeted not only by the tides of suburban forces but also by special interest currents exerting daily and even hourly pulls and tugs. This pressure is by no means improper—indeed, it is an essential component of the democratic process—but it may lead to decisions that respond to crises of the moment to the detriment of generations yet unborn. In matters concerning patterns of metropolitan settlement, adequacy of housing, and quality of the environment, for example, where present-day activities can yield long-term, potentially irreversible, and frequently incalculable harms, the court—as the most politically insulated branch of our democratic system—can act the most forcefully as guardian for the future.

Fourth, a judicial decision in matters of broad public concern can stimulate awareness and debate. As individuals invoke constitutional doctrine as a restraint on majority action, the trial and appellate process, traveling beyond conventional borders, can arouse a more generous vision of the social order. The outcome of a nascent judicial dispute does not turn on relationships or powers existing at the outset. After the debate, both within and outside the courtroom, the final result depends (to an often surprising extent) on the strength of the reasoning and the merits of the arguments on either side, as judges strive to interpret the mandate of the constitution or statute at issue. Judicial decrees can bring administrations, interest-group leaders, and legislators to approach from a fresh perspective issues that have either been taken for granted or simply ignored, even those that have long eluded solution. Passage of the FHA—even by a reluctant legislature—with its striking preamble adopting the constitutional obligation of a regional context for affordable housing, would have been impossible without the reasoned discourse of the Mount Laurel opinions.

But the mere fact that it is *appropriate* for the court to fashion judicial remedies may not be enough to support intervention. One must also ask whether intervention is *necessary*. Two major reasons can be advanced for an affirmative response in the New Jersey context.

First, there is no reason to believe—and, in fact, every reason to disbelieve, given the dreadful eight years between Mount Laurel I and Mount Laurel II—that housing segregation in New Jersey, enforced by local regulatory ordinances and sentiment, would stop of its own accord. Although in the abstract it may be preferable to achieve objectives through legislative rather than judicial intervention, this is not a choice always available. In New Jersey, the courts proved to be the only government institution able to alter the established course of local exclusionary zoning. Surely the failure of the legislative and executive branches to ensure equal access to suburban land was not the product of lack of awareness; indeed, many reports spoke eloquently to official concern. But whether owing to short-run views of self-interest, institutional ineffectiveness, or

## Residential Distribution

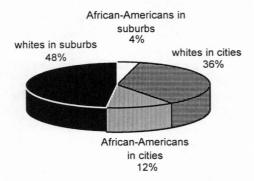

African-Americans in
suburbs
4%

whites in suburbs
48%

whites in cities
36%

African-Americans
in cities
12%

weakness of political will, the metropolitan areas remained unacceptably fragmented and encapsulated from the social and human points of view.

To this day, an interminable number of plans, proposals, and studies have emerged, but the necessary administrative reforms, the tangible dollars of funding, and the actual construction of houses are agonizingly slow in coming. Absent judicial conduct, it may become too late for any agency to repair the threatening schism in major metropolitan areas. The court, however, as a body of last resort, can break the logjam and then bear the criticisms and pressures that are likely to ensue. Nor should another useful by-product of the judicial presence be overlooked: it can be the scapegoat for local mayors and councils, who go back to the electorate, claiming that, opposed as they are to the change (even more adamantly than their constituents, they can argue), they have no choice but to comply with the judicial fiat. Judges provide wonderful political cover.

In New Jersey, the supreme court was asked to act in an area, zoning discrimination, where the other two branches of government were either unwilling or structurally unable to proceed. The high flame of a court remedy thawed the frozen pipes of the political system. So much for the debate as to whether courts are able to match the achievements of other branches of government; here, the alternative of other reform institutions and processes did not exist. The need to stir the powers of the other branches of government, gridlocked over a controversial issue, is the basic justification for judicial action in the reform of land-use regulation in New Jersey. The founding fathers did not think it natural that the judiciary would initiate, but given that it is a coequal branch, the founders would not eliminate the possibility that it might.

In Mount Laurel, the courts played out the difficult role assigned to them in a society governed by a written bill of rights: that of battling for unpopular causes and protecting the rights of minorities in cases of government law-breaking. This role obliges courts to operate as a safety valve when the rest of the governmental system is clogged. As Justice Brennan, himself once a justice of the New Jersey Supreme Court, pointed out, "Charged with the duty of enforcing the Constitution, courts are in the strongest position to insist that unconstitutional conditions be remedied."[3] In enunciating the Mount Laurel Doctrine, the courts spelled out for society the Sunday school teachings for a moral existence, imposing constitutional imperatives on the workaday world of jobs and living. They achieved change under the most difficult scenario imaginable, not in a head-on conflict with an entrenched bureaucracy insulated from public concerns but in direct hand-to-hand combat with the most elemental, local voice of popular will—the very personification of those passions the founding fathers so feared.[4] This localism, dominated by renascent segregationism and resurgent ethnicism, persists; neighborhoods are hardly reluctant to speak out resoundingly on local zoning matters.

Even if residents of suburban communities were aware of the true costs of exclusion, to themselves as well as to the residents of the inner cities, a collective action paradox prevents the formation of a coalition for effective remedies that could express itself through legislative or executive action. Since the public service costs of low-income housing are immediately felt in the locality, while its potential benefits—say, of availability of workers for the industries sought by those local governments—are not confined to the site, each locality has the incentive to wait for another to address the lack of affordable housing. Under the existing legal structure of local boundaries, no town can be certain that it can capture the benefits if it undertakes the expense; but it is clear that each one can benefit in the short term by shunting to its neighbor the obligation to house low-income families.

Illustrating the disparity between the ideal and the real, fostered by the courts' belief that political life must be brought as far as possible into accord with constitutional morality, the evolution of the Mount Laurel Doctrine reinforces an insight into a looming weakness of the political process of the 1990s: policy formulation, when entrusted to the elected instrumentalities of government, can become too easily identified with the interests of the economically powerful.[5] This is especially true of the small suburb with its insulated majority. And as Madison stressed in *The Federalist, No. 10*, the danger is exacerbated by the impossibility of a change in majority rule if exclusionary tactics bar would-be voters from entering the local precinct.

Thus the legitimacy of judicial intervention is even clearer in the context of exclusionary zoning than in the usual class of institutional restructuring litigation. Political malfunction attributable to a deeply ingrained,

## Children Under 18 in Poverty (1990)

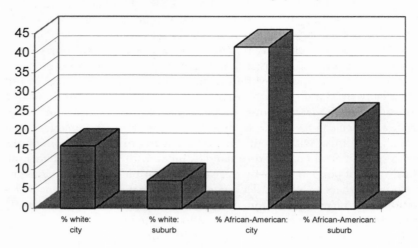

potentially permanent structural bias pervades the land-use scene. The broad argument made in *Baker v. Carr* (the one-person, one-vote decision), that courts must step in to correct a malfunctioning of the political system, applies forcefully in Mount Laurel.[6] Suburban governments operate on behalf of their own partisan considerations; their main interests reside in preserving tax ratables and in keeping densities low. Such local parochialism makes land scarce for housing, especially that destined for low-income families. Because it is easy for local homeowners to control the local council, a classic example of Madison's factionalist ghost appears. Entry of potentially dissenting voices is barred.

Owing to their poverty and small numbers, Ethel and Thomasene Lawrence, together with the other long-time residents of the Springville section of Mount Laurel, were as effectively disenfranchised in the local political process as were the plaintiffs who did not live in the township. Leadership of the locality came instead from the ranks of the new, moneyed arrivals who had their own ideas for the future of the township. The young professional who owned a home in one of the new developments became the standard-bearer for the zoning law that barred entry to others.

If the idea of a safety net is an accepted tenet of emerging welfare capitalism, judges cannot avoid responsibility, in the checks-and-balances system, for assuring its continued existence. Not all interests receive equal time in the legislative and executive forums. Buttressed by the value judgments of the politically and economically advantaged and legitimated by

## Unemployment for Central-City Males (aged 16-24)

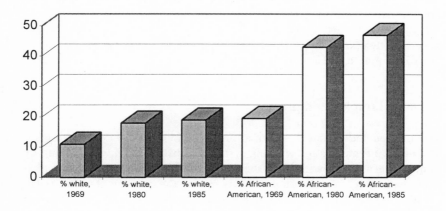

majoritarian support, local governments are free to act despotically within the sphere of their delegated land-use powers. By strict review of exclusionary regulations, courts permit the otherwise underenfranchised to contend for influence within the chaotic marketplace-of-ideas democracy that governs the United States.

A second reason supporting the necessity of the Mount Laurel judicial action emerges from the way political power is dispersed territorially in the United States. No one agency in front of the court, acting alone, has the governmental authority or ability to clear up the situation created by the multitude of local authorities responsible only to local constituencies.[7] Perhaps it is a case of too many cooks spoiling the efficient and equitable allocation of metropolitan land resources. Whatever the reason, the goal of making suburban land available for moderate- and low-income groups falls between the cracks of the many existing federal, state, and local agencies. At the same time, the economic realities of the real estate market jump over political boundaries; the courses followed by the spread of new jobs and transportation modes do not obligingly shape themselves to the artificial jurisdictional boundaries government bureaucracies would impose.

The state court, as an institution, is charged with overseeing the welfare of the state as a whole. As one New Jersey Supreme Court justice, applying hindsight to the matter, observed: "The court would be conducive to effectuating the substantive stance, which is to apply Mount Laurel on a regional basis. So we had three judges basically exercising statewide jurisdiction in the entire state and we could do it because we're a unified judiciary—every superior court judge basically has statewide jurisdiction." Acting in the holistic capacity of its equity jurisdiction, the state court can mitigate the administrative fragmentation and overlap that impedes solutions to continuous and systemic metropolitan area wrongdoing. Courts thereby can help spur the appropriate land-use authorities into fashioning comprehensive and realistic programs of action for revamping exclusionary local ordinances.[8]

## Remedial Implementation

Having concluded that it is both appropriate and necessary for it to fashion judicial remedies for ongoing systemic constitutional wrongdoing by other government institutions, the court should conduct itself reasonably and respectfully in fashioning and supervising the implementation of such remedies. Throughout, the New Jersey courts approached the question of relief with extreme caution; judges were mindful of municipalities' sensitivity to perceived outside meddling (remember, for instance, that Justice Hall's careful framing of the remedy in Mount Laurel I even drew a colleague's criticism for its naive reliance on the good faith of localities). The court's role is to establish performance standards for accomplishing goals, to see that the responsible authorities coordinate their work promptly and efficiently, and to goad into action those who fail to respond to the seriousness and urgency of the tasks before them. Clearly, the courts must not appropriate the administrative functions of the state's operating and regulatory agencies to a greater degree or for a longer duration than necessary; neither should they interfere with day-to-day decision-making processes nor attempt to replace or ignore the assembled expertise and experience of public officials and consultants. Instead, the courts should strive to fashion remedies that intrude as little as possible on the prerogative of the coordinate branches of government, leaving it up to the defendants themselves to determine how best compliance can be accomplished.

Enforcement is not an enviable burden imposed on the courts. But when administrative inertia or improper action leads to appreciable harm, the courts cannot dodge the obligation of seeing to the implementation of constitutional responsibilities. Somehow, the wrongful practice must be reconstructed in a way that satisfies the constitutional duty or simply be dismantled altogether. A remedy must be as broad and as detailed as needed to halt the wrongful conduct; in a fundamental sense, its magnitude and depth and the scope of the compliance mechanism must reflect the extent to which the systematic wrongdoing has upset social life.

Thus, after the eight years of neglect following the Mount Laurel I judgment, the mandate of Mount Laurel II, as expounded by the three

trial judges, created, defined, and maintained a reconstituted local practice that would guide transition to compliance with the substantive law.
A series of litigations would work out what a compliant world would
look like. New administrative mechanisms, specialized judges, deployment of professional experts and special masters, resort to negotiation
and mediation, and affirmative measures were the judicial tools employed
to set the framework for the fair share allocations of affordable housing
within the region. Because the exclusionary ordinances had been long
enduring, the court's jurisdiction entailed a complex proceeding with extensive monitoring. Hence the outcome of a typical Mount Laurel trial
provided the defendant locality with a blueprint detailing the ordinance
changes necessary to ensure sufficient suitable sites for moderate- and
low-income housing.

The remedies fashioned by the New Jersey Supreme Court, most recently exemplified in *Holmdel* and *Warren*, seek to strike that elusive
equilibrium between undue disruption of the balance in our political system and a guarantee of an aggressive program for affordable housing
within metropolitan areas. Through the very process of this advanced
form of institutional litigation—a participatory arrangement aimed at
creating a consensual remedial solution—the separation of powers doctrine is continuously reinterpreted in order to spur institutions to carry
out the functions delegated to them. Through concentrated effort, New
Jersey may yet accommodate the political, economic, and environmental
needs of its metropolitan areas. By breaking free from what are too often
nebulous restraints on their actions, the courts can apply legal logic to
evaluate social consequences directly. As the New Jersey courts act to
alleviate the structural deficiencies of the other political institutions operating within the metropolitan areas, often too easily overrun by majoritarian concerns, the difficult but inevitable future of the American judiciary's role in the large-scale restructuring of institutional breakdowns
begins to emerge.

Prominent jurists, perhaps best exemplified by Jerome Frank and Learned
Hand, extol the progressive judge as incorporating the evolving ethos of
the community she or he serves.[9] This vision is shattered, however, when
the norm is not already extant in the society but imposed by the legal
order. The Mount Laurel Doctrine articulated a fresh current of thought,
and the dominant public ethos rejected it. In light of the outraged opposition Mount Laurel aroused in local communities, what is one to make of
Judge Hand's statement that the profession of law "must feel the circu-
lation of the communal blood or it will wither and drop off, a useless
member"?[10] Does this mean that the courts must always capitulate to the
public will?

A minimalist argument readily presents itself for justifying the actions taken over two decades by the New Jersey courts. Even those who would confine judicial review to the policing of process should find little to fault in the New Jersey Supreme Court's intervention to formulate and enforce the Mount Laurel Doctrine.[11] "Physical access is indispensable to the constitutional norm of an individual's ability to participate in public discourse and to enact, reject, or modify laws. Without a voting presence within the boundaries of the local political unit endowed with the legislative power, how can the constitutionally essential political representation system be satisfied? When local laws of land-use control bar the entry of certain groups, there can be no public voice to present alternative policies to the body politic; minority interests will not be given the opportunity to persuade and prevail. Certainly, all would agree that protection of the political process is the province of the judiciary.

Thoughtful scholarship abounds about the need for judicial restraint, but the history of Mount Laurel, its means of coping with the remarkable scale and complexity of metropolitan relations, makes a powerful case for judicial action as a necessary element within the balance wheel of governance whenever official actions repeatedly offend constitutional principles. The actions of the Mount Laurel courts represent the evolution of a new system, a set of procedures adapted to meet the needs of the modern technological and industrial society with its novel patterns of population settlements within the metropolitan areas. When, however, is it appropriate for a court to move the boundaries (assuming they are fixed, even if only temporarily) that separate the powers? The proposition I advance here is that courts are obliged to intervene—to undertake the coercive reordering of major social institutions—when a wrongful social practice either impairs a group's ability to participate in the political process or when another branch of government is systematically delinquent in carrying out the mandates of the constitution.

In brief, before intervening in an institutional restructuring case, the court should find:

* law-breaking by the state or a unit of the state;
* illegality that affects a sizable segment of social life, with a detrimental impact on the legal interests of an indefinitely large number of persons;
* wrongdoing that is not isolated but systematic, indicating a persistent pattern of law-breaking over time;
* law-breaking that violates a constitutional provision, not simply an ordinary law;[12]
* wrongful practice that is entrenched, that means to project itself into the future, that the state refuses to correct, and that (probably for some political reason) the executive or the legislative body is structurally incapable of correcting.

Behind the elaborate procedural and remedial apparatus of Mount Laurel II is the sense that extant constitutional law is deeply critical of the existing suburban legal order as a whole and that the three trial judges, by specifying changes concretely and affirmatively, would help transform offending social practices. Since social energies are frustrated by out-of-date legal precepts, adjudication must assume new tasks in the collective suits. The resulting law, assuming that constitutional ideals have the power to guide large-scale reordering of institutional arrangements in metropolitan areas, goes deep into existing social arrangements, seeking to transform ongoing practices that violate the constitution. However, reconfiguration of offending practices by the judiciary still leaves municipalities with considerable leeway to choose among reordering alternatives, and remedies should be framed so as to leave room for local discretion.

In essence, Mount Laurel was a rescue operation—a restoration of justice in the metropolitan region, which had been subverted by the failure of New Jersey's municipalities to abide by fundamental principles of our social order. The resulting judicial remedies were intended to catalyze the latent reordering potential of the local government system. Once municipal powers were mobilized by a corrective goal, the New Jersey Supreme Court believed that the system could ameliorate the social consequences of constitutional illegality. Thus the Mount Laurel judges built into their decrees a probability of future compliance on the part of the municipalities by adding substantive prescription to injunctive restraint. This was the transformative vision.

# XII

## National Ramifications:
## Judges as Social Innovators

WHEN THE long-brewing crisis over local exclusionary zoning ordinances finally erupted, the constitutional responsibility to enforce public law norms forced the judiciary to undertake an extensive and, at times, coercive reordering of the way localities managed their land-use regulations. No longer would it be enough that the law "forbids rich and poor alike to sleep under the bridges, to beg in the streets, and to steal their bread."[1] The time for substantive equality had arrived. Each town had to establish land-use regulations that would offer opportunities for satisfying its obligation to provide a fair share of the regional need for low- and moderate-income housing, present and prospective. Traditional separation of powers doctrines did not furnish a pertinent guideline for the courts' efforts to remedy the deep wrongdoing of systemically misusing local regulatory powers.

The shifts in power among the judicial, legislative, and executive branches of the New Jersey government played out against the background of changes in the composition of the state supreme court, as well as of the executive and legislative branches. After the courts' initial intervention to protect minorities from majoritarian overreaching, the other departments of government responded almost immediately, first informally and then with formal barriers to unwelcome change. Recalcitrance triggered a vigorous counterthrust by the courts, which resisted both the disregard of their affordable housing decisions by the coequal branches of state government and the obstructionist actions of local governments.

Over the course of this point-counterpoint series, New Jersey seemed finally to come to terms with the courts' rulings by passing the Fair Housing Act, which created the Council on Affordable Housing as an alternative to the courts and led to administrative ordering of the regional fair share requirement. The state had agreed with the courts' elevation of low- and moderate-income housing to the level of a constitutional obligation. The latest judicial moves on the political chessboard—*Holmdel* and *Warren*—reinforce the promise expressed more vaguely in the earlier *Hills* opinion, which sustained the FHA's constitutionality. Nevertheless, the cycle of sporadic intervention by the various branches of government, a continuation of the policy tug-of-war, persists.

## An Instrument of Social Change

In the years preceding Mount Laurel I, the state of New Jersey had grown ever more susceptible to metropolitan separatism. Municipalities wielded local land-use law to keep rich and poor, blacks and whites far apart, separated by legal walls surrounding suburbia. The potential explosion of class and racial conflict and the risk of an open rift with local governments prevented the governor and the legislature from taking direct action. Even officials who disapproved of the discrimination refused to incur the political costs that action would bring. Should overwhelming difficulties of reform mean that the courts ought to withdraw as well—a recommendation made by more than a few commentators? As Cardozo wrote, a judge "is not a knight-errant, roaming at will in pursuit of his own ideal of beauty or of goodness. He is to draw his inspiration from consecrated principles."[2] But to what extent can society rely on these "consecrated principles"—presumably the statement of timeless verities—to act for themselves? Who will put them into practice? Ultimately, does Cardozo's dictum mean that agencies of government should never intercede, even where constitutional rights call out for vindication?[3]

Increasingly, the judiciary's role is to break institutional stalemate. Municipalities defy the law with exclusionary zoning regulations. Institutions do not reform themselves. Everyone has a veto over everyone else. Thus, within the reality of current American politics, it makes considerable sense for individuals, builders, and public interest groups to press for institutional restructuring by way of lawsuits. The New Jersey courts first responded to this pressure to adjust societal relationships with considerable hesitation, out of deference to other branches of government and because of their own too strict adherence to the traditional adjudicatory model. In particular, localities seized on the long delay between Mount Laurel I and Mount Laurel II, seeing in it a lack of will to enforce constitutional rights. Soon enough, however, the judicial system learned the need for firmness in remedy and the obligation, in New Jersey's political setting, to move quickly toward revising details of ordinances.

The totality of the experience shows how well the judiciary can respond to the abdication of responsibility by other institutions when there is a systemic breakdown in governmental behavior. Ultimately, it demonstrates the judiciary's skill in fashioning effective mechanisms for coping with governmental wrongdoing. Amid fierce criticisms by local politicians, the courts persevered. Their novel administrative framework, proving unexpectedly successful, has ramifications beyond its immediate context of exclusionary zoning. This general applicability can ease the job of judges in other types of institutional litigations. Mount Laurel puts to rest charges that judges lack the capacity to formulate and implement complex remedies. Moreover, it shows how the independent status of the courts—the basis of their legitimacy—is reinforced as they achieve institutional reforms without the support of political leaders and much of the public.

Creation of the three-judge court, inventive use of special masters and other expert assistance, the use of negotiation techniques, the evolution case by case of practical compliance mechanisms, and above all enlistment of the private market in solving a social problem made Mount Laurel–type injunctions more than hortatory.[4] At the time of Mount Laurel I, affordable housing in the New Jersey suburbs was an ever-retreating mirage. If some seer had predicted that in twenty years every New Jersey locality in a growth area would assume the presence of low- and moderate-income housing within its boundaries and that towns' master plans would incorporate a housing element for that purpose, the crowd would have hooted that Cassandra down in disbelief. Equally implausible would have been a prophecy conjuring up a state agency created to estimate housing needs, formulate a consistent and rational fair share allocation, and review local ordinances for compliance with affordable housing needs, not to mention the passage, however reluctantly, of a Fair Housing Act codifying the legislature's acknowledgment that regional housing consideration must be integrated into local zoning ordinances in order to satisfy "the constitutional obligation enunciated by the Supreme Court,"[5] an act reinforced by that court's assumption in 1993 that "the central goal" of the FHA "is to implement the Mount Laurel doctrine."[6]

Now, almost all localities in New Jersey have institutionalized planning for moderate- and low-income dwelling units.[7] The Mount Laurel opinions, controversial as they are, make the local process of considering housing needs a common routine that stands as a new norm in the political and administrative process. No municipality writes its local master plan without obeisance to its housing obligation, amplifying the community's statement of readiness to comply with fair share requirements. Municipal attorneys may argue in the courtroom that the obligation should be defined differently, but after Mount Laurel II they must accept the concept's basic validity. Today, no responsible local official is unaware of the obligations that the complex rulings have imposed. Affordable housing is brought up at every meeting of one planning board, a special master reports, and its provision is always a subject of discussion with developers seeking planning permission. Another official noted, "The mayor, turning the mike off, asks the town attorney, 'Where do we stand on the affordable housing requirement?'" Once woven into the fabric, the Mount Laurel Doctrine is there on a continuing basis. As judicial remedies force compliance in the real world, the illegality of abuse of local zoning power filters into public consciousness. Conformity is routinized. Proximity may not lead to cultural integration, but affordable housing in the suburbs is nevertheless a ticket to economic opportunity, mutual respect, and cultural understanding.

The dialogue among the New Jersey branches of government is instructive on yet another score. Judges often take extreme stands in institutional litigation so that the legislature, if and when forced to act, can assume a centrist position. In this way courts can force accountability from elected officials without causing them to lose face (or elections). That dialogue also furnishes a background for implementing the applicable legal and constitutional doctrines; until action is taken by the executive or legislative branches, much can be learned from the initial experience of the Mount Laurel judges in handling the problem. The supreme court's courageous interpretation of what the law required, followed by the hands-on experience of the three trial judges—a quasi-administrative agency cum court—combined with the expertise of the special masters in spelling out details and refining techniques, and culminating in the begrudging acceptance of the FHA by the legislature, constituted a more effective societal process, it can be argued, than would have been a hesitant legislature's initial authorization of an administrative agency to supervise the introduction of affordable housing into the suburbs.

## Producing Results

The quantifiable results of the Mount Laurel litigations are considerable, although they are only a start. In the six years from 1987 to 1993, the courts and COAH had overseen or influenced affordable housing at a rate of 11,000 land parcels a year, and New Jersey municipalities had zoned, rehabilitated, or built 54,000 dwelling units. New construction of affordable housing in the suburbs is placed at 14,000 units.[8] (This should be set in context: only 153,000 building permits were authorized in the entire state, so the Mount Laurel construction activities make up nearly 9 percent of the total, and its total parcel activity is 35 percent of all the authorizations in the state.) Rehabilitated units total 11,000, and the remainder is zoned, waiting to be built. Moreover, the building activity influenced by the court or COAH is much greater but impossible to quantify. Many communities have produced affordable housing as a result of lawsuits in process or settlements; others choosing not to go before COAH or follow its procedures have required developers to put up affordable housing or provided it themselves.

With better timing and luck—catching the boom-bust cycle in housing at the right phase—still more affordable units would exist. The courts removed the legal obstacles, but the economics of the market continued to post high barriers to entry. Yet even this obstruction may prove temporary. Projects cleared of exclusionary regulations are already in the pipeline, set to go as soon as the economic fog that misted the construction outlook from 1992 to 1994 lifts.[9] And the figure could even run higher than 54,000: the 270 municipalities certified by COAH or the courts have the potential of yielding 62,000 low- and moderate-income units. With the addition of 22,000 units in the 44 municipalities who have filed housing elements with COAH, the total would come to 84,000 units.[10]

The Mount Laurel decisions have enabled thousands of people in New Jersey to live in affordable housing units in attractive suburban communities that otherwise would have shut them out. But despite changes in local land-use law, many remain inadequately housed. COAH recalculated the need for affordable housing from 1993 to 1999 at 86,308 units. But in 1994 the New Jersey Department of Community Affairs estimated an overall statewide need for 20,000 additional affordable housing units annually for the next five years. In addition, some 25,295 eligible households still await their chance to own or rent Mount Laurel housing units.[11] Hence, in proportion to housing demand as a whole, the enhancement thus far—and the improvement still promised—is no more than a moderate step in the right direction. Moreover, the shortage derives from problems of income as much as a dearth of shelter. It would be misguided to pin all hopes of solution on changes in land-use practice; that would simply fob off responsibility from other potential income redistributors to the courts, COAH, and a market incapable of producing affordable unit increments without a major shift in wealth among households. But the expectation remains that establishing affordable housing in the suburbs

will make further advances in the next decade, as more attention is paid to the metropolitan dilemma and, under the joint aegis of COAH and the courts, to narrowing the gulf between proclaimed purposes and social realities.[12]

Any final summation of Mount Laurel's achievements must also allay a core doubt. Empowering minorities to move out of the inner cities was the original motive of Mount Laurel I and II (albeit never explicitly pushed to the forefront).[13] Did the intended beneficiaries—Camden or Newark lower-income families, for instance—actually move into affordable housing in the idyllic New Jersey countryside, or were the new units occupied by suburban elderly or others not specifically the target of the judicial opinions? Statistics are lacking, but thus far integration on a physical scale of African-Americans and Hispanic-Americans from inner-city neighborhoods has fallen short of expectations.

Conclusions on this score may be premature, however. There simply has not been enough time for social learning to occur, for new standards of social acceptability to form, or for corrective policies to coalesce. Whenever a town absorbs new low- and moderate-income housing and the sky does not come tumbling down, other communities will be that much more likely to take the leap themselves.[14] And here the empiric record is surprisingly auspicious: there has been no formal instance of hostility, altercations, or—perhaps most important to worried suburbanites—depreciation of property values. This is the case even when the Mount Laurel projects are right next to the market units. Apparently, the prospect of new neighbors is more frightening than the actuality. Another reason for optimism is that until recently, localities deliberately excluded inner-city residents from the new housing units; the outcome of the *Warren* case, which outlaws local residence and work preferences, was not announced until 1993, and its impact has yet to register.[15]

The issue of race, of course, remains intensely sensitive and uniquely difficult. The New Jersey Supreme Court acted against local exclusionary zoning at a time when many states were distancing themselves from housing and race issues. Indeed, the racial implications of the Mount Laurel decisions were barely addressed in any public forum, let alone in the text of the judicial opinions themselves. While remedies were framed and zoning ordinances revised, participants tiptoed around the racial implications of their agreements.[16] Aversion and resentment, even contempt, for minorities is not mentioned. Thus Justice Hall struggled to use economic discrimination as the suspect classification that triggered strict scrutiny, and despite the many references to the plight of the poor, there was no explicit mention of race in Chief Justice Wilentz's lengthy Mount Laurel II opinion.[17] *Holmdel*, for its part, focused on affordable housing. Class divisions were used as a euphemism for racial animosity and managed to obscure the whole race issue. Groups representing minorities preferred to skirt silently around what seemed to them a minefield.

As Mount Laurel gradually moves forward through one business cycle to the next, it may find itself representative of a new period in which class actually does preempt race, forcing New Jerseyites (and other Americans) to confront the underlying reality of class divisions in the United States and to question the destructive myth of a classless society.[18]

## How Widely Does All This Apply?

It has taken decades of experience, culminating in the pioneering work of the Mount Laurel judges, to point up the fundamental role of exclusionary zoning in reinforcing metropolitan segregation. Not that discrimination is unknown to the law of real property, of course. Purchasing a home is a complex transaction, and the occasions to suffer misfeasance are many—from the first encounter with a realtor to the closing with a mortgage lender. Grasping that prejudice flows from the seemingly neutral setting of the local land-use control system requires a subtler understanding, however, in part because exclusionary zoning is not so clearly linked to the violation of individual rights as is direct discrimination in real estate transactions. Understandably, then, in view of our blindness to the problem itself, the public policies necessary to end racially segregated land-use patterns at the metropolitan area level are neither easily recognized nor extensively deployed in antidiscrimination strategies.

The Mount Laurel decisions highlight two basic and interrelated issues: under the legal order, legally separate communities enjoy autonomous power over local land uses; and accordingly, they use land-use regulations to carry out constituents' desires not to live next to households commanding a lower income or social status than their own, in the same fashion that homeowners employed private restrictive covenants to exclude minorities from mostly all-white neighborhoods—until the U.S. Supreme Court outlawed the practice in 1948.[19]

As presently constituted, no public body represents the interests of metropolitan areas as a whole in implementing regional housing opportunity. Nor is this likely to change, since there is no community motivation to formulate ordinances (or the legal powers to adopt them) aimed at overcoming the self-serving policies of narrow groups of residents. With such fragmentation of legal power within the metropolitan area, communities are free to construct land-use ordinances to uphold the interests of individuals seeking to maintain social status through position in the stratified hierarchy of place. Because the bulk of undeveloped land is clustered in suburban communities, this power gives suburbs tremendous control over metropolitan development, especially as it affects residential and employment opportunities. But if the fate of inner-city neighborhoods rests with the suburbs growing up around them, so too, in an economy that poses common risks and shared opportunities, a dying city will hold back an entire region.

Here lies the contribution of the New Jersey courts as different states are forced to revamp their zoning laws in the face of intensifying central city–suburban conflict.[20] Foremost is the New Jersey Supreme Court's broad redefinition of the term *general welfare*, which emphasizes that the welfare that confers validity on police power regulations is, at a minimum, that of the region.[21] In other words, the perspective for considering external impacts extends beyond local borders; a locality may not use zoning power, a police power of the state, to maintain itself as an enclave of affluence or of social homogeneity. In *Warren*, the court reemphasized that outlook: "To repeat, that doctrine recognizes that each community bears an obligation to provide its fair share of housing *for the region*."[22] It reminded the public that in terms echoing the judicial decisions, the legislature, in the FHA, had expressly recognized the need to deploy local regulations in order to meet a fair share of regional housing needs.[23]

The upshot is that towns may not refuse to confront the future by building moats around themselves and pulling up the drawbridge through enacting prohibitory land-use controls. Now they must deploy their land-use powers with an eye to regional costs and benefits so that the burden of affordable housing can be distributed equitably. No longer is our prime task to tend our own gardens—unless we take a more expansive view of the garden's extent.

The significance of this standard is not confined to residential exclusion. The Mount Laurel opinions foreshadow a willingness to modify the desultory minimum rational basis analysis, under which an ordinance is upheld if it bears any reasonable relation to the ends of health, safety, or welfare. At the least, questions of fundamental import will find themselves in an expanding category of intensified judicial scrutiny, with significant consequence for outcomes. There is no reason the regional logic of the Mount Laurel Doctrine could not extend to other issues of metropoliswide concern, such as air pollution, the location of waste treatment plants, or the building of hospitals, sewer systems, or other major facilities. Taking their cue from the courts, public interest groups and developers could now react less deferentially to the historically presumptive authority of localities to formulate policies with an eye only to local welfare. Strictly insular regulation could become a relic of the past.

The Mount Laurel cases also offer a fresh baseline for evaluating other municipal actions that bear extralocal implications. If carried to their logical conclusion, these cases transform the nature of judicial review of local enactments; legal rules that exclude groups from prime necessities of life—affordable housing is but one example—should not be accorded the time-honored presumption of legislative validity.[24] In addressing the issue of discrimination, the court made it clear that the critical point of concentrated judicial attention was effect rather than motive and intent; the almost impossible burden of proving a desire to exclude gave way to ascertaining the impacts of a challenged regulation. The court also banished other traditional barriers to plaintiffs invoking judicial jurisdiction, most importantly by giving nonresidents standing to bring actions.

As a corollary to its formulation of a constitutional right of access to moderate- and low-income housing, the New Jersey Supreme Court broadened the equal protection clause of the state's constitution to encompass discrimination based on wealth. Suspect classification, in New Jersey at least, now goes beyond race to include poverty in a broad sense. The very first Mount Laurel decision noted that poor minorities were not the only category of citizens excluded because of restrictive zoning. "We have reference to young and elderly couples, single persons and large, growing families not in the poverty class," Justice Hall emphasized, "but who still cannot afford the only kinds of housing realistically permitted in most places."[25] Hall then went on to place discrimination against the poor (defined so broadly as to encompass households above the official poverty line) under special judicial supervision. By striking out on a jurisprudential road far afield from federal interpretations, by introducing economic disparities as suspect classifications, with an unstated underlying theme that, for purposes of judicial review, the urban poor are of special significance among the class of persons disadvantaged by discriminatory practices, the court created a new avenue to constitutional protection in areas one can as yet only dimly discern.

Together, Mount Laurel I and II represent a concerted effort by judges to bring rational regional planning to troubled metropolitan areas, a program to balance the competing land uses of suburban sprawl and open space, of housing density and natural resource enhancement.[26] They elevate regional planning to a new status in the future administration of metropolitan areas in the United States.[27] In moving toward increased interrelation of the inner city and the suburb by linking affordable housing to population growth, jobs, and transportation requirements, the need (and potential) for a coordinated metropolitan urban approach emerges. Experts and lawyers briefed the judges well on the nature of urban growth in New Jersey, the overall need of regions to be economically competitive, the relation of residences to jobs, as well as on the land, construction, and financing costs of affordable housing. And the judges absorbed the information. By placing their weight behind the formulation of comprehensive regional plans, the courts incorporated the insights of planning experts and administrators into decision making and propelled the regional planning profession to the forefront in the resolution—and preemption—of critical land use issues. Imposing heavy responsibility on the related professions followed from the courts' decision to give physical facility planning legal impact and to build judicial decrees on that basis. Fair share housing procedures introduced by the judges are critical because they inject the concept of location into affordable housing responsibility.

Of compelling interest to lawyers is the sub silentio reversal of the New Jersey Supreme Court's earlier decisions regarding the role of the master plan as a constitution for reviewing local land-use ordinances. The justices had always been aware of the significant assistance that state and locally adopted comprehensive plans could render courts in measuring the validity of exercises of the regulatory power; in addition, they were cognizant of the benefit of increased consistency and coherence brought about by long-term planning. As early as *Kozesnik v. Township of Montgomery*, the supreme court had mused aloud, "No doubt good housekeeping would be served if a zoning ordinance followed and implemented a master plan," but it concluded that "the history of the subject dictated another course."[28] Presumably this has now changed: as part of the regional affordable housing mandate, the court found that a regional comprehensive plan is the controlling land-use instrument, and it bolstered the role of locally adopted master plans. Housing allocation planning—determining present and prospective needs—became an integral part of regional planning. The Mount Laurel II opinion reached out for the SDGP—and its later version, the SDRP—as a definitive statement of the long-range strategy for New Jersey's future growth that deserved actualization.[29] With the passage of time, the compliment was reciprocated: the Mount Laurel precedent was cited and incorporated as an undergirding for the SDRP in its enabling legislation.

The Mount Laurel courts tested remedies and compliance mechanisms in the laboratory of litigations affecting different municipalities. They fostered affirmative actions in the pursuit of clearing away legislative impediments to equal opportunity; and the delicate role of special masters in revising ordinances and monitoring implementation was shaped case by case. How best to collaborate with developers and the private market can also be traced in the evolving line of precedents. Elaborated from the learning process of trial and error, the New Jersey administrative machinery for joint ventures can be applied to other fields of complex institutional restructuring.

Other striking achievements also emerge from the Mount Laurel cases. The decisions are impressive examples of the flexibility of the federalist system in the United States, in which state courts retain the power to interpret their state constitutions more expansively (or, for that matter, more restrictively) than a conservative U.S. Supreme Court reads analogous provisions of the Constitution. Justice Hall was careful (and prudent) to base his decision in the first Mount Laurel case on the state constitution and on state grounds. In part a means of immunizing the New Jersey rulings from subsequent review by the U.S. Supreme Court, this approach also allowed him to shield developing doctrine from existing federal precedent during a time of extensive federal judicial retreat in these areas. By holding that housing was a fundamental personal interest and that economic status rose to the level of a suspect classification, Justice Hall created quite a different environment for his decision than could have existed in a federal court. In doing so, he also provided another outlet for reform: state constitutional requirements may be more demanding than those of the U.S. Constitution.[30] More than one avenue of petition for judicial relief exists to bring about the changes necessary to break political deadlock and revitalize social institutions. The pendulum of reform swung back to the state judiciary.

## The Environmental Balance

With its fairness-inspired requirement for land-use policies, Mount Laurel can be said, in more than a symbolic way, to be a forerunner of the environmental justice movement. Justice Hall's discussion anticipated the quest for environmental justice that has slowly pressed itself on the national consciousness. Surprisingly, only recently has it become apparent that the burden of pollution caused by industry, waste dumps, incinerators, and other high-risk activities falls disproportionately on the neighborhoods of the poor and minorities.[31] As one response, President Clinton required federal agencies to monitor whether their regulations affect minorities unequally and to determine the extent to which "environmental racism" is a national problem.[32] With similar fairness concerns in mind, New Jersey chose in Mount Laurel II to address more traditional environmental concerns arising from subdivisions—focusing on water quality, soil erosion, or impacts on features of natural beauty—for reasons of balance, not simply as pretexts for keeping land scarce and away from the unwanted. This approach allowed for an assessment of both the environmental justice concerns that might arise because of inner-city concentrations of poverty and the potential damage to environmental resources caused by unplanned development in the suburbs.[33]

This metropolitan perspective on environmental impact should be contrasted with the actions of a typical suburb: Mount Laurel itself, for example, when compelled by Justice Hall's decision to rezone sites for affordable housing, chose to place low-income housing in the unsafe industrial area. The Mount Laurel decisions, on the other hand, by encouraging higher-density development in areas of the state planned for growth, further encouraged environmental considerations by mitigating the otherwise rapacious sprawl of some suburban developments elsewhere: with well-designed garden apartments and row houses, less land is consumed, thereby decreasing the need for roads, infrastructure, and the spreading of utilities that leads to increasing costs and a declining quality of life.

But how finely calibrated was the balancing? Since the provision of land suitable for affordable housing was the driving concern of the Mount Laurel judges, they tended—despite acknowledging the significance of environmental factors—to favor builders. Justice Hall, in the first Mount Laurel opinion, brushed aside the environmental defenses so readily advanced by municipalities in defense of restrictive zoning. In the course of balancing interests, he raised the question of whether exclusionary effects should be tolerated for the sake of environmental quality. Although recognizing its claims, he (and the trial judges in their assessment of site suitability) was inclined to give weight to environmental impact only if the harm was avoidable and the consequences substantial. And the courts continued to be generally skeptical of environmental claims. In 1985, for example, Judge Serpentelli began his discussion of Warren Township's assertion that proposed projects would have a negative impact on a river by saying, "Mount Laurel places a heavy burden on the defendant raising [the environmental] defense to prove that the danger is substantial and very real."[34]

Especially in *Orgo Farms and Greenhouses v. Township of Colts Neck* did Judge Serpentelli wrestle with his angel in harmonizing the conflicting goals of growth and preservation of resources. In the end, he resorted to a condensed three-pronged balancing test: he would take into account ecological and environmental concerns, yet the regulations could not be used to thwart growth, and as the synthesis of the two contraries, the restrictions could be only those reasonably necessary for public protection of a vital element.[35] For *Orgo*, he formulated the test in a slightly different fashion: "The impact of the proposal on the environment or other substantial planning concerns must not be clearly contrary to sound land use planning."[36] But the approach was essentially pragmatic. A builder's remedy would not be allowed in areas designated "agricultural" or "conservation" by the SDGP, and only under special circumstances would it be permitted in "limited growth areas."[37] Otherwise, however, the builder's remedy would prevail.

This was conceived as a way of sharing the burden of controlling pollution and restricting the development of environmentally critical land. After all, the Division of State and Regional Planning—the group that formulated the SDGP—has better access to scientific data on those issues, as well as the capability to evaluate that data. In addition to the general evaluation of environmental impact, specific narrower issues—relating primarily to increased expenses of public services—implicitly affected the outcome of other opinions that addressed potential difficulties confronting a municipality in providing water, sewer, and other utility services to proposed developments.[38]

While paying respect to the expertise of the state agencies, the judges nevertheless subjected their conclusions to cross-examination. In *AMG*, for example, the court pointed out that the state plan for avoiding water pollution was based on expected water flow that, in turn, was extrapolated from population projections—a planning process that was rejected by Judge Serpentelli because the projections assumed and embodied existing zoning patterns, some of which were exclusionary. "To permit Warren to hide behind a state policy which incorporates exclusionary zoning," the judge wrote, "is to permit Warren to do indirectly what it cannot do directly."[39]

In general, then, the strong upholding of the Mount Laurel Doctrine tipped the scales toward affordable housing even at the expense of alleged environmental harms, despite repetition of the statement that neither factor was to outweigh the other initially—and despite the belief that comprehensive planning on a regional basis could reconcile the incipient conflicts between growth and the natural environment by way of trade-offs and accommodations. The very newness of the idea made affordable housing take precedence for the moment. By and large, the judges sought to confine the builder's remedy to growth areas and to shield the other areas of the SDGP from unfettered development.[40] However, by placing a "heavy" burden on defendant municipalities raising the environmental defense, rather than putting the onus on the builders to prove the suitability of their sites, the judges were inclined to dismiss claims of environmental disruption; in some instances, they may have gone so far as to refuse to face up to environmental problems posed by particular projects. In this phase of the evolution of remedies, striking a balance between ecological and economic systems may not have been all that even.[41]

Admittedly, another factor might also have contributed to the seeming imbalance in the New Jersey courts' analyses of suburban environmental concerns: the scope of environmental regulation was much narrower in the immediate post–Mount Laurel II years. Environmental protection was in its infancy; the Army Corps of Engineers, the agency that made most of the environmental regulatory decisions at the time, was primarily concerned with streambeds, floodplains, water quality, and steep slopes.[42] Many of the builder's remedies that were easily found—and without a significant evidentiary basis—not to be environmentally problematic under the third part of the Mount Laurel II balancing test might not pass environmental muster in the 1990s, given the extensive wetland

and air quality regulations that now complement soil and water quality regulations.

Another lesson of the Mount Laurel litigations that is transferable to other complex institutional litigations is the effective interaction of lawyers with scientists and other professionals. The success in this area confounded critics who argued the incompetence of the judiciary as an institution for gathering and analyzing complex data or, for that matter, absorbing the skills of other disciplines. After considerable experimentation, the New Jersey trial judges, with liberal resort to special masters, proved themselves fully capable of dealing with the difficult methodologies of economic projections, estimates of job availability, projections of housing need, environmental impact statements, and planning criteria for the suitability of sites. The judicial troika was able to fashion methodologies that could be successfully implemented in the real world of investing and building.

## The Moral Base

Nonexclusion sums up the aspirational norms of the society. The national goal embodied in section 2 of the National Housing Act of 1949—providing "a decent home and a suitable living environment for every American family"—still resounds.[43] Fed up with politics as usual, suburbanites as much as inner-city residents, in seeking permanence in their political lives, look to the enduring nature of constitutional promises. While perhaps not the first priority, the ideals embodied in Mount Laurel are congenial to many members of the majority.[44] Surveys of public opinion—the determinant of many public policies—are beginning to show a significant change in the attitudes of the white majority. Instead of lumping all minorities together under one massive stereotypic umbrella, the racial issue is increasingly broken down into component questions designed to elicit distinct individual responses.[45] Outlooks differ, depending on the particular issue and how it is posed, but despite deep divisions, surveys indicate that whites are open to persuasion by counterarguments in many of the problem areas. No matter their attitudes about the use of the affirmative power of government to ensure equal treatment of groups, few, if any, found moral justification for encroachment by sovereign power that precludes choice and bars minorities from achieving what they could otherwise attain on their own.

Removing exclusionary local zoning—and other governmental land-use controls devised to increase housing costs unnecessarily—is a cause that might win over public opinion on grounds of careful analysis and traditional sentiments. Like the Mount Laurel judges, most Americans see their country as a land of opportunity in which fixed barriers (especially in the form of adopted public policy) do not stand in the way of upward mobility. Indeed, the underlying principle behind this nation's founding was that ideas and people should be accepted or rejected on their own merits, not on the basis of prejudice or stereotypes. Even the more conservative mind is not totally at ease with opposition to Mount Laurel I and II. Exclusionary zoning is, after all, the assertion of delegated public power by a local community to the detriment of a cherished assumption of the society: the individual's subjective pursuit of happiness and well-being.

But there is a need to span the disparity between what we like to think of ourselves and how we act. In a deep sense, the Mount Laurel judges could not escape the divisive dilemma of race and class; they sought to prescribe societal values of nonexclusion that would be integrated into individual living, where subjectivities inevitably dominate outlook. Living with this conflict between daily individualist claims and high moral precepts—so powerfully captured by Gunnar Myrdal in *An American Dilemma*—is rendered more tolerable by the courts' mediation.[46]

By the petition of the Mount Laurel plaintiffs, the New Jersey courts were shoved center stage in a political morality play. Bearing not just statewide but nationwide ramifications was the doctrine's impact on the consciousness of the American people. The call for territorial freedom in the pursuit of housing intensified with experience. Where Mount Laurel I emphasized the constitutional obligation of municipalities and looked to them to assume the initiative, Mount Laurel II stressed the moral imperative for judicial intervention when other government agencies failed to realize the goals that Justice Hall had derived from constitutional guarantees. Because constitutional wrongs needed to be remedied, Justice Wilentz argued, because social injustices could not be allowed to persist, the court was morally obliged to alleviate the affordable housing crisis created by abuse of public political power. Ideology combined with doctrine. "The government that controls this land represents everyone," he declared, and "while the state may not have the ability to eliminate poverty, it cannot use that condition as the basis for imposing further disadvantages."[47] He further emphasized, "We shall continue—until the Legislature acts—to do our best to uphold the constitutional obligation that underlies the *Mount Laurel* doctrine."[48]

Thus the New Jersey Supreme Court invoked the claims of conscience to justify the substance of the doctrine and the active role of the court. "I've always hoped," observed Ethel Lawrence, the original Mount Laurel plaintiff, "[that] the courts would find a way to bring economical housing to Mount Laurel and other towns where people just can't afford to be anymore, but I support my hope with prayer, too. I say, 'God, you know what I'm talking about, you know what we need.' I leave the rest up to him."[49] This assertion of faith is not too far removed from the court's legal position. The Mount Laurel opinions send an urgent message that the court will do everything in its power to improve the suburban housing situation for the state's low- and moderate-income residents. "That is our duty," they solemnly concluded.[50] When it comes to the basic interest of affordable housing, the court's vigilance expands, driven by its derivation of what the constitution requires. And the moral aspects of this line of decisions are rarely challenged publicly. This represents an opening—perhaps a fleeting one—to forge a new kind of majority coalition.

## National Urban Policy

Clearly, the Mount Laurel struggle for regional housing mobility is interwoven with the national domestic policies of its time. In its perception of how American society functions, the Reagan Revolution (even as modified by the Gingrich gloss) hypothesized that government actions, far from being the solution, were themselves the problem—too costly and too intrusive.[51] Its guiding image of action and responsibility therefore sought to reduce government intervention by substituting the private economic market and untrammeled individual initiative. This shift in outlook bore curious, contradictory implications for the responsibilities of municipalities. On the one hand, all functions of government were to be curtailed; at the same time, under the New Federalism of the Reagan administration, decentralization was the formulaic key; hence, local governments were to take over whatever public authority over affairs that could not be avoided.[52] In other words, as part of the program to enfeeble the national levels of urban expenditures, municipalities' functions were made greater than ever.

But with the new mandates and obligations came no additional funding. Federal support for state and local comprehensive land-use planning was removed. The administration limited the budget of the Department of Housing and Urban Development, slashed grants for sewer and water systems, set a ceiling on tax-exempt housing bonds, eliminated low-income housing support for nonprofit community groups, chose to ignore needs for infrastructure, services, environmental programs. One federal program after another that had supported local government functions was cut or allowed to lapse.

Inevitably, localities were left strapped for funds. Their inability to finance the infrastructure needed by growing populations forced the financially embarrassed suburbs to resort to exclusionary regulatory ordinances to reduce expenditures for public services and facilities. The privatization of social capital became the dominant theme in the absence of federal income tax funds, and developers became targets for fees and land contributions—which led to a notable increase in housing costs.

This chain of events provoked yet another paradox: the supply-side approach that heralded trust in the private market and belief in growth brought about increased governmental restrictions on the market and on metropolitan land when it came to suburban life. In seeking to bar government from interfering with the workings of the market's invisible hand, the national federalist agenda pushed local governments to interfere with the private building industry and, through regulation and taxation, to counter the ordinary operations of the real estate world. Developers who would have built for the affordable housing market were stopped in their tracks by excessive local government regulations and permit requirements. The private building sector was not allowed to adjust supply to demand through the pricing mechanism; restrictive regulations impeded the equilibrium that would otherwise have occurred. Municipalities limited the availability of land for low- and moderate-income housing.

The typical suburbanite's attitude reflected and was reinforced by the individualistic conception of society that predominated in Washington. The fencing off of neighborhoods was applauded in the national capital—and made manifest in the 1994 congressional elections. The emergence of gated and walled communities was a taken-for-granted component of local existence. They were an apt manifestation of the Reagan-era philosophy that vaunted individual interest and left little room for social responsibility.[53]

Periodically, there are deep shifts in prevailing assumptions and in shared patterns of thought. The United States is emerging from a decade in which the social compact was sharply modified: neglect of a major segment of the society was conspicuous in urban policy; scant thought was paid to conditions in the segregated central city with limited hope and high unemployment; meager resources were allocated to the provision of affordable housing in suburbia. This pervasive disregard embodied in national policy left a deep and cumulative mark on Americans' vision of the nature of society—on how and where people live and on the extent and direction of population and job growth. It left the poor and striving crowded into densely populated urban centers as suburban laws and ordinances barred opportunities to better their existence by moving to the suburbs. Privatization of community space was an assumed goal.

Once Ethel Lawrence and her family invoked their jurisdiction, however, the Mount Laurel courts sought to redress the geographic fracture of the metropolis. And in doing so, the justices, guided by Enlightenment ideas, endeavored to shape the future. Their work is not done. Although Clinton's election in 1992 seemed at the time to herald a new political era, the Republican landslide of 1994 signals a turning back; the pendulum swing of the political cycle once again has moved toward reduced government and greater delegation of federal power to the states and localities. Because of this trend the courts will likely be called on to persevere in keeping a public focus on the goals of Mount Laurel I and II, invoking state constitutional standards to remain a beacon of constancy amid the two-year ebbs and flows of political moods.

Land is inescapably the stage where life's activities are pursued, the foundation of the economic and emotional life of the citizenry. The land issue—more precisely, in the American system of social stratification, the suburban land issue—could become a potential focus for consensus: the availability of suburban land, on an equal basis unrestricted by the exercise of local regulatory power, is crucial to fulfilling the fundamental equal opportunity mission of our country. Fully achieving the Mount Laurel Doctrine involves recognition that economic development hinges on adequate physical infrastructure, awareness of the interdependence of central city and suburb in the metropolitan area, and support for government joint ventures with the private housing market. Suburban government can be a positive force in peoples' lives. The excesses of localism and the denial of a common civic culture subvert that mission; walled enclaves are a repudiation of the American experiment in social integration and intensify the pathologies of concentrated poverty. Incorporating more traditional ideas of moral and social interdependence can reset the terms of the debate over the aspiration of class and racial mix and foster the realization of the goals set forth by the New Jersey courts.

In reviewing the history of the Mount Laurel Doctrine, one is struck by the enormous power of the judicial branch to act as a catalyst for change. Too often existing governmental institutions fail to address the social conflicts endemic to a complex industrial society. Noble efforts tend to get bogged down by the often contradictory interests of elected officials, regulators, representatives of business, and private citizens. At times, the political joints become frozen. Institutional restructuring by way of a lawsuit thaws the political ice. Indeed, the genius of the judicial system is its capacity to function as an alternative, complementary route out of a social impasse.

It is as important that the court be seen as possessing the requisite authority and freedom to exercise it as it is that it exercise that authority in a particular way. Critics are distressed when a judge finds it necessary to take over a public housing authority,[54] for example, or to supervise the details of local zoning ordinances in New Jersey municipalities. But how else are persisting walls of indifference and neglect to be pierced? One can state the heart of the controversy over the Mount Laurel courts' reach with chilling bluntness: the intense local opposition to the generally wise and able handling of suburban exclusionary zoning by the New Jersey judges is not based on distrust of an imperial judiciary, on purported distortion of accepted procedures, on dread of abuses of discretion, on fears that heavy-handed solutions wreak havoc with cherished suburban character, or on jurisprudential concerns about the separation of powers. Essentially, what disturbs some local officials and some state legislators is the substance of the court's decree: that systemic law-breaking by suburban localities must cease.

The Mount Laurel courts' battle with popular sovereignty is intended to restore the American dream of home ownership to its constitutional dimensions. The New Jersey judiciary ushered in a constitutional order at the state level (with broad implications for other states and the nation as a whole) to remove barriers to regional mobility, address housing discrimination in the suburbs, begin to deconcentrate poverty in central cities, and move toward more effective and harmonious development of metropolitan areas. With luck, work, and time perhaps the intransigence, contention, and relatively high cost of exclusionary litigation will be supplanted by a reconciliation of the public with its constitutional norms.

Once upon a time, what a suburb did in its own backyard was nobody's business but its own. After Mount Laurel, the state, primarily through the courts, is likely to be watching and responding. The Mount Laurel judges affected local official behavior by breaking the bonds of confining legal conventions and the stereotyped adjudicatory model that fostered them; in so doing, they impressed on New Jerseyites a new understanding of what constitutes an overriding state and regional interest. The judges transformed the adjudicatory model of litigation by instilling meaningful remedies for institutional restructuring without harming the fairness of the legal process itself.

As things stand, the suburbs are in retreat from their original isolationist posture. So are the courts, if only to a certain degree. With a bow to political realities, the New Jersey Supreme Court has recognized that it and the FHA deal "with one of the most difficult constitutional, legal and social issues of our day."[55] Though it has acceded to the state legislature's intervention, it reserves the right to reenter the fray as necessary. Judicial review of localities' exercise of the state-delegated regulatory power for consonance with the general welfare—newly interpreted as the welfare of the state as a whole—is the law today.[56]

The law compels New Jerseyites, sensitized to their own possible culpability, to redefine their idea of community and their understanding of social reality. The interdependence of inner city and suburb is not easy to grasp, much less to accept in some of its implications, and recognition of the existence of a racially or income stratified society requires swallowing a bitter dose of realism. Individuals and governments are forced to consider the many Americans living in impoverished conditions in the inner city, lacking the services, guideposts, and familial support available in suburban districts, and to respond to a fresh vision of a unified metropolitan area—one that provides equal access for all to land, jobs, and housing.

There is a danger in all this of exaggerating the iniquities of suburbanites, the benevolence of the courts, and the impending arrival of the millennium of universal love. Through almost daily encounters with the human passions enveloping litigation, the three trial judges did not confuse desires with those actions necessary to bring them into actuality. Opposition by middle-class people to entry of inner-city residents into their community may be motivated by genuine concern for safety, good schools for children, preservation of housing economic values, and freedom to choose neighbors, as much as by rank prejudice. And courts, like many other elites, may be taking the easy way of calling for sacrifices by others, not by themselves. Such are the pains of maturation that Mount Laurel II added to Mount Laurel I in dealing with the political imbalances of choice and access brought about by local governmental abuse of the zoning power.

Political resistance to the courts' role in institutional litigation undoubtedly will persist. In *The Federalist* James Madison warned, "But it is the reason, alone, of the public, that ought to control and regulate the government. The passions ought to be controlled and regulated by the government."[57] The Reagan domestic isolationism has its emotional roots in suburbia. Local land-use controls harness and stimulate popular sentiments based on a "we" that excludes a larger "them." Nevertheless, although the parameters are limited within which judicial review realistically operates, New Jersey is in the midst of a historic transition away from the unquestioned supremacy of local government in formulating land regulations. All now depends on how well the promises of mutual understanding and respect across group and class lines—based on the mandate of the state constitution as enunciated and implemented in the Mount Laurel cases—and the bargain struck with the legislative branch in the FHA are converted into day-to-day operations.

COAH, the most direct descendant of the social compromise, is an administrative start to the arduous task of curbing zoning and other regulatory abuses that place artificial limits on housing supply in the suburbs that market and demographic growth forces would otherwise demand.[58] Unfortunately, thus far the agency continues to be seen as a vestige of antimajoritarianism and needs judicial bolstering, as in *Holmdel*, or un-comfortable support as the lesser of two evils.[59] As one municipal attor-ney exclaimed, "Everyone is scared to death of going back to the courts!"

By repeatedly stating the constitutional ideal and by shaping, paring, and phasing remedies, the courts achieved a synthesis of proclamation and deed in a protracted process that lasted a quarter of a century. They were determined to train public attention on abuses of local political power. Consequently, the courts offered a semblance of solidarity at a time when so much was keeping New Jerseyites apart. In sum, the judicial system forged a minimum consensus that society was unable to achieve on its own. The Mount Laurel II opinion did not expect the racial and ethnic fragmentation and stratification of the metropolitan landscape to change overnight, but it insisted that the process begin in earnest and it tolerated neither benign neglect nor systemic exclusion.

In its inquiry into human good, the court has history on its side; the venerable theme of freedom based on equality of access to land returns in modern dress. Fears expressed by some that an aggressive judicial posi-tion might undermine the cause (and the court itself) primarily mask the discontent of special interests: the unfolding of the Mount Laurel sub-urban experience demonstrates that judicial action can unleash forces stronger than a pious declaration of intent. By mounting coherent strate-gies, litigation can develop into a workable instrument of social change.

And metropolitan social change is imperative. The need for affordable housing within metropolitan areas is a national crisis that demands force-ful judicial leadership. Public transportation is absent or insufficient to enable inner-city poor to work at job centers in suburban locations. As the inner city–suburb commute changes to an intersuburb network and as the edge cities in suburbia attract independent and self-contained spatial concentrations of cultural, financial, and business activity, the physical separation of people in metropolitan areas along class or racial lines in-creases, as do misunderstandings and conflicts.[60] Residential segregation affects the schools children attend, the friends they and their parents make, the job networks to which people have access, even the quality of food and merchandise available for them to buy.[61]

If our divided society is not to break asunder from such deepening geographic division, the link between inner city and suburb must be re-paired. The plight of the Lawrences—hardworking people who could not afford to live in the place of their birth—and of other Americans trapped within the crumbling inner cities was a call to action for the New Jersey courts. Thousands of people are forced by the clannishness of affluent suburbs to live without hope and without opportunity. Thousands of people are precluded from realizing the dream of a home in a suitable

living environment where jobs, safety, and the culturally enjoined pursuit of happiness exist. And all because of exclusionary zoning. The appalling conditions of concentrated inner-city neighborhoods underlie civil unrest and other social ills, most especially the sheer waste of able workers—a group disproportionately composed of minorities—who are unable to exploit the job opportunities in the expanding service and financial centers of metropolitan areas. The New Jersey Supreme Court recognized that some of this nation's most pressing concerns over society's cohesion will never be solved, and some of its gravest injustices never redressed, until Americans begin to break down the ghetto walls and deal with the intertwining of race segregation with land-use planning.

In focusing on the invidious discrimination that can result from local community regulatory power, the Mount Laurel decisions can serve as a vibrant and capacious vehicle for social justice and advancement. Future waves of home building will test how far the recognition of the common goals of inner city and suburb can be carried. Will history conclude that without the intervention of the courts the metropolitan United States would have gone the way of other societies buried under their own contradictions and destroyed by an inability to correct imbalances too glaring and injustices too painful?

# Notes

All unattributed quotations in the text are from interviews conducted by the author with judges, lawyers, special masters, local officials, and others from March 1992 to May 1995.

## Chapter I
## Breaking New Ground

1. Legal services for those without the ability to pay the going rate have enabled the poor to go to court in order to redress social and economic injustices. This dramatic shift in the availability of legal talent has procured extensive judicial review of executive and legislative actions. See Charles M. Haar and Daniel W. Fessler, *The Wrong Side of the Tracks* (New York: Simon and Schuster, 1986), 31–36.

2. For an example of its use as precedent, see Brian W. Blaesser, Susan M. Connor, Eric Damian Kelly, Stuart Meck, John M. Payne, James M. Rubenstein, Charles F. Tucker, and Norman Williams, Jr., "Advocating Affordable Housing in New Hampshire: The *Amicus Curiae* Brief of the American Planning Association in *Wayne Britton v. Town of Chester*," *Washington University Journal of Urban & Contemporary Law* 40 (1991): 3.

3. Social scientists are still absorbing the consequences of the new urban geography. Indeed, Robert Fishman argues that the whole terminology of "suburb" and "central city" deriving from the era of the industrial metropolis has become obsolete. *Bourgeois Utopias: The Rise and Fall of Suburbia* (New York: Basic Books, 1987). On the history of suburbs, see Kenneth T. Jackson, *Crabgrass Frontier: The Suburbanization of the United States* (New York: Oxford University Press, 1985).

4. Rural areas account for the balance.

5. See Joel Garreau, *Edge City: Life on the New Frontier* (New York: Doubleday, 1991). Cf. Charles M. Haar, ed., *The President's Task Force on Suburban Problems* (Cambridge, Mass: Ballinger, 1974).

6. In general, see "Discrimination in the Housing and Mortgage Markets," *Housing Policy Debates* 3, no. 2 (1990).

7. The slightly increased rate of black suburbanization is more an extension of city neighborhoods into the suburbs, with those areas closest to the central city's core experiencing increased population density. According to a Census Bureau analyst of racial data, "Nearly 25 percent of blacks who live in suburban areas are below the poverty line." "Blacks Moving to Suburbs, but Significance Is Disputed," *New York Times*, August 15, 1982, sec. 1, p. 18. See also Richard D. Alba and John R. Logan, "Variations on Two Themes: Racial and Ethnic Patterns in the Attainment of Suburban Residence," *Demography* 28 (1991): 431–513.

8. An increase from 9.8 percent in 1970 to 14 percent in 1980 to 15.4 percent in 1987. See Paul Peterson, "The Urban Underclass and the Poverty Paradox," in Christopher Jencks and Paul Peterson, eds., *The Urban Underclass* (Washington, D.C.: Brookings Institution, 1991), 7. See Harry J. Holzer, "The Spatial Mismatch Hypothesis: What Has the Evidence Shown?" *Urban Studies* 28 (1991): 105–22.

9. Benjamin Disraeli, *Sybil: or The Two Nations* (1845; London: T. Nelson, 1957), bk. 2, chap. 5.

10. John F. Kain, "The Spatial Mismatch Hypothesis: Three Decades Later," *Housing Policy Debate* 3, no. 1 (1992): 371, 450. In general, see Anthony Downs, "Policy Directions concerning Racial Discrimination in U.S. Housing Markets," *Housing Policy Debate* 3, no. 2 (1992): 685–745; and John F. Kain and John M. Quigley, *Housing Markets and Racial Discrimination: A Microeconomic Analysis* (New York: National Bureau of Economic Research, 1975). But cf. Christopher Jencks and Susan Mayer, "Residential Segregation, Job Proximity and Black Job Opportunities," in Laurence E. Lynn, Jr., and Michael G. H. McGeary, eds., *Inner-City Poverty in the United States* (Washington, D.C.: National Academy Press, 1990).

11. In general, see Kain and Quigley, *Housing Markets*; Keith R. Ihlanfeldt and David S. Sjoquist, "Job Accessibility and Racial Difference in Youth Employment Rates," *American Economic Review* 80 (1990): 267–76; Jonathan S. Leonard, "The Interaction of Residential Segregation and Employment Discrimination," *Journal of Urban Economics* 21 (1987): 323–46.

12. One study concludes that "residential segregation in Detroit imposes irremediable spatial disequilibrium on black workers." Jeffrey S. Zax and John F. Kain, "Commutes, Quits, and Moves," *Journal of Urban Economics* 29 (1991): 164. When workers must commute long distances, companies either face high turnover and absenteeism or incur the costs of providing transportation or housing for employees. George H. Douglas traced the origins of the modern suburb to the streetcar and interurban railroads in *All Aboard: The Railroad in American Life* (New York: Paragon House, 1992).

13. The suburbanization of jobs is well documented in Douglas S. Massey and Mitchell L. Eggers, "The Ecology of Inequality: Minorities and the Concentration of Poverty, 1970–1980," *American Journal of Sociology* 95 (1990): 1153–88.

14. Felicity Barringer, "Hire City Poor in the Suburbs, a Report Urges," *New York Times*, December 4, 1992, sec. D18.

15. Justice Hall, writing of Camden, stated that "what has happened to that city is depressing indeed." *Southern Burlington County NAACP v. Township of Mount Laurel*, 67 N.J. 151, 172, 336 A.2d 713, 724 (1975), cert. denied, 423 U.S. 808, 96 S.Ct. 18 (1975) (Mount Laurel I). Between 1950 and 1970 the number of jobs in Camden fell from 43,267 to 20,671, while overall jobs in the area's labor market increased from 94,507 to 197,037.

16. Iver Peterson, "Job Growth in Region's Suburbs Outpaces Cities'," *New York Times*, December 21, 1992, sec. B1.

17. For a recent overview, see Anthony Downs, *New Visions for Metropolitan America* (Washington, D.C.: Brookings Institution, 1994). See Charles M. Haar

and Dimitri Iatridis, *Housing the Poor in Suburbia: Public Policy at the Grass Roots* (Cambridge, Mass.: Ballinger, 1974).

18. William Julius Wilson, *The Truly Disadvantaged: The Inner City, the Underclass, and Public Policy* (Chicago: University of Chicago Press, 1987); Michael H. Schill, "Deconcentrating the Inner City Poor," *Chicago-Kent Law Review* 67 (1992): 795. But see John C. Weicher, "How Poverty Neighborhoods Are Changing," in Lynn and McGeary, *Inner-City Poverty in the United States.*

19. The street culture "presents early sexual experience and promiscuity as a virtue. For many such girls who have few other perceivable options, motherhood, accidental or otherwise, becomes a rite of passage to adulthood." Elijah Anderson, "Neighborhood Effects on Teenage Pregnancy," in Jencks and Peterson, *The Urban Underclass,* 375. See also Dennis P. Hogan and Evelyn M. Kitagawa, "The Impact of Social Status, Family Structure, and Neighborhood on the Fertility of Black Adolescents," *American Journal of Sociology* 90 (1985): 825–55; Frank F. Furstenberg, Jr., S. Philip Morgan, Kristin A. Moore, and James L. Peterson, "Race Differences in the Timing of Adolescent Intercourse," *American Sociological Review* 52 (1987): 511–18.

20. John M. Quigley, "New Directions for Urban Policy," *Housing Policy Debates* 5, no. 1 (1994): 100–101. But cf. John Charles Boger, "Race and the American City: The Kerner Commission in Retrospect—an Introduction," *North Carolina Law Review* 71 (1993): 1289.

21. See Advisory Commission on Regulatory Barriers to Affordable Housing, *"Not in My Backyard": Removing Barriers to Affordable Housing* (Washington, D.C.: U.S. Department of Housing and Urban Development, 1991); Henry O. Pollakowski and Susan M. Wachter, "The Effects of Land-Use Constraints on Housing Prices," *Land Economics* 66 (1990): 315–24; William A. Fischel, *Do Group Controls Matter?: A Review of Empirical Evidence on the Effectiveness and Efficiency of Local Government Land Use Regulation* (Cambridge, Mass.: Lincoln Institute of Land Policy, 1990).

22. One criticism of the role of the courts in Mount Laurel litigation is that land-use issues involve basic public policies that, in a democracy, the legislature should resolve. This oversimplifying notion of democratic theory would place all consideration of "value" into one branch of government alone: the legislature. Its chief justification is that basic public policy questions should be made with public hearings, open debate, compromise, and, more questionably, constituents' ability to decide not to reelect.

## Chapter II
## Launching the Mount Laurel Doctrine

1. *Lionshead Lake, Inc. v. Township of Wayne,* 10 N.J. 165, 89 A.2d 693 (1952), appeal dismissed, 344 U.S. 919, 73 S.Ct. 386 (1953). The decision concluded: "So long as the zoning ordinance was reasonably designed, by whatever means, to further the advancement of a community as a social, economic and political unit, it is in the general welfare and therefore a proper exercise of the zoning power." 10 N.J. 172, 89 A.2d 697. See Charles M. Haar, "Zoning for

Minimum Standards: The *Wayne Township* Case," *Harvard Law Review* 66 (1953): 1051.

2. *Fischer v. Township of Bedminster*, 11 N.J. 194, 93 A.2d 378 (1952); *Vickers v. Township Committee of Gloucester Township*, 37 N.J. 232, 181 A.2d 129 (1962). The frequently cited case of *Duffcon Concrete Products, Inc. v. Borough of Creskill*, 1 N.J. 509, 64 A.2d 347 (1949), invoked regionalism to uphold the right of the borough to determine what was in its best interests. The court first concluded: "What may be the most appropriate use of any particular property depends not only on the conditions, physical, economic and social, prevailing within the municipality and its needs, present and reasonably prospective, but also on the nature of the entire region in which the municipality is located and the use to which the land in that region has been or may be put most advantageously." 1 N.J. 513, 64 A.2d 349–50. It then went on to uphold the exclusion of a concrete plant on the ground that it could find a location elsewhere in the region. See also *Guaclides v. Borough of Englewood Cliffs*, 11 N.J. Super. 405, 78 A.2d 435 (1951), concerning rezoning all multifamily zones to single-family zones, and *Fanale v. Borough of Hasbrouck Heights*, 26 N.J. 320, 139 A.2d 749 (1958), regarding the exclusion of apartment houses.

3. *Lionshead Lake*, 10 N.J. 173, 89 A.2d 697.

4. In his own words, "The judicial branch does not meet its full responsibility when, as here, its concept of review gives unquestioning deference to the views of local officials." *Vickers*, 37 N.J. 261, 181 A.2d 145 (Hall, J., dissenting).

5. NJSDC, *1990 Census Publication, New Jersey Population Trends, 1790 to 1990* (April 1991).

6. The trial court noted other regulations that had exclusionary effects. In one instance, the developer had been required to insert a clause in the leases "that no school-age children shall occupy any one-bedroom apartment and that no more than two such children shall reside in any two-bedroom unit." *Southern Burlington County NAACP v. Township of Mount Laurel*, 119 N.J. Super. 164, 290 A.2d 465 (1972).

7. The township's growth had been spurred by the construction of main highways, including the New Jersey Turnpike, I-295, and Routes 70 and U.S. 130.

8. Mount Laurel I, 67 N.J. 151, 336 A.2d 713. The trial court below invalidated the zoning ordinance in toto, although the judgment did not take into account regional needs. The township appealed to the appellate division but was certified, on the supreme court's own motion, before argument in the division.

9. Here Justice Hall followed the route of broader state constitutional law prescribed by Justice William Brennan, which states that "our liberties cannot survive if the states betray the trust the Court has put in them." "State Constitutions and the Protections of Individual Rights," *Harvard Law Review* 90 (1977): 503.

10. Mount Laurel I, 67 N.J. 174, 336 A.2d 724.

11. Ibid.

12. Ibid., 67 N.J. 187, 336 A.2d 732.

13. Reported in the *Trenton Evening Times*, March 6, 1973, p. 11.

14. See *San Antonio Independent School District v. Rodriguez*, 411 U.S. 1, 93 S.Ct. 1278 (1973).

15. Thus the legal question as defined by the court charged with resolving it became a broad one: "Whether a developing municipality like Mount Laurel may validly, by a system of land use regulation, make it physically and economically impossible to provide low and moderate income housing in the municipality for the various categories of persons who need and want it and thereby, as Mount Laurel has, exclude such people from living within its confines because of the limited extent of their income and resources." Mount Laurel I, 67 N.J. 173, 336 A.2d 724.

16. *Lindsey v. Normet*, 405 U.S. 56, 74, 92 S.Ct. 862, 874 (1972).

17. Mount Laurel I, 67 N.J. 178, 336 A.2d 727.

18. Earlier, in his *Vickers* dissent, Hall had argued that the prior cases of *Lionshead* and *Fischer* had rationalized exclusionary results

by reference to the statutory zoning purposes of "conserving the value of property" and "encouraging the most appropriate use of land" and in the name of preservation of the character of the community or neighborhood. I submit these factors are perverted from their intended application when used to justify Chinese walls on the borders of roomy and developing municipalities for the actual purpose of keeping out all but the "right kind" of people or those who will live in a certain kind and cost of dwelling. . . . To reiterate, all the legitimate aspects of a desirable and balanced community can be realized by proper placing and regulation of uses, as the zoning statute contemplates, without destroying the higher value of the privilege of democratic living. (*Vickers*, 37 N.J. 266, 181 A.2d 147)

19. Minutes of township committee meetings that were introduced into evidence expressed attitudes of indifference to poor housing conditions, including desires to clear out substandard areas "and thereby get better citizens": "We must be as selective as possible . . . we can approve only those development plans which will provide direct and substantial benefits to our taxpayers." *Southern Burlington County NAACP*, 119 N.J. Super. 169–70, 290 A.2d 468.

20. In *Arlington Heights*, for example, decided in 1977, the U.S. Supreme Court refused to protect minorities without a clear showing of discriminatory motive. See *Village of Arlington Heights v. Metropolitan Housing Development Corp.*, 429 U.S. 252, 97 S.Ct. 555 (1977). Cf. *Huntington Branch NAACP v. Town of Huntington*, 844 F.2d 926 (2d. Cir. 1988), aff'd, 488 U.S. 15, 109 S.Ct. 276 (1989) (upholding exclusionary zoning claims under the federal Fair Housing Act). See also *Washington v. Davis*, 426 U.S. 229, 96 S.Ct. 2040 (1976), a decision that dealt a devastating blow to plaintiffs seeking strict judicial review of legislation that enforced and perpetuated patterns of racial inequality. Cf. *Rogers v. Lodge*, 458 U.S. 613, 102 S.Ct. 3272 (1982). The standing requirement to invoke the federal forum for exclusionary zoning litigation was made almost impossible to satisfy in *Warth v. Seldin*, 422 U.S. 490, 95 S.Ct. 2197 (1975).

21. Writing for the majority in *McDonald v. Board of Election Commissioners of Chicago*, 394 U.S. 802, 807, 89 S.Ct. 1404, 1407–8 (1969), Chief Justice Warren declared: "A careful examination . . . is especially warranted where lines are drawn on the basis of wealth or race . . . two factors which would indepen-

dently render a classification highly suspect and thereby demand a more exacting judicial scrutiny." This course was stopped abruptly in *Dandridge v. Williams*, 397 U.S. 471, 90 S.Ct. 1153 (1970).

22. The first decision of the U.S. Supreme Court upholding the validity of comprehensive zoning, *Village of Euclid v. Ambler Realty Co.*, 272 U.S. 365, 389–90, 47 S.Ct. 114, 119 (1926), contains suggestive dicta on the issue of regionalism: "But the village, though physically a suburb of Cleveland, is politically a separate municipality, with powers of its own and authority to govern itself as it sees fit. . . . It is not meant by this, however, to exclude the possibility of cases where the general public interest would so far outweigh the interest of the municipality that the municipality would not be allowed to stand in the way."

23. Mount Laurel I, 67 N.J. 179, 336 A.2d 727–28.

24. Ibid., 67 N.J. 179, 336 A.2d 728.

25. A six-sentence concurring opinion by Justice Mountain argued that "the term, 'general welfare' . . . can and should properly be interpreted with the same amplitude" by reference to the state enabling acts, "without resort to the Constitution." Mount Laurel I, 67 N.J. 193, 336 A.2d 735 (Mountain, J., concurring).

26. Mount Laurel I, 67 N.J. 192, 336 A.2d 734.

27. Ibid., 67 N.J. 191, 336 A.2d 734.

28. The trial court had ordered the township to prepare within ninety days a detailed plan of implementation to meet the housing needs of present low- and moderate-income residents and employees. See *Southern Burlington County NAACP*, 119 N.J. Super. 164, 290 A.2d 465.

29. Mount Laurel I, 67 N.J. 192, 336 A.2d 734. The realism of this aspiration was sharply questioned in a series of articles by Jerome G. Rose. See, e.g., "The *Mount Laurel* Decision: Is It Based on Wishful Thinking?" *Real Estate Law Journal* 4 (1975): 61, in which the author averred that the decision was "based upon the wistful hope of an idealistic but credulous court"; and "The *Mount Laurel II* Decision: Is It Based on Wishful Thinking?" *Real Estate Law Journal* 12 (1983): 115, where Rose observes, "[The] weakness of the decision may emerge in time, not from its ethical principles, but from the economic and political assumptions on which it rests."

30. Justice Pashman returned to this central theme in another long opinion, concurring in part and dissenting in part, in *Oakwood at Madison, Inc. v. Township of Madison*, 72 N.J. 481, 371 A.2d 1192 (1977):

> I differ with the majority, however, as to the nature and scope of judicial remedies made available for the trial court during the remedial stages of the litigation. In cases of this nature, I conceive that powerful judicial antidotes may become necessary to eradicate the evils of exclusionary zoning. For this reason, I would proceed less gingerly than the majority; I would go farther and faster in outlining for the trial judge the full arsenal of judicial weaponry available for this purpose. . . .
>
> The failure to clarify ambiguities and to formulate guidelines for effective judicial review serves to strip the principles laid down in *Mt. Laurel* of all practical effect. Town officials who believe that courts will equivocate in enforcing municipal obligations to meet regional housing needs have no reason to

act voluntarily in satisfying the mandate of Mt. Laurel, especially where such action faces strong local opposition. Under these circumstances, judicial timidity merely encourages municipal officials to yield to local prejudices and await the filing of law suits by low income persons and frustrated developers. (72 N.J. 563, 371 A.2d 1233)

31. Mount Laurel I, 67 N.J. 179, 336 A.2d 727.

32. Ibid., 67 N.J. 190, 336 A.2d 733. The housing conditions of the plaintiffs—as found by the trial court—had an undoubted influence. The electrical wiring in the residence of one of the plaintiffs "is in an exposed condition and she often gets shocks from the outlets; one space heater by the front door provides inadequate intermittent heat and she must use the gas stove to provide sufficient heat; cold air comes through the windows; drains do not work on occasion and the cesspool backs up into the toilet." Another dwelling of a family with four children was "heated by a single kerosene heater; there was little or no hot water; the cesspool backed up and the place was infested with vermin." *Southern Burlington County NAACP*, 119 N.J. Super. 166–67, 290 A.2d 466–67.

## Chapter III
## The View from the Mount

1. Whether a state constitution, in allocating power among the different levels of government, reserved land-use functions solely to municipalities (sometimes splicing minutely according to different population ranges for cities, towns, and villages) was the subject of debate for the greater part of this nation's existence.

2. *Duffcon Concrete Products, Inc. v. Borough of Cresskill*, 1 N.J. 509, 64 A.2d 347 (1949); *Fischer v. Township of Bedminster*, 11 N.J. 194, 93 A.2d 378 (1952).

3. *Vickers v. Township Committee of Gloucester Township*, 37 N.J. 233, 81 A.2d 129 (1962).

4. *Southern Burlington County NAACP v. Township of Mount Laurel*, 161 N.J. Super. 317, 343, 391 A.2d 935, 948 (1978).

5. In response to Mount Laurel I, the township calculated its indigenous need to be 103 units and its regional need as 515 units and amended its zoning ordinance to permit construction of 131 units of low- and moderate-income housing. The court was forced to conclude that this revision "fails completely to comply with the mandate of *Mount Laurel I*." *Southern Burlington County NAACP v. Township of Mount Laurel*, 92 N.J. 158, 302, 456 A.2d 390, 464 (1983) (Mount Laurel II).

6. *Southern Burlington County NAACP*, 161 N.J. Super. 329, 391 A.2d 941. The trial judge even embraced the much-debated "filtering down" theory, which maintains that the construction of new (and relatively expensive) housing causes older housing, vacated by those moving on to more luxurious units, to become available for poorer residents. True, almost as an afterthought, the trial court did take the cue of the upper court's directives by striking down selected provisions of the local zoning ordinance, such as its conditioning of zoning changes on the adoption of similar amendments in the ordinances of adjacent towns. In addition,

with some demurrers, the judge forbade bedroom limitations and caps on numbers of children as too obviously exclusionary for even him to swallow.

7. Robert Hanley, "After 7 Years, Town Remains under Fire for Its Zoning Code," *New York Times*, January 21, 1983, 31.

8. Of those new units, 80 percent had to be one-bedroom and 20 percent two-bedroom.

9. *Oakwood at Madison, Inc. v. Township of Madison*, 72 N.J. 481, 371 A.2d 1192 (1977).

10. The process "involves highly controversial economic, sociological and policy questions of innate difficulty and complexity. Where predictive responses are called for they are apt to be speculative or conjectural." *Oakwood at Madison*, 72 N.J. 533, 371 A.2d 1218.

11. Mount Laurel II, 92 N.J. 252, 456 A.2d 438.

12. *Oakwood at Madison, Inc. v. Township of Madison*, 117 N.J. Super. 11, 283 A.2d 353 (1977). The Middlesex County Planning Board's comprehensive master plan and housing element covered Madison Township and all constituent towns, including low- and moderate-income housing needs, production goals, strategies, and programs.

13. Mount Laurel II, 92 N.J. 158, 456 A.2d 390.

14. Ibid., 92 N.J. 201, 456 A.2d 411.

15. Ibid., 92 N.J. 209, 456 A.2d 415.

16. Ibid.

17. The plan, formulated by the state's Department of Community Affairs as the guide for the future growth and development of New Jersey, divided the state into six types of areas: growth, limited growth, agriculture, conservation, pinelands, and coastal zones.

18. Mount Laurel II, 92 N.J. 247, 456 A.2d 435.

19. Ibid., 92 N.J. 226, 456 A.2d 424.

20. Despite this provision, the revised plan due by 1985—designated as the State Development and Redevelopment Plan—was not completed until June 12, 1992, and even at that late date fears were expressed that it would never see the light of day. A May 1990 version was never formally adopted by the executive branch, merely tacitly accepted by the governor's cabinet. Delays were also attributable to foot dragging—especially when it came to appropriations—by the state legislature.

21. In *Orgo Farms and Greenhouses, Inc. v. Township of Colts Neck*, 192 N.J. Super. 599, 471 A.2d 812 (1983), however, Judge Serpentelli, balancing housing and environmental factors, refused to deny a remedy within an area designated in the SDGP as limited growth. In such situations, he suggested, it would be appropriate to reverse the standard burden of proof and to put the onus on the builder to prove the absence of detrimental environmental and planning effects.

22. See Charles M. Haar, "The Master Plan: An Impermanent Constitution," *Law and Contemporary Problems* 20 (1955): 353.

23. *Oakwood at Madison*, 72 N.J. 498, 371 A. 2d 1200.

24. Mount Laurel II, 92 N.J. 251, 456 A.2d 438.

25. Acknowledging the criticism that without federal or state subsidy it is impossible to build low-income housing, *Madison Township* substituted the re-

quirement of "least-cost housing." It also expressed doubts as to the validity of inclusionary zoning that grants a bonus of increased density over what is normally permitted as an incentive for affordable housing in New Jersey.

26. Mount Laurel II, 92 N.J. 252, 456 A.2d 438.

27. Ibid., 92 N.J. 251, 456 A.2d 438.

28. See, e.g., *Glenview Development Co. v. Township of Franklin*, 164 N.J. Super. 563, 397 A.2d 384 (1978), which held that fair share requirements need not be applied to rural areas not undergoing development, and *Pascack Ass'n, Ltd. v. Mayor of Washington*, 74 N.J. 470, 379 A.2d 6 (1977), where the township contended that it had no obligation to provide for multifamily housing because it was a small municipality, already built up, and thus was not "developing" within the understanding of Mount Laurel I. The supreme court agreed.

Justice Pashman's dissent in this second case was as impassioned as it was pessimistic:

> The Court's characterization of some communities as "developed" allows municipalities which have already attained "exclusionary bliss" to forever absolve themselves of any obligation for correcting the racial and economic segregation which their land use controls helped to create. By rewarding the past unlawful use of the zoning power to accomplish racially and economically discriminatory planning, we encourage future abuse of land use planning controls. The existence of developed, insular communities which are allowed to reap the benefits of their illegality without being required to share in the costs is a constant reminder to developing communities of the benefits to be gained from illegal and exclusionary zoning. Similarly, remaining communities and inner cities will be required by today's decision to take more than their "fair share" of low and middle-income multi-housing; that specter can only encourage municipalities to avoid the label of "developing." . . .
> . . . Society as a whole suffers the failure to solve the economic and social problems which exclusionary zoning creates; we live daily with the failure of our democratic institutions to eradicate class distinctions. Inevitably, the dream of a pluralistic society begins to fade. (74 N.J. 505–6, 518, 379 A.2d 24, 31)

29. Mount Laurel II, 92 N.J. 275, 456 A.2d 450.

30. This also constituted a reversal of the *Madison Township* court, which had refused a request to order the township to take affirmative action by way of tax concessions or sponsoring public housing projects. The court declared that affirmative measures may include requiring the use of available federal or state subsidies. Overzoning to allow for more than the fair share is another measure a municipality must consider.

31. Mount Laurel II, 92 N.J. 217, 456 A.2d 419.

32. *Fairfax County v. DeGraff*, 214 Va. 235, 198 S.E.2d 600 (1973).

33. Mount Laurel II, 92 N.J. 272–73, 456 A.2d 449.

34. Adopting resolutions of need is a condition precedent to obtaining federal public housing subsidies.

35. Mount Laurel II, 92 N.J. 222, 456 A.2d 421 n. 8.

36. Ibid., 92 N.J. 222, 456 A.2d 422.

37. Ibid., 92 N.J. 261, 456 A.2d 443.

38. Ibid., 92 N.J. 201, 456 A.2d 411.

39. Ibid., 92 N.J. 337, 456 A.2d 483.

40. *Oakwood at Madison*, 72 N.J. 551, 371 A.2d 1227.

41. Mount Laurel II, 92 N.J. 280, 456 A.2d 452 n. 37.

42. The court also insisted on conditioning the construction of higher-priced units on the building of lower-income units to ensure that developers would actually deliver the promised lower-income housing.

43. This six-year cycle coincides with (1) the revision cycle of municipal master plans in the related statutes, (2) the capital improvement program cycle for underlying infrastructures, and (3) the recurring update of the state plan.

44. Mount Laurel II, 92 N.J. 293, 456 A.2d 459.

45. Ibid., 92 N.J. 199, 456 A.2d 410.

46. Ibid., 92 N.J. 218, 456 A.2d 420.

47. Ibid., 92 N.J. 219, 243, 456 A.2d 420, 433.

48. By pointing to municipal palliatives to the perceived fiscal consequences of inclusionary zoning, such as developer fees and self-building by a locality—something it did not do until much later in *Holmdel Builders Ass'n v. Township of Holmdel*, 121 N.J. 503, 583 A.2d 277 (1990)—the court could have spared itself much grief. Yet other arguments about increased infrastructure costs could also have been used. For example, the programs of state aid to education, coming from an income tax not in effect at the time of the original Mount Laurel decision in 1975, could have been used to reduce the differential tax burden between municipalities that accepted development and those that did not.

49. Mount Laurel II, 92 N.J. 289–90, 456 A.2d 458.

50. As Wilentz acknowledged in *Hills* in 1986, "It was the total disregard by municipalities of the judiciary's attempts to enforce the obligation, and the interminable delay where litigation was in process" that spurred his most outspoken comments. *Hills Development Co. v. Township of Bernards*, 103 N.J. 1, 41, 510 A.2d 621, 642 (1986). Despite the urgent judicial mandates, Mount Laurel and other communities like it had succeeded in excluding the poor. "To the best of our ability, we shall not allow it to continue. . . . The obligation is to provide a realistic opportunity for housing, not litigation. We have learned from experience, however, that unless a strong judicial hand is used, Mount Laurel will not result in housing but in paper, process, witnesses, trials and appeals." Mount Laurel II, 92 N.J. 199, 456 A.2d 410.

Chapter IV
Judges into the Fray

1. As in other fields of endeavor, Mount Laurel soon developed its own obscure technical jargon: *region, fair share,* and *past and prospective need* became terms of common usage. Such abstractions would decide what a town's zoning ordinance and consequent physical landscape would be.

2. *AMG Realty Co. v. Township of Warren*, 207 N.J. Super. 388, 504 A.2d 692 (1984).

3. One of the planners recalls how, "as drafts were produced, the judge was right on top of that whole process and talking with those of us whom he had

appointed about the impact of this approach or that, and he was just thoroughly involved in the whole proceeding."

4. Mount Laurel II, 92 N.J. 256, 456 A.2d 440 (citing *Oakwood at Madison, Inc. v. Township of Madison*, 72 N.J. 481, 537, 371 A.2d 1192, 1219 (1977)). In the words of the distinguished authority Charles Abrams, "The geographic area within which dwelling units are closely substitutable for one another." *The Language of Cities: A Glossary of Terms* (New York: Viking, 1971), 142.

5. Regions should encompass a mix of rural and urban areas, housing types, and socioeconomic characteristics; ideally, they should be balanced so that one region is not significantly different in housing types or quality.

6. In the subsequent *J. W. Field Co., Inc. v. Township of Franklin*, Judge Serpentelli stated that the determination of the functional center "leaves room for some subjective evaluation by the court." 206 N.J. Super. 165, 179, 501 A.2d 1075, 1083 (1985). At the conclusion of that case, "the court was left with substantial doubt as to location" and appointed an expert to render an independent judgment. After his report, the court was still undecided: "The evidence in this case remains in equipoise." Ibid., 206 N.J. Super. 180, 501 A.2d 1083. Finally, as a fair resolution, Judge Serpentelli averaged the figures that emerged from the two configurations and split the obligations. 206 N.J. Super. 180, 501 A.2d 1083–84. It should be noted that this mechanism of regional designation has several hundred possibilities as a different region radiates from the center of each municipality.

7. The opinion further specifies that

The thirty minute drive will be measured by the following speeds:
1. 30 miles per hour on local and county roads,
2. 40 miles per hour on state and federal highways,
3. 50 miles per hour on interstate highways, the Garden State Parkway and the New Jersey Turnpike. (*AMG*, 207 N.J. Super. 400, 504 A.2d 698)

8. See John M. Payne, "Rethinking Fair Share: The Judicial Enforcement of Affordable Housing Policies," *Real Estate Law Journal* 16 (1987): 20–44.

9. As Douglas Opalski, executive director of the Council on Affordable Housing from 1988 to 1992, put it, the Fair Housing Act "embraces" the court's definition of present need obligation.

10. "Overcrowding" was defined as more than 1.01 persons per room. *AMG*, 207 N.J. Super. 401, 504 A.2d 699.

11. Vacant developable land was put forward as a more desirable measure, but no reliable data existed; in addition, much of growth area acreage is located in already developed cities and older suburbs not suitable for new development.

12. Owing to the frequently advanced notion that if a municipality takes jobs it should provide housing for the workers, an argument can be made that employment measures should be weighted more heavily than other factors. Judge Serpentelli noted that this factor may "reflect a policy of exclusion which has existed for many years because some towns have invited factories but excluded the workers." *AMG*, 207 N.J. Super. 433, 504 A.2d 716.

13. Unlike the other two factors, median income is first expressed as a ratio and then transformed into a percentage by averaging the growth area and present

employment percentages, with the resulting average used to multiply the median income ratio; the derived median income percentage is then added to the first two percentages of growth area and existing employment; the resulting sum is divided by three to derive an average local allocation percentage that is applied to the regional tally of present-need housing units to determine the local share.

In rejecting objections to the use of this factor, Judge Serpentelli stated that he had some reservations as to whether experience would demonstrate its usefulness, but "these concerns are overridden by the importance of having an economic indicator which mirrors fiscal capacity, prior exclusion, and most importantly, past inclusion." Ibid., 207 N.J. Super. 435, 504 A.2d 717.

14. Ibid., 207 N.J. Super. 459, 504 A.2d 730.

15. A sample application for Warren Township that illustrates the methodology was given by the court itself:

1. Region
The present need region for Warren (Region I) consists of eleven counties. . . . The prospective need region for Warren consists of . . . six counties. . . .

2. Regional Need
The indigenous need for Warren is 52. The eleven county reallocated present need pool is 35,014 and the six county prospective need pool is 49,004.

3. Allocation Factors
—Present Need
Using the eleven county present need region, Warren's fair share of the reallocation pool of 35,014 is 162 for the decade of 1980–1990 based upon the following calculation.
Warren's present need percentage of the present regional need is 1.126% which is arrived at as follows:
Growth Area = 1.780%
Present Employment = .179%
Median Income Ratio = 1.45
$(1.780 + .179)/2 = .9795 \times 1.45 = 1.420\%$
([this] represents the percentage modified by the ratio)
$(1.780 + .179 + 1.420)/3 = 1.126\%$
Reallocation Excess Pool = $35,014 \times 1.126$ (fair share %)
Municipal Share = 394
Phased in by one third $(394/3) = 131$
Additional 20% reallocation $(131 \times 1.2) = 157$
Vacancy Allowance $(157 \times 1.03) = 162$
Total Present Need is
(Indigenous) 52 + (Reallocated Present) 162 = (Total) 214
—Prospective Need
Warren's fair share of the prospective regional need of 49,004 is 732 units for the decade of 1980–1990.
Warren's prospective need percentage of the prospective regional need is 1.208%, computed as follows:
Growth Area = 2.556%
Present Employment = .304%

Employment Growth = .428%
Median Income Ratio = 1.41
(2.556 + .304 + .428)/3 = 1.096% × 1.41 = 1.545%
([this] represents the percentage modified by the ratio)
(2.556 + .304 + .428 + 1.545)/4 = 1.208%
Prospective Regional Need = 49,004 × 1.208 (fair share %)
Municipal Share = 592
Additional 20% reallocation (592 × 1.2) = 710
Vacancy Allowance (710 × 1.03) = 732
SUMMARY
(Total Present Need) 214 + (Total Prospective Need) 732 = (Total Fair Share)
946. (Ibid., 207 N.J. Super. 410–11, 504 A.2d 703–4)

16. *Countryside Properties, Inc. v. Mayor of Ringwood*, 205 N.J. Super. 291, 500 A.2d 767 (1984).

17. Ibid., 205 N.J. Super. 294, 500 A.2d 768.

18. Center for Urban Policy Research of Rutgers University, *Mount Laurel II: Challenge and Delivery of Low-Cost Housing* (New Brunswick: Rutgers University, 1983).

19. Final numbers are, of course, of the highest interest. Whereas the *AMG* methodology would translate into a total statewide need of 150,000 lower-income units, the report put the figure at only 120,000. By Judge Serpentelli's count, the *AMG* approach, now modified through the percentage provided by the computer tapes, produced a statewide number of lower-income units of 112,000, and when further modified by the addition of a separate identification of over-crowding—as required by Judge Skillman in *Countryside Properties*—a total of 148,000. On a regional basis (that covered both Warren and Franklin townships), the adjusted *AMG* approach identified 82,000 units, the Rutgers Report 90,000, and with the Skillman overcrowding surrogate, 113,000. At the same time, it is claimed that the *AMG* procedure overcounts Mount Laurel households for prospective-need purposes by nearly 14,000. Robert W. Burchell and David Listokin, *Response to the Warren Report: Reshaping Mount Laurel II Implementation* (report prepared for the New Jersey State League of Municipalities, December 10, 1984).

20. The report set up a two-level analysis of deficiency. If the unit was built before 1940, it is considered deficient if it has any one of the other six deficiencies; if built after 1940, it is substandard if it has any two deficiencies.

21. *Countryside Properties*, 205 N.J. Super 303, 500 A.2d 773.

22. Judge Skillman pointed out that the Tri-State Report encompassed the entire New York metropolitan area, including New York City's population, and besides this glaring distortion, was based on old data. In *Van Dalen v. Township of Washington*, 205 N.J. Super. 308, 500 A.2d 776 (1984), Judge Skillman lowered the figure to 67.5 percent to reflect the units considered not to be occupied by lower- and moderate-income families.

23. That is, 142.49 divided by 2,317 equals 6.15 percent, which multiplied by 1,020 equals 63.

24. *J. W. Field*, 206 N.J. Super. 165, 501 A.2d 1075.

25. Ibid., 206 N.J. Super. 173, 501 A.2d 1079.

26. Of course, this required a recreation of the excess pool arrived at in *AMG*, with the percentage of deficient units to standard units lower on a regional basis. The modification also required a change in identifying a municipality's indigenous need.

27. *J. W. Field*, 206 N.J. Super. 173, 501 A.2d 1079.

28. In particular, he questioned the lack of an elevator in a four-story structure as a factor, and the lack of central heating. He also pointed out that while the multisurrogate approach had the greater possibility of identifying truly deficient units it was weakened by the subsequent need to disaggregate the numbers to the local level. Ibid., 206 N.J. Super. 176, 501 A.2d 1081.

29. *AMG*, 207 N.J. Super. 453, 504 A.2d 726.

30. In *Morris County Fair Housing Council v. Township of Boonton*, the court stated flatly, "In fact, a master probably should be appointed as a matter of course in any case where a developer is the only party representing lower income persons." 197 N.J. Super. 359, 371 n. 2, 484 A.2d 1302, 1309 n. 2 (1984).

31. Ibid., 197 N.J. Super. 365, 484 A.2d 1305. The court added that it was "satisfied" that it could adequately safeguard against judgments of compliance being entered improvidently through use of procedures similar to those used by federal courts in class actions.

32. In Mount Laurel II, the supreme court went on to consider a still more remote possibility: if removal of excessive restrictions and the employment of affirmative devices failed to produce an adequate number of low-income housing units, a municipality could satisfy its fair share obligations through the construction of least-cost housing—the more lenient standard that the court had temporarily adopted in the *Madison Township* case.

33. *Allan-Deane Corp. v. Township of Bedminster*, 205 N.J. Super. 87, 115–16, 500 A.2d 49, 63 (1985).

34. Ibid., 205 N.J. Super. 103, 500 A.2d 56.

35. Ibid., 205 N.J. Super. 103, 500 A.2d 56. *Morris County Fair Housing Council v. Township of Boonton*, 230 N.J. Super. 345, 356–57, 553 A.2d 814, 820–21 (1989), featured the Mount Laurel judge's power to waive a fifty-foot buffer requirement. Judge Skillman also concluded that a local board's decision could not be justified on the ground that plaintiff refused to commit itself to a particular architectural style.

36. Interestingly, in reviewing project feasibility, the court examines whether the rezoning, density bonuses, mandatory set-asides, fee waivers, tax abatements, and other actions would still bring sufficient profit to the bottom line to make the project a likelihood.

37. *Allan-Deane*, 205 N.J. Super. 122, 500 A.2d 66.

38. Other subsidiary issues also required early resolution. One of the earliest facing Judge Gibson was the court's ability to bind independent agencies, such as a sewer authority over which a municipality with an exclusionary zoning code had no direct linkage. On what legal theory could they be held accountable?

39. In *Allan-Deane*, Judge Serpentelli rejected the claim of a competing landowner who did not intervene in the action until after the ordinance had been found noncompliant. He also emphasized the need "to choose any reasonable

combination of realistic sites or realistic mechanisms that will produce the required result—the likelihood." 205 N.J. Super. 114, 500 A.2d 62. A gradation of likeliness is not an element of the evaluation; Serpentelli rejected a weighing of suitability between included and excluded sites.

40. In the more conciliatory arena of Judge Gibson's court, this and the subsequent questions were raised, but "they never became a contested issue in the cases I had. . . . That isn't to say we didn't discuss these things, but they were resolved with my assistance, sometimes without my assistance."

41. *Morris County Fair Housing Council*, 230 N.J. Super. 345, 553 A.2d 814. The law division's other opinion is to be found in 220 N.J. Super. 388, 532 A.2d 280 (1986).

42. A striking variant occurred in *J. W. Field*, 204 N.J. Super. 445, 499 A.2d 251, where eleven plaintiff builders sought builder's remedies for low-income housing that exceeded the fair share number of the municipality. Judge Serpentelli created a four-step prioritization plan. First, a builder had to meet the threshold test of entitlement. The builder who had first filed a complaint received the first award, but only if located within a growth area of the SDGP. Remedies were then awarded to builders based on the date of filing, subject to modification based on whether any project was clearly more likely to result in construction than others were and whether any project was clearly more suitable from a planning viewpoint than others were. Only if a need for more parcels to satisfy the fair share remained would parcels in limited growth areas be considered.

43. Ibid., 204 N.J. Super. 468, 499 A.2d 263.

44. *Van Dalen*, 205 N.J. Super 308, 500 A.2d 776. In that case, although Judge Skillman was deciding the validity of an amended ordinance, uncertainties over the construction of lower-income housing in the new PUD district, the difficulty of providing sewage disposal facilities in the mobile home zone, and the impracticality of developing at a density of eight units per acre in the third zone led him to conclude that the revised zoning still did not create a realistic opportunity for building low-income housing. He ordered Washington Township to rezone (with the assistance of a special master) within ninety days.

45. Critics of the Mount Laurel Doctrine argue that the question should be whether the *forum* is suitable to determine whether the site is suitable. Some believe that the popularly elected state legislature, rather than the state courts, should be making determinations of suitability and that the Mount Laurel Doctrine causes judges to overstep their proper role and usurp the legislative function.

46. *J. W. Field*, 204 N.J. Super. 463, 499 A.2d 261. See also *Orgo Farms and Greenhouses, Inc. v. Township of Colts Neck*, 192 N.J. Super. 599, 471 A.2d 812 (1983), where a builder's remedy was granted within a "limited growth" area of the SDGP.

47. COAH, the agency established by the Fair Housing Act in 1985, has generously acknowledged this on many occasions since its establishment.

48. For one professional planner's overview of methodological approaches to fair share determinations, see George M. Raymond, "Berenson: An Obligation Undefined Is an Obligation Unfulfilled," *Pace Environmental Law Review* 4 (1986): 131–54.

Chapter V
Of Special Masters and the Front Line

1. For the early history of masters in state courts, see J. W. Dilworth, "Master in Chancery," *Baylor Law Review* 5 (1953): 374. See also Debra Dobray, "The Role of Masters in Court Ordered Institutional Reform," *Baylor Law Review* 34 (1982): 581–603.

2. According to Rule 53(a) of the Federal Rules of Civil Procedure,

The order of reference to the master may specify or limit the master's powers and may direct the master to report only upon particular issues or to do or perform particular acts or to receive and report evidence only and may fix the time and place for beginning and closing the hearings and for the filing of the master's report. Subject to the specifications and limitations stated in the order, the master has and shall exercise the power to regulate all proceedings in every hearing before the master and to do all acts and take all measures necessary or proper for the efficient performance of the master's duties under the order. The master may require the production before the master of evidence upon all matters embraced in the reference, including the production of all books, papers, vouchers, documents, and writings applicable thereto. The master may rule upon the admissibility of evidence unless otherwise directed by the order of reference and has the authority to put witnesses on oath and may examine them and may call the parties to the action and examine them upon oath. When a party so requests, the master shall make a record of the evidence offered and excluded in the same manner and subject to the same limitations as provided in the Federal Rules of Evidence for a court sitting without a jury.

3. One of the rare instances of a judge disagreeing with the master's conclusions occurred in *Allan-Deane Corp. v. Township of Bedminster*, 205 N.J. Super. 87, 123, 500 A.2d 49, 67 (1985), where the master agreed with the conclusions of the municipality that a site be accepted as providing a realistic opportunity, subject to expansion of a sewage treatment plant, but the judge rejected the plan.

4. This is also true when the appointed master is a generalist rather than a professional scientist. In the Boston Harbor litigation, for example, the reliance of the special master, a lawyer, on the expert advice of his engineers and professors was open and manifest. See Stewart T. Seward, "The Boston Harbor Dispute: Judicial Strategy and Legislative Deadlock," in Charles M. Haar, ed., *Of Judges, Politics and Flounders: Perspectives on the Cleaning Up of Boston Harbor* (Cambridge, Mass.: Lincoln Institute of Land Policy, 1986), 1–50.

5. See David I. Levine, "The Authority for the Appointment of Remedial Special Masters in Federal Institutional Reform Litigation: The History Reconsidered," *UC Davis Law Review* 17 (1984): 753. For excellent discussions of this idea by Judges David L. Bazelon and Harold Leventhal, see *Ethyl Corp. v. EPA*, 541 F.2d 1 (D.C.Cir. 1976). See also the analysis in depth by David L. Kirp and Gary Babcock, "Judge and Company: Court-Appointed Masters, School Desegregation, and Institutional Reform," *Alabama Law Review* 32 (1981): 313.

Similar questions are raised by the relatively new profession of conflict management and mediation. See the insightful article by Michael Wheeler, "Regional Consensus on Affordable Housing: Yes in My Backyard?" *Journal of Planning,*

*Research, and Education* 12 (January 1993): 139–49, in which he discusses the profession's disquieting effects on existing institutions, noting specifically that negotiated settlements can deprive courts of their function of articulating and confirming fundamental rights. But see Lawrence Suskind and Susan Podziba, *Mediating Affordable Housing Disputes: The Capitol Region Case Study* (Cambridge, Mass.: Lincoln Institute of Land Policy, 1989).

6. Major concerns are spelled out in Elizabeth Montgomery, "Force and Will: The Use of Special Masters to Implement Judicial Decrees," *University of Colorado Law Review* 52 (1980): 105. She writes, "Unless the powers and responsibilities of extrajudicial assistants are carefully prescribed, the activities of these assistants may violate the provisions of article III." Ibid., 122.

7. In their shuttle diplomacy, the elite group of hybrid masters proved to be best at resolving disputes between developers and municipalities, where the parties could at least quantify their compromises in dollars.

8. See Charles M. Haar, "The Role of the Special Master: A Helpful Judicial Tool," *National Law Journal*, January 11, 1982, 11.

9. As Dr. Johnson framed the dilemma, "You cannot help paying regard to their argument, if they are good. If it were testimony, you might disregard it, if you knew that it were purchased." He went on to quote a beautiful image of Bacon: "Testimony is like an arrow shot from a long bow; the force of it depends on the strength of the hand that draws it. Argument is like an arrow from a cross-bow, which has equal force though shot by a child." James Boswell, *Life of Johnson* (1791; Oxford University Press, 1953).

10. Both Judge Paul Garrity in the Boston Harbor case and Judge Joseph L. Tauro in the mental retardation case took the other parties' viewpoints into account when selecting masters. *Quincy v. Metropolitan District Commission*, Civil Action No. 138477 (1983); *Ricci v. Okin*, 823 F.Supp. 984 (D.Mass. 1993).

11. Rule 53(b) specifies that "reference to a master shall be the exception and not the rule. In actions to be tried by a jury, a reference shall be made only when the issues are complicated; in actions to be tried without a jury, save in matters of account and of difficult computation of damages, a reference shall be made only upon a showing that some exceptional condition requires it." The New Jersey rule is more expansive. It provides for appointment of a master "upon approval by the Chief Justice . . . or under extraordinary circumstances." N.J. Civil Practice Rule 4:41–1. In 1993, it was relaxed even further.

12. See David N. Kinsey, "A Special Master Remembers the Decade after Mount Laurel II," *Housing New Jersey* 2 (February 1993): 5.

13. *Brown v. Board of Education of Topeka, Kansas*, 349 U.S. 294, 300, 75 S.Ct. 753, 756 (1955). Again, in *Swann v. Charlotte-Mecklenburg Board of Education*, 402 U.S. 1, 15, 91 S.Ct. 1267, 1276 (1971), the court declared "breadth and flexibility are inherent in equitable remedies."

14. For an interesting contrast, see the analysis of the public politician role exemplified by the master in the Milwaukee School desegregation case in Kirp and Babcock, "Judge and Company," 342.

15. Footnote 40 orders: "Given the sensitive nature of the function, the master should not communicate privately with the court." Mount Laurel II, 92 N.J. 285 n.40, 456 A.2d 455 n.40.

16. The experience of two colleagues at the Columbia Law School, who—

remarkably—still remain close friends, provides an ominous warning against too strict a following of the letter of the law on consultation. See Curtis J. Berger, "Away from the Court House and into the Field: The Odyssey of a Special Master," *Columbia Law Review* 78 (1978): 707.

## Chapter VI
## The Legislature Strikes Back . . .

1. *Hills Development Co. v. Township of Bernards*, 103 N.J. 1, 64, 510 A.2d 621, 654 (1986) (Sometimes referred to as Mount Laurel III).

2. *In re Egg Harbor Assocs.*, 94 N.J. 358, 464 A.2d 1115 (1983). The appellate division held that CAFRA empowered it to impose fair share housing conditions. *In re Egg Harbor Assocs.*, 185 N.J. Super. 507, 449 A.2d 1324 (1982).

3. The state did ease the developer's burden by allowing him to construct the required affordable housing in a separate development off the site.

4. *Egg Harbor*, 94 N.J. 366, 464 A.2d 1119.

5. Mount Laurel II was cited for its holding of fundamental fairness with respect to the power of municipalities to zone in furtherance of the general welfare and for its approval of mandatory set-asides. 94 N.J. 366–67, 464 A.2d 1119–20.

6. Ibid., 94 N.J. 370, 464 A.2d 1121.

7. Ibid., 94 N.J. 374, 464 A.2d 1123–24.

8. Ibid., 94 N.J. 383, 464 A.2d 1128.

9. *New Jersey Statutes Annotated* 13:19–11.1 (St. Paul, Minn.: West, 1986).

10. Wynona M. Lipman, "The Fair Housing Act?" *Seton Hall Legislative Journal* 9 (1986): 572.

11. Joseph F. Sullivan, "A Housing Bill to Aid the Poor Passed in Jersey," *New York Times*, March 8, 1985, B2.

12. Senator Stockman had the following to say about the veto:

The ten-page conditional veto message severely threatened the integrity of the legislation. Both Senator Lipman and I felt compelled to attempt to defeat the final version of the bill in the Senate. We met with no success. We argued that the Governor's proposal, among other things, threatened to deprive persons who need housing from representation on the board; established fair share housing criteria that easily could be used to reward those affluent municipalities that have been most blatantly exclusionary; reduced the commitment of resources so that the proposed financial program after the first year was largely illusory and introduced provisions into the act which clearly raised serious constitutional questions. (Gerald R. Stockman, "The Art of the Possible," *Seton Hall Legislative Journal* 9 (1986): 583).

The major change recommended by Governor Kean was a small funding mechanism to pay for affordable housing. His amendment also included the requirement to take into account historic, environmental, and farmland preservation in determining a region's fair share need.

13. United Press International, June 27, 1985.

14. The act stipulates that four members must be elected officials representing local government; two must represent low- and moderate-income households, one also representing builders; and three must represent the public interest.

15. *New Jersey Statutes Annotated* 52:27D-302(a).

16. One factor the act emphasizes is the use of the State Development and Redevelopment Plan (SDRP), the overall master plan for the state, in determining where development is to be encouraged or limited and what kinds of development are appropriate.

17. The housing element has to contain at least a detailed inventory of existing housing, a future projection of the housing stock for the next six years, a demographic analysis, an analysis of present and future employment, the municipality's present and future fair share of low-income housing, and an analysis of land suitable for low-income housing. See *New Jersey Statutes Annotated* 52:27D-310.

18. The act specifies economic viability through mandatory set-asides, density bonuses, tax abatements, infrastructure expansion and rehabilitation, and municipality-generated funds. *New Jersey Statutes Annotated* 52:27D–311. Any municipality, after filing a resolution of participation, a housing element plan and a proposed fair share housing ordinance implementing the housing element plan, may then petition the council for "substantive certification." The council is required to issue certification if no objection is filed within forty-five days of publication of notice and if it finds that the fair share plan "is consistent with the rules and criteria adopted by the council" and makes "the achievement of the municipality's fair share of low and moderate income housing realistically possible." If an objection is filed, the council is required to mediate the dispute. Ibid., 52:27D-314.

19. Ibid., 52:27D-317(a). This has never occurred. This section of the FHA is a return to the presumption of validity of legislative acts, which reverses the Mount Laurel shift of the burden of proof to the municipality whose ordinance is challenged. COAH will also codefend against subsequent allegations of exclusionary zoning.

20. The FHA also established a new source of funds—2.5 percent of the state's realty transfer fee—to assist municipalities in implementing their fair share obligations. This was in addition to a one-time appropriation of $15 million to the New Jersey Mortgage and Housing Finance Agency (MHFA) to underwrite down payments and closing costs.

21. *Hills*, 103 N.J. 1, 510 A.2d 621. Twelve appeals were pending before the supreme court; it selected five for oral argument designed to cover all the issues; two of them were part of the public advocate's lawsuit against municipalities in Morris County.

22. Specifically, the court upheld the constitutionality of (1) the act's temporary moratorium on the builder's remedy; (2) delays in the fulfillment of fair share obligations resulting from the establishment of the council; and (3) the procedure for reviewing zoning ordinances, insofar as it did not preclude ultimate judicial review. It also rejected the argument of the act's unconstitutionality because it interfered with the supreme court's exclusive control over actions in lieu of prerogative writs.

Earlier, Judge Skillman, in upholding the constitutionality of the act on its face, had observed, "The council will find itself walking through a constitutional minefield when it undertakes, in conformity with the act" to establish criteria and guidelines for determining municipal fair share allocations and for establishing

housing regions. He also remarked on the difficulties posed by review of municipal petitions for substantive certification of housing elements. "However," he
concluded, "appropriate respect for the legislative branch of government, and the
council, precludes the court from assuming that the council will be unsuccessful
in traversing the difficult course which lies before it." *Morris County Fair Housing Council v. Township of Boonton*, 209 N.J. Super. 393, 435, 507 A.2d 768,
791 (1985).

23. *Hills*, 103 N.J. 65, 510 A.2d 655. The implications of the interplay of
judges and legislators is illuminatingly discussed in Alan B. Handler, "Jurisprudence and Prudential Justice," *Seton Hall Law Review* 16 (1986): 571. Cf. *Abbot
v. Burke*, 100 N.J. 269, 495 A.2d 376 (1985).

24. *Hills*, 103 N.J. 40–41, 510 A.2d 642.

25. Ibid., 103 N.J. 21, 510 A.2d 632.

26. Ibid., 103 N.J. 49, 510 A.2d 647.

27. Judge Serpentelli, who had denied motions to remove in several of the
cases, ruefully and half-amusedly stated that never had he suffered so many rejec-
tions of his opinion in one day.

28. He chose to stress the intrinsic advantages of a legislative approach—"this
cooperative effort," he termed it—over the more limited options available under
judicial enforcement. "By virtue of the Act," he asserted, "the three branches of
government in New Jersey are now committed to a common goal." *Hills*, 103 N.J.
63, 510 A.2d 654.

29. Ibid., 103 N.J. 22, 510 A.2d 632. A sigh of relief was almost audible as he
continued his overall endorsement of the legislature's action:

> The municipalities of this state, and the State itself, are about to have the benefit
> of a coherent, consistent plan to provide a realistic opportunity for lower in-
> come housing. That legislative solution may work well. It certainly may differ
> from the prior judicial solution. Regions, regional need, fair share, all may be
> different; the locus of the obligation may be different; the timetable different;
> the method of satisfying the obligation different; and compliance may in fact
> become voluntary. As lower income housing is produced, the state will be de-
> veloped in accordance with a rational comprehensive land-use state plan. It
> may be that the method of providing lower income housing will be more effec-
> tive both in the total output and the speed of construction. When all of the
> standards of the Council are in place, *Mount Laurel* cases may move expedi-
> tiously: the expertise of administrators, and their power to make decisions
> binding on all municipalities, and to modify them, has a potential of being
> significantly more effective than case-by-case judicial disposition. (Ibid., 103
> N.J. 51–52, 510 A.2d 648)

30. As Judge Skillman put it, he had a difficult time seeing how it could "be
reconciled with the prohibition of the New Jersey Constitution against legislative
interference with judicial remedies." *Morris County Fair Housing Council*, 209
N.J. Super. 418, 507 A.2d 782.

31. *Hills*, 103 N.J. 21, 43, 510 A.2d 632, 644.

32. Ibid., 103 N.J. 23, 510 A.2d 633.

33. Ibid., 103 N.J. 65, 510 A.2d 655.

34. Ibid., 103 N.J. 47, 510 A.2d 645.

35. Ibid.

36. *New Jersey Statutes Annotated* 52:27D-316.

37. Before the supreme court issued this sweeping opinion, the trial courts had been adamant about not permitting transfers.

38. *New Jersey Statutes Annotated* 52:27D-313. Originally, municipalities could petition any time within two years of November 30, 1990. The council is required to decide certification only for towns that petition it or are transferred to it from the courts.

39. *Hills*, 103 N.J. 36, 510 A.2d 640. Within the not too distant future, Chief Justice Wilentz opined, most municipalities subject to Mount Laurel obligations would enact conforming ordinances providing a realistic opportunity for construction of their fair share. Ibid., 103 N.J. 36–37, 510 A.2d 640.

40. In addition to the municipalities remaining under the court's jurisdiction, another eleven had a precredited need of zero and thirty-two more are central cities. This leaves some two hundred towns, many of which are covered by sewer bans or environmental constraints, are outside growth areas, or are corridors in the state.

41. Provisions exist both in the act, as interpreted by the court in *Hills*, and in the council's own procedural regulations under which cases may be taken out of the jurisdiction of the council and placed in the forum of an appropriate Mount Laurel judge. Thus far, at least two towns have reverted to the courts from COAH.

42. The act empowers the MHFA to administer rent controls, resale price controls, and eligibility lists for purchasers and renters of inclusionary developments. *New Jersey Statutes Annotated* 52:27D-324.

43. On February 3, 1993, for instance, COAH cut by more than 34 percent the total number of affordable housing units municipalities must now address in order to comply with the FHA. Reaction to the new numbers is mixed. By 1995, COAH's phase II (1993–99) calculations reduced prior projections of need by 48 percent, primarily because 1990 Census numbers confirmed that Phase I overestimated prospective need.

44. *AMG Realty Co. v. Township of Warren*, 207 N.J. Super. 388, 504 A.2d 692 (1989). Counsel in *Borough of Carteret*, 142 N.J. Super. 11, 359 A.2d 526 (1976), requested that the planners involved in the case attempt a consensus approach, which was subsequently adopted in *AMG*.

45. The formal methodology does differ, however, from that originally created by Judge Serpentelli, in that the council's figures diverge from the courts' by type of dwelling unit and other measures and shadings. In addition, the trial courts are now under an obligation to conform their rulings to the council's. Thus, despite the concern COAH shares with the judiciary about statewide need, it has undone some of the courts' work.

46. Of a total of 242,760 units, *AMG* assigned 199,665 (82 percent) to the suburbs and 43,095 to the central cities, whereas COAH assigned 114,000 (78 percent) to the suburbs and 31,707 to the central cities, out of a total of 145,707.

47. In its 1994 codification for calculating the fair share obligation, COAH continued to steer a midway course between the Mount Laurel mandates and the suburban pressures expressed in its enabling legislation. The calculation

continues past practices. The first step is to determine "precredited need," the cumulative 1987–99 housing obligation. It represents the combination of indigenous need, derived from 1990 Census counts of substandard housing units for the region where the municipality is located, and present need reallocated if the need, as a percentage of its total housing units, is greater than the region's substandard percentage. This is added to prospective need, the projections of future low- and moderate-income household formation; the projected amount was reduced in light of the experience that the 1987–93 projections had overestimated population growth.

Reallocating to the municipal level differs in some aspects from the previous approach and includes three factors: the regional share of nonresidential ratables, which COAH has found to be a superior surrogate for employment; an income factor, based on the assumption that wealthier localities have greater responsibility and financial capacity; and the availability of undeveloped land having infrastructure capacity.

The next step is estimating how secondary sources—demolitions, filtering, conversions, and spontaneous rehabilitation—enhance and diminish the obligation during the prospective six-year certification period.

The final step is to determine "calculated need," the local housing obligation remaining after COAH has recognized the municipal response to the precredited need by a variety of credits, caps, and adjustments. These include a one-for-one deduction based on a fair share plan to construct low- and moderate-income units, transfer of units via an RCA, and zoning that implements a housing element certified by the council or the superior court.

The obligation is separated into a "rehabilitation component," indigenous need minus spontaneous rehabilitation, and an "inclusionary component," all of the calculated need that remains after subtracting the rehabilitation component. A municipality may fulfill its inclusionary components through various compliance mechanisms: "municipality sponsored construction; inclusionary zoning; regional contribution agreements; alternative living arrangements; the creation of accessory apartments; the purchase of housing units that have never been occupied; and the purchase of housing units that have been vacant for 18 months or more." Laura Preston, "Understanding Your Fair Share Obligation," in COAH, "The COAH Handbook . . . Getting through the Maze" (1994, mimeographed). See "Summary of Public Comments and Agency Responses," *New Jersey Register* 26 (June 6, 1994): 2301.

48. Jesus Rangel, "Jersey Tells Town to Plan Housing Despite Lack of Open Land," *New York Times*, October 19, 1988, B1.

49. Editorial, *New York Times*, November 5, 1988, A26.

50. *Paramus Substantive Certification No. 47*, 249 N.J. Super. 1, 591 A.2d 1345 (1991).

51. See *AMG*, 207 N.J. Super. 388, 504 A.2d 692. Currently the classifications are: (1) metropolitan planning area, (2) suburban planning area, (3) fringe planning area, (4) rural planning area, (5) rural/environmental sensitive planning area (agricultural preservation district), and (6) environmentally sensitive planning area.

52. See *New Jersey Statutes Annotated* 52:27D–304(b). It did specify that re-

gions consist of no more than four and no less than two contiguous counties that comport to standard metropolitan statistical areas as much as possible.

53. On February 3, 1993, for the first time COAH proposed to realign several of its housing regions, configuring each so that it would have enough undeveloped land to meet regional needs, and to provide each region with a center city in order to facilitate regional contribution agreements (RCAs).

54. The FHA does not deal with indigenous need at all; COAH borrowed this principle from the judiciary.

55. The basic projection method used by both the SDRP and COAH is an averaging of results from the historic trends of migration (tending to favor less developed areas) with an economic demographic approach building off a base of job growth (tending to favor built-up areas). Furthermore, COAH relies on the SDRP to weight various planning area designations for new unit need allocation purposes. Designated centers are the preferred mechanism for accommodating growth in each planning area.

56. In the introduction to its rules detailing the procedures and data employed to calculate lower-income housing need, COAH acknowledges the heavy influence of the three Mount Laurel judges.

57. There was a sense at COAH that judges and masters have not adequately considered the potential of filtering down upper-income housing units to lower-income people. The formula the agency ultimately adopted took this factor into account in satisfying a locality's fair share obligation, an action that, not incidentally, helped to produce a lower ceiling on fair shares. In its work on the post-1993 projections, the council followed its earlier methodology, with certain revisions.

58. *New Jersey Statutes Annotated* 52:27D-307(c)(2)(f) requires COAH to adopt criteria and guidelines for "municipal adjustment of the present and prospective fair share . . . whenever . . . vacant and developable land is not available in the municipality."

59. *In re Borough of Roseland*, 247 N.J. Super. 203, 588 A.2d 1256 (1991).

60. *Calton Homes, Inc. v. Council on Affordable Housing*, 244 N.J. Super. 438, 582 A.2d 1024 (1990).

61. *Roseland*, 247 N.J. Super. 203, 588 A.2d 1256.

62. *Allan-Deane Corp. v. Township of Bedminster*, 205 N.J. Super. 87, 106, 500 A.2d 49, 58 (1985).

63. Ibid. As a further example, in *J. W. Field Co. v. Township of Franklin*, 204 N.J. Super. 445, 499 A.2d 251 (1985), the court held that it would not insist on rigid adherence to its fair share methodology when there were voluntary efforts at compliance.

64. In the *Township of Hillsborough* case, the appellate division, by way of dictum, states: "Although there is some merit to the Public Advocate's criticism of the formula by which COAH assigns credits to reflect filtering, he has failed to demonstrate that the formula is arbitrary and capricious." *In re Petition for Substantive Certification filed by the Township of Hillsborough*, A-6118-87T3 (1987).

65. A municipality may request a "phase-in schedule," *New Jersey Statutes Annotated* 40:55D-61, and the act affords ample "good faith" time to plan and

construct inclusionary developments. See Justin M. Monaghan and William Penkethman, Jr., "The Fair Housing Act," *Seton Hall Law Journal* 9 (1986): 585.

66. They had already begun to use phase-in schedules. Manalapan Township is an example of this. But reducing the number of required units to 999 within six years is hardly an incentive to comply. If all come under the inclusionary cover, this amounts to nearly five thousand more units just to meet the obligation, and upwards of fifteen thousand population increase.

67. *Van Dalen v. Township of Washington*, 120 N.J. 234, 576 A.2d 819 (1990).

68. The moratorium inspired an intense debate between the executive and legislative branches. In its original draft, the act nullified any judgments levying the builder's remedy after January 20, 1983. The governor questioned the constitutionality of such action. The final draft leaves a "final judgment" effective but suspends nonfinal judgments for the five-month period. See "Governor's Reconsideration Statement," *1985 New Jersey Session Law Service* (St. Paul, Minn.: West, 1985), 83–84.

69. Mount Laurel II had said that trial courts could relieve a municipality of its immediate duty where the requisite housing would be in "such quantity as would radically transform the municipality overnight." Mount Laurel II, 92 N.J. 219, 456 A.2d 420.

70. "The small reduction in need that this capping procedure provides," the council's rule explains, "prevents the smaller communities in a region from experiencing significant change while complying with the state's low- and moderate-income housing mandate."

71. *Calton Homes*, 244 N.J. Super. 447, 582 A.2d 1029.

72. Ibid., 244 N.J. Super. 453, 582 A.2d 1033.

73. Thus the cap dropped Middletown Township's obligation of 13.3 percent of Monmouth County's obligation to 7.8 percent. Comparing Middletown Township to other municipalities in the county revealed another inequity: as a result of the cap, Middletown's fair share would be only slightly higher (937–1000 units) than that of Freehold Township, although it had 3.3 times more households to share the obligation.

74. *Calton Homes*, 244 N.J. Super. 438, 582 A.2d 1024. On January 31, 1993, the governor signed an amendment to the FHA that reinstated the thousand-unit cap.

75. *Orgo Farms and Greenhouses, Inc. v. Township of Colts Neck*, 192 N.J. Super. 599, 605, 471 A.2d 812, 815 (1983).

76. An unfair criticism by some academics is that the builder's remedy can also be described as a judicial technique to encourage litigation (the old sin of champerty and maintenance) that gives the judiciary jurisdiction to make legislative policy decisions.

77. *New Jersey Statutes Annotated* 53:27D-312(a). A locality's plan to enter into an RCA must be submitted to COAH in its housing element plan and must include its reasons for entering into the agreement, the agreement itself, the number of units to be transferred, the compensation to be paid by the sending municipality to the receiver, and the nature and source of the compensation. The

amount of compensation must be based on "a weighted average of the costs of rehabilitation and new construction." There are no provisions for transferred funds to go to the inner cities with the greatest need for low-income housing.

A major rule, adopted in 1995, requires a minimum RCA payment of $20,000 per unit, with any money not needed for a particular housing unit to be used for additional housing.

78. The contentions of the public advocate were swept aside by several court opinions. See, especially, *Morris County Fair Housing Council*, 209 N.J. Super. 393, 507 A.2d 768, where Judge Skillman upheld the act's RCA provisions, primarily on the assumption that COAH would exercise its approval power "in a manner which appropriately implements the objectives of the Mount Laurel Doctrine." Ibid., 209 N.J. Super. 432, 507 A.2d 790.

79. *In re Township of Warren*, 247 N.J. Super. 146, 155, 588 A.2d 1227, 1232 (1991). Judge Skillman pointed out "that the particular RCA . . . makes good planning sense. Warren is a sprawling suburban municipality with no public transportation and with employment opportunities limited to an area along Route 78. On the other hand, New Brunswick is well served by bus and rail transit which provides ready access to employment opportunities." Ibid., 247 N.J. Super. 164, 588 A.2d 1236–37.

80. *New Jersey Statutes Annotated* 52:27E-31.

81. As long as the base allows for it, some 3,270 units are committed for transfer out of 48,493 units covered by COAH and the courts as of March 1993. This is 6.7 percent of total fair shares. At $20,500 per RCA, $64.3 million has been committed to fifteen urban-aid cities. If they had RCA'd to the limit, 24,250 units and $497 million would have been transferred.

82. The other side of the picture is that approximately $60 million has been transferred to urban areas to rehabilitate nearly 2,500 deficient units and to construct over 700 new units. Douglas Opalski, "COAH Summary" (paper prepared for Senate Community Affairs Committee, March 1992, mimeographed).

83. By January 31, 1995, Newark led the rest of the state in acquiring RCAs: 6 RCAs transferred 732 affordable housing units at an average cost of $18,335 per unit. (The average cost of constructing a new affordable housing unit or substantially rehabilitating an existing unit is estimated at $80,000.) Through February 1995, the highest price paid under an RCA was $27,500 per unit, paid by Hopewell to Trenton and by Franklin to Perth Amboy. The lowest price was $11,500 per unit, paid by Hamilton to Trenton.

84. In general, see Harold A. McDougal, "From Litigation to Legislation to Exclusionary Zoning Law," *Harvard Civil Rights—Civil Liberties Law Review* 22 (1987): 623; Rachel Fox, "Selling Out of *Mount Laurel*: Regional Contribution Agreements in New Jersey's Fair Housing Act," *Fordham Urban Law Journal* 16 (1988): 535.

85. The Fair Housing Act does provide appropriations, albeit of a minimal nature, for housing rehabilitation and for new low-cost rental units. To put a more positive spin on the use of RCAs, one could argue that they work like regional tax-base sharing, where two towns mutually agree to pool their resources and needs.

Chapter VII
. . . And the Judiciary Responds

1. See the cases and explanatory notes in Charles M. Haar and Michael Allan Wolf, *Land-Use Planning*, 4th ed. (Boston: Little, Brown, 1989), 629–45.

2. Ibid. *Pioneer Trust and Sav. Bank v. Village of Mount Prospect*, 22 Ill.2d 375, 176 N.E.2d 799 (1961), laid down the most stringent standard, allowing only those exactions "specifically and uniquely attributable" to the development. To the contrary is *Associated Home Builders v. Walnut Creek*, 4 Cal.3d 633, 484 P.2d 606 (1971), which requires only a reasonable connection between the growth caused by the development and the need for additional facilities. There are many variants between these extremes. The cases were lumped together in Justice Scalia's opinion in *Nollan v. California Coastal Commission*, 483 U.S. 825, 107 S. Ct. 3141 (1987). The U.S. Supreme Court has yet to speak directly on the issue, although *Dolan v. City of Tigard*, __ U.S. __, 114 S.Ct. 2309 (1994), moves it toward strict scrutiny.

3. *Nollan*, 483 U.S. 836, 107 S.Ct. 3148; *Dolan*, __ U.S. __, 114 S.Ct. 2317 (1994).

4. *Holmdel Builder's Ass'n v. Township of Holmdel*, 121 N.J. 550, 583 A.2d 277 (1990).

5. Ibid., 121 N.J. 557, 583 A.2d 280. The affordable housing fees ranged from $0.25 to $0.75 per square foot in Chester Township to $0.80 to $1.80 per square foot in Middleton Township. The townships of Chester and South Brunswick imposed a mandatory development fee on all new noninclusionary developments, and their ordinances did not give developers a density bonus in exchange for the fee. Holmdel Township gave developers a density bonus if they contributed to an affordable housing trust fund.

6. *Holmdel Builder's Ass'n v. Township of Holmdel*, 232 N.J. Super. 182, 195, 556 A.2d 1236, 1242 (1989).

7. The FHA does allude to fees in section 311(8), and municipal attorneys have pointed to other sections of the act as supporting this mechanism.

8. *Holmdel*, 121 N.J. 579, 583 A.2d 291.

9. Ibid.

10. Ibid.

11. The court's language skirts one difficult issue raised at the trial level—is the fee a kind of tax? If so, a different set of constitutional and legislative tests would have to be applied, testing developer fees under the uniformity standards in the constitution regarding comparable burden within a use category.

12. The court referred extensively to the studies of the linkage programs of Boston and San Francisco. See the pathbreaking analysis by Jerold S. Kayden and Robert Pollard, "Linkage Ordinances and Traditional Exactions Analysis: The Connection between Office Development and Housing," *Law and Contemporary Problems* 50 (1987): 127.

13. *Holmdel*, 121 N.J. 573, 583 A.2d 288.

14. Ibid., 121 N.J. 571, 583 A.2d 287. The relation called for in Justice Scalia's well-known *Nollan* opinion, 483 U.S. 825, 107 S.Ct. 3141, is not mentioned. Reasons commonly advanced for the strong causal nexus are that it en-

sures that a developer pays for the externalities necessitated by the development at the same time that it protects a developer from paying a disproportionate share of the costs of an improvement that also benefits others.

15. This is the basis for COAH's determination of the fees such that they equate with internal subsidies on inclusionary developments. By extension, the burden is spread more evenly among all new uses that help trigger the need for affordable housing, enjoy its provision (labor supply, for example), and also absorb the capacity for its provision. The court left open the constitutionality of nonresidential development fees not counterbalanced by density bonuses, reserving the question to itself—after advising COAH that it "might well choose to follow this approach." *Holmdel*, 121 N.J. 580, 583 A.2d 292. The court also invited (although maintaining silence as to how it might rule) future consideration of the right of individuals to seek refunds of fees that localities had collected prior to *Holmdel*. But a realistic opportunity for affordable housing in the metropolitan context will be the lodestar. The plaintiff New Jersey Builders Association sought a refund of the monies paid into the Chester Township affordable housing trust fund plus accrued interest. However, the appellate division ruled that COAH should be given a chance to decide the issue before judicial remedies become appropriate. See *Frank A. Greek & Sons, Inc. v. Township of South Brunswick*, 257 N.J. Super. 94, 607 A.2d 1359 (1992).

16. This will vary according to where the fees are set over time. COAH set the fees at 0.5 percent for noninclusionary residential uses. Some at the public hearings on the fees argued that the nonresidential fees may be consistently too low.

17. *Holmdel*, 121 N.J. 580, 583 A.2d 292. The appellate division had ruled that, as opposed to a voluntary fee, a "mandatory development fee applied indiscriminately as a price to build within a municipality has no 'real and substantial relationship to the regulation of land.'" *Holmdel*, 232 N.J. Super. 194–95, 556 A.2d 1242.

18. Since then, COAH has developed a position that localities must petition for substantive certification in order to collect developer fees. This indirect method of expanding its jurisdiction was attacked by the Department of Community Affairs: "Why deny one tool in an arsenal of tools to municipalities when some simple standard would suffice?"

19. *Holmdel*, 121 N.J. 580, 583 A.2d 292. A more typical example of judicial deference to COAH's competence is Judge Skillman's earlier ruling in *Warren Township* that although there is no express legislative authorization for occupancy preference for local residents, COAH "has the implied power to adopt regulations which authorize this preference." *In re Petition for Substantive Certification Filed by Warren Township*, 247 N.J. Super. 146, 171, 508 A.2d 1227, 1240 (1991). Nonetheless, in 1993 the supreme court struck down the balanced regulation issued by COAH in the *Warren* case of that year. See *In re Petition for Substantive Certification Filed by Warren Township*, 132 N.J. 1, 622 A.2d 1257 (1993).

20. *Van Dalen v. Township of Washington*, 120 N.J. 234, 244–45, 576 A.2d 819, 825 (1990).

21. *Holmdel*, 121 N.J. 573, 583 A.2d 288.

22. True, there is the statement in *Holmdel* that "it cannot be overstressed that the Legislature, through the FHA, intended to leave the specific methods of

compliance with Mt. Laurel in the hands of COAH and the municipalities, charging COAH with the singular responsibility for implementing the statute and developing the state's regulatory policy for affordable housing." Ibid., 121 N.J. 576, 583 A.2d 290. But the court offered its own policy readings, regardless.

23. Throughout the *Holmdel* opinion, the court stressed the similarities between development fee ordinances and mandatory set-asides and relied on Mount Laurel II to hold both exercises as legitimate regulatory measures. A more reticent approach may be adopted in other situations: standard off-site improvements, for example, while essential for land processing, are outside the realm of affordable housing and therefore may not be a subject on which the court presently desires to take a lead.

24. *Warren*, 132 N.J. 1, 622 A.2d 1257.

25. Ibid., 132 N.J. 28, 622 A.2d 1270.

26. Ibid., 132 N.J. 39, 622 A.2d 1277.

27. Ibid., 132 N.J. 30, 622 A.2d 1272.

28. In *Warren*, it should be noted, the racial characteristics of commuters to the towns were not available and not definitive. Ibid., 132 N.J. 41, 622 A.2d 1278. Had they been, the court might have reached a different conclusion. For some towns, for example, anecdotal data shows a relatively higher share of jobs held by minorities in the town than in the region overall; indeed, many entry-level jobs happened to be for security guards and custodial personnel. Thus minorities might well have benefited from the overturned standards setting aside half of all new units for people living *or working* in the municipalities.

29. The court pointed out that, assuming the regional obligation pursuant to the FHA is not diluted, a municipality may zone for additional affordable housing reserved exclusively for local needs.

30. Justice Stewart G. Pollock, in a concurring opinion, based invalidation of COAH's regulation on its internal inconsistency. He observed, "I believe it is unnecessary and unwise for the Court to proceed to decide that the regulation is unconstitutional . . . because a constitutional decision may inhibit other branches and levels of government from taking action to vindicate the *Mount Laurel* obligation without judicial intervention." *Warren*, 132 N.J. 43, 622 A.2d 1279.

31. *Holmdel*, 121 N.J. 562, 583 A.2d 283.

32. Ibid., 121 N.J. 577, 583 A.2d 290.

33. Ibid., 121 N.J. 578, 583 A.2d 291.

34. See also *Alexander's Department Stores of New Jersey, Inc. v. Borough of Paramus*, 125 N.J. 100, 592 A.2d 1168 (1991).

35. *Holmdel*, 121 N.J. 580, 583 A.2d 292.

36. The council issued its development fee regulations on January 21, 1992. It now requires an expanded version of the housing element, which must include a spending plan with a detailed schedule of how fees will be used to promote affordable housing and including mechanisms for meeting shortfalls. There is a 20 percent limit on administrative costs and a 30 percent minimum for affordability assistance, which means that only 70 percent (even of in-lieu payments) can be channeled into housing programs, such as funding an RCA. For example, if a town negotiates a $20,000-per-unit development fee in lieu of construction, only $14,000 per unit would be available, which is still substantially above the $9,500

unit cost of the twenty-nine RCAs executed as of June 1992. See Philip B. Caton and Karen Kaminsky, "Urban Development Fees to Render Housing Affordable," *Housing New Jersey* 2 (June 1992): 3.

The regulations follow the court in insisting that there be a comprehensive and defensible plan and program for converting funds into affordable housing and in requiring a plan for spending revenues derived from the fees. On the reciprocal requirement, a maximum fee applies where there is no compensatory benefit; the rules allow higher fees of up to 6 percent of equalized assessed valuation on non-inclusionary residential development by allowing a compensatory benefit (such as a density bonus). COAH is motivated partly by fears that excessive fees could become a new exclusionary device. See Douglas Opalski, "COAH's Emerging Mandatory Development Fee Rule" (paper prepared for New Jersey Conference of Mayors, August 15, 1991, mimeographed). It nonetheless estimates that fees could generate up to $38 million per year for low-income housing—nearly quadruple the annual amount New Jersey receives from the federal government for housing. See Douglas Opalski, "COAH Summary" (paper prepared for Senate Community Affairs Committee, March 1992, mimeographed).

37. *Warren*, 132 N.J. 40, 622 A.2d 1277.

38. Recall the court's admonition in Mount Laurel III that "if . . . the Act . . . achieves nothing but delay, the judiciary will be forced to resume its appropriate role." *Hills Development Co. v. Township of Bernards*, 103 N.J. 1, 23, 510 A.2d 621, 633 (1986). It is also useful to remember that the legislative branch expects and invites courts to participate in the evolution of statutory guidelines as unforeseen or unacknowledged realities intrude. See Irving R. Kaufman, "Anatomy of Decisionmaking," *Fordham Law Review* 53 (1984): 1.

39. *Warren*, 132 N.J. 41, 622 A.2d 1278.

40. As noted by the court itself,

We understand the enormous difficulty of achieving a political consensus that might lead to significant legislation enforcing the constitutional mandate better than we can, legislation that might completely remove this Court from those controversies. But enforcement of constitutional rights cannot await a supporting political consensus. So while we have always preferred legislative to judicial action in this field, we shall continue—until the legislature acts—to do our best to uphold the constitutional obligation that underlies the *Mount Laurel* doctrine. That is our duty. We may not build houses, but we do enforce the Constitution. (Mount Laurel II, 92 N.J. 212, 456 A.2d 417)

41. Benjamin N. Cardozo, *The Nature of the Judicial Process* (New Haven, Conn.: Yale University Press, 1921), 94.

## Chapter VIII
## The New World of Judicial Remedies

1. *Davis v. Board of School Commissioners of Mobile County*, 402 U.S. 33, 37, 91 S. Ct. 1289, 1292 (1971).

2. See Donald L. Horowitz, *The Courts and Social Policy* (Washington, D.C.: Brookings Institution, 1977), for a pessimistic analysis of the ability of courts to

reorder institutional breakdowns; cf. Paul L. Rosen, *The Supreme Court and So-cial Science* (Urbana: University of Illinois Press, 1972).

3. Gerald N. Rosenberg, *The Hollow Hope: Can Courts Bring about Social Change?* (Chicago: University of Chicago Press, 1991). Rosenberg suggests that courts can never be effective producers of social reform.

4. See Albert O. Hirschman, *The Rhetoric of Reaction: Perversity, Futility, Jeopardy* (Cambridge, Mass.: Belknap Press, 1991).

5. See the testimony of Robert W. Burchell before the Assembly Housing Committee, Trenton, New Jersey, November 23, 1992 (mimeographed), 9.

6. There are always indirect effects on whose quantification experts disagree. For example, a group of New Jersey towns, mostly in Bergen and Essex counties, is producing affordable units even though not yet bound to do so by either COAH or the courts, induced by the presence of fair share requirements. This "gray" inventory is not included among the achievements of Mount Laurel.

7. The opinions have been invoked more recently to support legislation for enhancing rental housing construction. See, for example, N.J. Assembly AHO Committee, Amendments to Assembly no. 89, June 7, 1993.

8. *The Federalist, No. 78*, ed. Benjamin Fletcher Wright (Cambridge, Mass.: Belknap Press, 1961), 489.

9. This pattern had been consistent ever since the local ability to zone was clarified in the New Jersey Constitution of 1947.

10. See Charles M. Haar, "Zoning for Minimum Standards: The *Wayne Township* Case," *Harvard Law Review* 66 (1953): 1051.

11. For examples of such charges, see Archibald Cox, "The New Dimensions of Constitutional Adjudication," *Washington Law Review* 51 (1976): 791; Colin S. Diver, "The Judge as Political Powerbroker: Superintending Structural Change in Public Institutions," *Virginia Law Review* 65 (1979): 43; Nathan Glazer, "Should Judges Administer Social Services?" *Public Interest* 50 (1978): 64; Horowitz, *The Courts and Social Policy*; Jerome G. Rose, "Waning Judicial Legitimacy: The Price of Judicial Promulgation of Urban Policy," *Urban Lawyer* 20 (1988): 801; and Rosenberg, *The Hollow Hope*.

12. Cited by Milton Katz, *A Service in Memory of Paul Abraham Freund, 1908–1992* (Cambridge, Mass.: Harvard Law School, 1992), 30.

13. See Isaiah Berlin, *The Crooked Timber of Humanity: Chapters in the History of Ideas*, ed. Henry Hardy (London: John Murray, 1990).

14. Rosenberg discusses the difficulty of generalizations about the efficacy of courts in his perceptive book *Hollow Hope*. He suggests that constraints limit courts, but when political, social, and economic conditions support change, courts can effectively produce significant social reform. Yet the Mount Laurel type of institutional litigation is interesting precisely for its demonstration of the reverse: the courts' confrontation, indeed disregard, of the popular will neverthe-less permitted significant changes. Even Rosenberg's prima facie reasonable argu-ment that litigation must be well grounded in precedent and elite support for such outcomes is not true of the Mount Laurel situation. Nor, finally, can criticism turn on the courts' lack of implementation powers since they developed when necessary—and more than adequately to meet the problem of recalcitrance.

15. See Thomas O. Sargentich, "The Contemporary Debate about Legislative-

Executive Separation of Powers," *Cornell Law Review* 72 (1987): 430. The separation of powers is part of the New Jersey governmental structure. N.J. Constitution, art. 3, par. 1. This is elucidated in *Knight v. Margate*, 86 N.J. 374, 387–88, 431 A.2d 833, 840 (1981):

> Governmental checks and balances are an integrated feature of our fundamental organic law. . . . It is a constitutional axiom that each branch of government is distinct and is the repository of the powers which are unique to it; the members or representatives of one branch cannot arrogate powers of another branch. The constitutional spirit inherent in the separation of governmental powers contemplates that each branch of government will exercise fully its own powers without transgressing upon powers rightfully belonging to a cognate branch. Each branch of government is counseled and restrained by the constitution not to seek dominance or hegemony over the other branches.

16. There is comity, however. The judiciary relied on that principle to fashion an inclusionary solution by default, encouraged judicial action, and then condoned administrative solutions in tandem with its own.

17. In *The Federalist, No. 47*, Madison wrote, "On the slightest view of the British Constitution, we must perceive that the legislative, executive, and judiciary departments are by no means totally separate and distinct from each other." He continued, "Likewise in no state constitution has a competent provision been made for maintaining in practice the separation delineated on paper" (337).

18. For a stimulating view of the appropriateness of judicial intervention, see Philip Bobbitt, "Is Law Politics?" *Stanford Law Review* 41 (1989): 1233.

19. Roger J. Traynor, "La Rude Vita, la Dolce Giustizia; or, Hard Cases Can Make Good Law," *University of Chicago Law Review* 29 (1962): 223. As he observed of the judge, "As continuity editor of a hodgepodge of materials he must be alert to the exaggerations and understatements of the script writers as he distills the plot from their thick adversary versions of what is past and not forgotten but unfortunately distorted by the tricks of memory." Ibid.

20. In an interview, a federal judge, with some hesitation, conceded that adhering too slavishly to tradition and overlooking the altered circumstances posed by institutional litigation caused him—mistakenly—not to discuss matters with his master away from the parties and their lawyers.

21. See the perceptive work of Susan Sturm, "Resolving the Remedial Dilemma: Strategies of Judicial Intervention in Prisons," *University of Pennsylvania Law Review* 138 (1990): 805.

22. See Peter H. Schuck, *Suing Government: Citizen Remedies for Official Wrongs* (New Haven, Conn.: Yale University Press, 1983), 28.

23. Horowitz, *The Courts and Social Policy*, 34.

24. See, e.g., Alexander M. Bickel, *The Supreme Court and the Idea of Progress* (New York: Harper and Row, 1970).

25. Despite surface appearances, remedies for exclusionary land-use regulations may be easier for the judiciary in terms of institutional capacity than are other types of complex litigation.

26. Some have even complained that the court's failure to specify its constitutional mandate "slowed voluntary compliance by municipalities because the

municipalities remained uncertain as to what their obligations entailed." G. Alan Tarr and Russell S. Harrison, "Legitimacy and Capacity in State Supreme Court Policymaking: The New Jersey Court and Exclusionary Zoning," *Rutgers Law Journal* 15 (1984): 519. An interesting speculation into the tempting world of might-have-beens arises from the long delay between Mount Laurel I and Mount Laurel II. Had Justice Hall's ruling been implemented sooner, would the racial composition of those occupying the affordable housing been different? Had Mount Laurel I been effective from the start, it might have mitigated extensive improvements to intrasuburban and interstate access by requiring better transportation matches locally between consumer income and housing costs. New Jersey's most recent long-range state transportation plan, done in 1984, suggests intrasuburban and intersuburban improvements to both Philadelphia and New York City, as opposed to a focused urban-suburban pattern of access improvements within the state itself. Some key transportation officials believe that the access system has been playing catch-up—that is, simply relieving the major backlog of congestion—and thus following, not leading, land use. In other words, the market forces of suburbanizing jobs and the middle class—especially after the recession of 1981–82—have driven the access pattern and continue to do so. In the period between the two Mount Laurel decisions, for example, the transportation system shifted so that professional and financial service groups could commute readily from the suburbs to the major central cities, a pattern that rendered economically and logically feasible the movement of yuppies into the Mount Laurel units built after the second supreme court opinion.

Regarding the issue of speed, *In re Paramus Substantive Certification No. 47*, 249 N.J. Super. 1, 591 A.2d 1345 (1991), provides a warning of a different sort. There, the appellate court chastised COAH by raising legal considerations of site plan–planning board relief at the expense of a fair share plan. Based on the decision, inclusionary site issues would be bifurcated into constitutional fair share issues for COAH and related legal issues for judicial litigation, the realistic opportunity of sites notwithstanding. Under this order, COAH certification and housing production can be undermined with a subsequent lawsuit raising claims of spot zoning, which up until the decision had been viewed as a make-weight argument. Since towns are vulnerable to this allegation every time a disgruntled property owner not included in the local fair share plan takes exception to a neighbor who may benefit under the municipal housing element, *Paramus* encourages litigation and delay and discourages compliance and voluntary participation with COAH.

This is the sort of issue that runs counter to the comity one hopes to see between the judicial and administrative branches. It is ironic that in *Hills* the supreme court assigned to COAH the quasi-judicial job of reviewing resource restraints (and balancing related equities with respect to access to sewer, water, transportation services, and thus development), whereas the appellate court in *Paramus* is very careful to reserve for the judiciary fairness and equality issues involving the selection of sites that may involve claims of spot zoning.

27. See Theodore Eisenberg and Stephen C. Yeazell, "The Ordinary and the Extraordinary in Institutional Litigation," *Harvard Law Review* 93 (1980): 466.

28. "One of the most important considerations governing the exercise of equitable power is a proper respect for the integrity and function of local govern-

ment institutions." *Missouri v. Jenkins*, 495 U.S. 33, 51, 110 S.Ct. 1651, 1663 (1990).

29. See Stephen C. Yeazell, "Intervention and the Idea of Litigation: A Commentary on the Los Angeles School Case," *UCLA Law Review* 25 (1977): 244. For a study of the most common area of institutional restructuring, see David L. Kirp, "Legalism and Politics in School Desegregation," *Wisconsin Law Review* (1981): 924. See also Vincent M. Nathan, "The Use of Masters in Institutional Reform Litigation," *University of Toledo Law Review* 10 (1979): 419.

30. See Wayne D. Brazil, "Special Masters in Complex Cases: Extending the Judiciary or Reshaping Adjudication?" *University of Chicago Law Review* 53 (1986): 394.

31. Cf. *White v. Weiser*, 412 U.S. 783, 794–97, 93 S.Ct. 2348, 2354–56 (1973).

32. For example, Chief Justice Wilentz might have been able to muster support by permitting the payment of fees to public interest lawyers who succeeded in the litigation. Since he did not do so, the private bar had another reason for not rallying around the issue.

33. See Timothy G. Little, "Court-Appointed Special Masters in Complex Environmental Litigation: *City of Quincy v. MDC*," *Harvard Environmental Law Review* 8 (1984): 435.

34. Mount Laurel II, 92 N.J. 287, 456 A.2d 456.

## Chapter IX
## Discretion and Its Discontents

1. The most discerning effort yet to construct boundaries around the setting of remedies is Susan P. Sturm, "A Normative Theory of Public Law Remedies," *Georgetown Law Journal* 79 (1991): 1355.

2. Cf. Chief Justice Burger's statement in *Swann v. Charlotte-Mecklenburg Board of Education*, 402 U.S. 1, 31, 91 S. Ct. 1267, 1283 (1971): "In seeking to define the scope of remedial power of courts . . . words are poor instruments to convey the sense of basic fairness inherent in equity. Substance, not semantics, must govern."

3. See Charles M. Haar and Michael Allan Wolf, *Land-Use Planning*, 4th ed. (Boston: Little, Brown, 1989). In general, these are devices aimed at overcoming the rigidities of the districting employed by traditional Euclidean zoning.

4. Normally, the possibility of reversal by an appellate court haunts the lower courts as they wield their remedial powers, exerting a substantial moderating influence on excess. In interviews, the trial judges asserted this more than once, especially in the light of the numerous reversals brought about by the *Hills* case.

5. See Frank M. Coffin, "The Frontier of Remedies: A Call for Exploration," *California Law Review* 67 (1979): 983.

6. See Lon L. Fuller, "The Forms and Limits of Adjudication," *Harvard Law Review* 92 (1978): 353. But cf. Abram Chayes, "The Role of the Judge in Public Law Litigation," *Harvard Law Review* 89 (1976): 1281; Owen M. Fiss, "Foreword: The Forms of Justice," *Harvard Law Review* 93 (1979): 1; and Judith Resnik, "Managerial Judges," *Harvard Law Review* 96 (1982): 374.

7. *Hart v. Community School Board*, 383 F. Supp. 699, 766–67 (E.D.N.Y. 1974).

8. Ibid., 766.

9. There is a paradoxical contention that institutional litigation remedies stress theory over practice: since the judiciary errs in relying too heavily on theoretical concepts offered by academic experts, it ignores recommendations supplied by practitioners. This argument is raised in strongest terms by Nathan Glazer, "Should Judges Administer Social Services?" *Public Interest* 50 (1978): 78–79.

10. See, e.g., Abraham Lincoln's address at Springfield, Illinois, on July 17, 1858, in Roy P. Basler, ed., *The Collected Works of Abraham Lincoln* (New Brunswick, N.J.: Rutgers University Press, 1953), 2:517.

11. The very idea of American exceptionalism rests on the special role of the courts and their power to declare unconstitutional or ultra vires acts of the majority; a source of friction and consolation, this role underlies the great debates over recent appointments to the U.S. Supreme Court.

12. See the pathbreaking work by Peter H. Schuck, *Suing Government: Citizen Remedies for Official Wrongs* (New Haven, Conn.: Yale University Press, 1983), especially chap. 7.

13. Cf. Ronald Dworkin, *Taking Rights Seriously* (Cambridge, Mass.: Harvard University Press, 1978); William A. Fletcher, "The Discretionary Constitution: Institutional Remedies and Judicial Legitimacy," *Yale Law Journal* 91 (1982): 635; and Glazer, "Should Judges Administer Social Services?" 64.

## Chapter X
## Leadership in Institutional Reform

1. One exception to the rule of political inertia is the public interest segment of the New Jersey bar. It can act quickly because it is dominated by a unitary purpose and its national role, after all, is to support the court. But when carrying the burden of a large message, the voice of the public interest bar often is too shrill to be truly effective.

2. Mount Laurel II, 92 N.J. 198, 456 A.2d 410.

3. Ibid., 92 N.J. 295, 456 A.2d 460.

4. Poking behind the scene in one case reveals a story with a twist. The COAH-precredited need for Cherry Hill was initially put at 2,295. With a cap of 1,000 units and additional credits, it was further mediated down to 819. Then Cherry Hill refused to accept even this since the whole town had only some 1,500 dwelling units. Back in court, its fair share was set at 1,000, but a lack of vacant developable land ended in there still being no compliance plan. The emerging COAH methodology would now put the township's precredited need at 1,215.

5. See the engrossing description by Marcia Steinberg, *Adaptations to the Activist Court Ruling: Aftermath of the Mount Laurel II Decision for Lower Income Housing* (Cambridge, Mass.: Lincoln Institute of Land Policy, 1989). See also Robert C. Holmes, "A Black Perspective on Mount Laurel II: Toward a Black Fair Share," *Seton Hall Law Review* 14 (1984): 944.

6. Some have pointed out the price of this success: "Black electoral success alone cannot transform the depressed political and economic state of the black community, especially given that blacks are concentrated in politically impotent and economically isolated parts of urban metropolitan areas where racial polarization continues." Lani Guinier, "The Triumph of Tokenism: The Voting Rights Act and the Theory of Black Electoral Success," *Michigan Law Review* 89 (1991): 1131–32.

7. Some, discouraged by the results, have criticized COAH for not actively encouraging affirmative marketing and for leaving outreach to developers, so that prospective applicants never hear of the program. See Ellen Lovejoy, "Mount Laurel Scorecard," *Planning* (May 1992): 10.

8. The situation is not too different from the difficulty plaintiffs encountered in the famous *Gautreaux* litigation, *Hills v. Gautreaux*, 425 U.S. 284, 96 S.Ct. 1538 (1976), in persuading public housing tenants to stay in projects in Chicago at a time when people did not believe the rehabilitation promises the government made. Cf. Drew S. Days III, "School Desegregation Law in the 1980's: Why Isn't Anybody Laughing?" *Yale Law Journal* 95 (1986): 1737.

9. See Charles M. Haar, *Between the Idea and the Reality: A Study in the Origin, Fate, and Legacy of the Model Cities Program* (Boston: Little, Brown, 1975).

10. The paucity of the results may be due to a failure of imagination. Lack of knowledge is hard to believe, in view of the widespread political repercussions of Mount Laurel, but marketing and applicant-screening activities also affect the demographic makeup of the set-aside units; rather than the region, especially the inner cities, the applicant pool is drawn from the immediate area of the development.

11. See Jane Wheatley, "Marketing, Long-Term Planning Key to Mount Laurel Success," *Housing New Jersey* 3 (February 1994): 6.

12. While the equitable decree has to be tailored to the extent of the violation, its primary purpose is to make success possible. A court may have to add broad-based education and community relations programs, even when the immediate violation before it relates only to affordable housing. The Mount Laurel remedies, to their detriment, lacked a broader structure. Without a full panoply of social efforts—education, day care, job training—lower- and upper-income residents continue to feel estranged from one another, generating greater social distance even as geographical distance is reduced. More specifically, the antidiscrimination statutes—especially the laws dealing with lending practices—require strenuous efforts by all branches. See "Discrimination in the Housing and Mortgage Markets," *Housing Policy Debate* 3, no. 2 (1992): 185.

13. *Hills Development Co. v. Township of Bernards*, 103 N.J. 1, 24, 510 A.2d 621, 634 (1986).

14. Melinda Hennberger, "A Yonkers Street: Whites, Blacks, and Silence," *New York Times*, October 15, 1992, A1.

15. See John Robert Meyer and Jose A. Gomez-Ibanez, *Autos, Transit, and Cities* (Cambridge, Mass.: Harvard University Press, 1981).

16. This approach differs from that of Owen Fiss. Both approaches agree,

however, on the judge's obligation to participate in a dialogue. See Owen M. Fiss, "Objectivity and Interpretation," *Stanford Law Review* 34 (1982): 739.

17. Mount Laurel II, 92 N.J 209, 456 A.2d 415.

18. American Bar Association, *Model Code of Judicial Conduct*, Canon 3(b)(9) (Chicago: American Bar Association, 1990).

19. Quoted in the *Bergen Record*, February 14, 1983, B1.

20. Advisory Commission on Regulatory Barriers to Affordable Housing, *"Not in My Back Yard": Removing Barriers to Affordable Housing* (Washington, D.C.: U.S. Department of Housing and Urban Development, 1991).

## Chapter XI
## The Last Recourse

1. Cf. the well-known comment by Justice Jackson during oral argument in *Brown v. Board of Education*: "I suppose that realistically the reason this case is here is that action couldn't be obtained from Congress." Bureau of National Affairs, *U.S. Law Week* 22 (1953): 3161.

2. This simply elaborates a traditional insight. As John Gray put it, judges "determine duties and the corresponding rights upon the application of persons claiming those rights." John Chipman Gray, *The Nature and Sources of the Law*, 2d ed. (New York: Macmillan, 1931), 114.

3. *Rhodes v. Chapman*, 452 U.S. 337, 359, 101 S.Ct. 2392, 2406 (1981) (Brennan, J., concurring).

4. *The Federalist, No. 57*, 383.

5. For a cogent analysis of the political difficulties inhering in restraining the exclusionary practices of suburban municipalities, see Michael H. Schill, "The Federal Role in Reducing Regulatory Barriers to Affordable Housing in the Suburbs," *Journal of Law and Politics* 8 (1992): 703.

6. *Baker v. Carr*, 369 U.S. 186, 82 S.Ct. 691 (1962).

7. In theory, a state could reorder municipal boundaries, even wipe them out, but the political reality of local sovereignty makes this more illusion than reality.

8. The broader perspective is already manifest in the recent cases requiring localities to take regional needs into account when enacting local land-use controls. Cf. *Golden v. Planning Board of Town of Ramapo*, 30 N.Y.2d 359, 285 N.E.2d 291 (1972).

9. See, e.g., Robert Jerome Glennon, *The Iconoclast as Reformer: Jerome Frank's Impact on American Law* (Ithaca, N.Y.: Cornell University Press, 1985), 102–28.

10. Learned Hand, *The Spirit of Liberty*, 3d ed. (New Haven, Conn.: Yale University Press, 1960), 15.

11. John Hart Ely, *Democracy and Distrust: A Theory of Judicial Review* (Cambridge, Mass.: Harvard University Press, 1980). Cf. the critiques of Frank I. Michelman, "Process and Property in Constitutional Theory," *Cleveland State Law Review* 30 (1982): 577; and Paul Brest, "The Substance of Process," *Ohio State Law Journal* 42 (1981): 131.

12. In cases of ordinary law-breaking, legislative amendment can easily reconcile the norm to the social practice.

Chapter XII
National Ramifications

1. Anatole France, *The Red Lily* (New York: Modern Library, 1917), 75.

2. Benjamin N. Cardozo, *The Nature of the Judicial Process* (New Haven, Conn.: Yale University Press, 1921), 141. One school of political scientists agrees: "It would appear to be somewhat naive to assume that the Supreme Court either would or could play the role of Galahad." Robert A. Dahl, "Decision-Making in a Democracy: The Supreme Court as a National Policy-Maker," *Journal of Public Law* 6 (1957): 284.

3. Cf. Michael Walzer, *Spheres of Justice: A Defense of Pluralism and Equality* (New York: Basic Books, 1983).

4. Another word is necessary regarding the builder's remedy. The FHA does not empower COAH to act on its own to enforce the fair share requirement affirmatively. Nor does the agency have power to impose sanctions for failure to provide the appropriate number of affordable housing units. In the end, the ability to invoke the court to issue a builder's remedy serves as the defense against local recalcitrance.

5. *New Jersey Statutes Annotated* 52:27D-303. What would have been believable is that the FHA took a few steps back from the remedies proposed in Mount Laurel II. Specifically, there is the mixed motivation of the RCA and the reduction in the number of low- and moderate-income housing units a town must provide.

6. *In re Petition for Substantive Certification Filed by Warren Township*, 132 N.J. 1, 41, 622 A.2d 1257, 1278 (1993).

7. Environment restrictions in the Pinelands, sewer bans, and built-up "Fanwood" municipalities are still entrenched to a large degree.

8. Robert W. Burchell, David Listokin, and Arlene Pashman, *Regional Housing Opportunities for Lower-Income Housing* (New Brunswick, N.J.: Center for Urban Policy Research of Rutgers University, 1994), 23.

9. There are contradictory signs, however. The demand for market housing may not be as intense as it was with the baby boomer generation, so the four-to-one Mount Laurel ratio may not work: with the need for affordable housing increasing and the household formation rates of the well-to-do going down, it may not be possible for significant low-cost units to be carried by sufficient market units. If increased density will not suffice to make a project feasible for a private developer, other sources of subsidy will be required to offset the developer's costs.

10. Douglas Opalski, "COAH Progress Report" (March 19, 1992, mimeographed).

11. New Jersey's total housing stock increased 10.9 percent between 1980 and 1990, with some 234,000 sale units and 13,000 rental units added to the state's inventory.

Of the 2.8 million households in the state, 251,000 very-low-income renter households devote more than 30 percent of their income to rent and utilities, while 94,000 very-low-income households that do own their homes devote more than 50 percent of their income to housing and utilities, and an additional 73,000 households devote between 30 and 50 percent to these purposes. Put another way, the majority of poor families in New Jersey spend over 35 percent of their income for housing, a figure that rises to over 50 percent in many cases.

12. Federal and state subsidies will be a necessary component of any overall comprehensive housing program intended to address this issue.

13. See Justice Pashman's concurring opinion in *Oakwood at Madison, Inc. v. Township of Madison*, 72 N.J. 481, 558, 371 A.2d 1192, 1230 (1977). Cf. Martha Lamar, Alan Mallach, and John M. Payne, "Mount Laurel at Work: Affordable Housing in New Jersey, 1983–1988," *Rutgers Law Review* 41 (1989): 1199.

14. This, apparently, has been the effect of the decree in the *Gautreaux* litigation. See Henry G. Cisneros, ed., *Interwoven Destinies: Cities and the Nation* (New York: Norton, 1993).

The siting of public housing in the Chicago area has been the center of one of the longest metropolitan land-use battles. See *Hills v. Gautreaux*, 425 U.S. 284, 286–92, 96 S.Ct. 1538, 1541–44 (1976), which describes the litigation history, and *Gautreaux v. Landrieu*, 523 F.Supp. 665, 667–69 (N.D.Ill. 1981), which sets forth the consent decree. The program provides continuing support—psychological and social, as well as financial—to help minority households move to the suburbs. Studies of the program show that, thus far, adults are able to locate and keep jobs and children do much better in suburban schools. See James E. Rosenbaum, Nancy Fishman, Alison Brett, and Patricia Meaden, "Can the Kerner Commission's Housing Strategy Improve Employment, Education, and Social Integration for Low-Income Blacks?" *North Carolina Law Review* 71 (1993): 1519.

15. *Warren*, 131 N.J. 1, 622 A.2d 1257. In their 1989 Study, "Mount Laurel at Work," Lamar, Mallach, and Payne found that most residents of Mount Laurel units came from either the same municipality or a nearby municipality ten miles or less away (1257).

16. Mount Laurel I accepted the defense's representation that the township was not motivated by intent or desire to exclude on the basis of race. In later litigations, the public advocate introduced evidence of racial bias to counter townships' arguments that African-Americans and Hispanic-Americans did not want to move out of the familiar surroundings of inner cities.

17. As Hall framed the legal issue, it was whether Mount Laurel could "make it physically and economically impossible to provide" affordable housing "for the various categories of persons who need and want it and thereby" exclude people "because of the limited extent of their income and resources." Mount Laurel I, 67 N.J. 173, 336 A.2d 724.

18. The number of inner-city neighborhoods with non-Hispanic whites in the majority and with poverty rates of at least 40 percent grew by 141 percent between 1979 and 1989. See Urban Institute, *Policy and Research Report* 11 (Fall 1993).

19. *Shelley v. Kraemer*, 334 U.S. 1, 68 S.Ct. 836 (1948).

20. The New York courts, for example, have followed the Mount Laurel Doctrine, though only in part, leaving considerable confusion in their wake. *Berenson v. Town of New Castle*, 38 N.Y.2d 102, 378 N.Y.S.2d 672 (1975), ruled that local zoning had to consider the effect on regional housing needs. New York is

closer to Mount Laurel I than II in its refusal to impose specific unit goals or affirmative obligations. Instead of fair share, it uses "some general notion of [a town's] expected [housing] contribution." *Blitz v. Town of New Castle*, 94 A.D.2d 92, 98, 463 N.Y.S.2d 832, 836 (1983). Unlike New Jersey municipalities, New York's are not directly required to eliminate regulations resulting in costs over and above those required by health and safety. In *Suffolk Housing Services v. Town of Brookhaven*, 70 N.Y.2d 122, 517 N.Y.S.2d 924 (1987), the court required the identification of a specific site and a particular developer before it would grant relief. Cf. *Britton v. Town of Chester*, 134 N.H. 434, 445, 595 A.2d 492, 498 (1991), which found the local ordinance to be "blatantly exclusionary" of affordable housing and even ordered a builder's remedy. See John M. Payne, "From the Courts: Exclusionary Zoning and the 'Chester Doctrine,'" *Real Estate Law Journal* 20 (1992): 366.

The Pennsylvania Supreme Court was influenced by Mount Laurel I in *Township of Willistown v. Chesterdale Farms, Inc.*, 426 Pa. 445, 341 A.2d 466 (1975), which found a failure to zone for a fair share of the regional need for a particular form of housing, and in *Surrick v. Zoning Hearing Bd. of Upper Providence Township*, 476 Pa. 182, 382 A.2d 105 (1977), which declared the ordinance invalid because it did not provide a regional fair share of multifamily housing. In three post-*Surrick* cases, however, a sharply divided supreme court struggled with the implications and scope of its fair share mandate. In *In re Appeal of M. A. Kravitz Co.*, 501 Pa. 200, 460 A.2d 1075 (1983), the plurality found that the board of supervisors for Wrightstown Township—given the absence of major employers within the township, the lack of major highway links with Trenton and Philadelphia, and expert testimony that the "area has experienced little growth in the past and is designated as an area slated for little growth in the future"—had legitimately denied a zoning amendment that would have allowed the plaintiff to create a town house development on its ninety-six-acre parcel. 501 Pa. 214, 460 A.2d 1082. Justice Hutchinson, one of three dissenters, was disturbed by the township's "total exclusion of townhouses." 501 Pa. 221, 460 A.2d 1086.

Two days later the court decided *In re Appeal of Elocin, Inc.*, 501 Pa. 348, 461 A.2d 771 (1983). In another plurality opinion, the court wrote: "We do not agree that a municipality must necessarily provide for every conceivable use. Where a municipality provides for a reasonable share of multi-family dwellings [semi-detached homes, two-family homes, and apartment homes with up to four units] as Springfield has done [12 percent of its housing units], it need not provide for every conceivable subcategory of such dwellings." 501 Pa. 353, 461 A.2d 773. Thus the town's rejection of Elocin's proposal "to construct 567 mid- or high-rise apartment units and 305 townhouse units" was not unconstitutional. 501 Pa. 350, 461 A.2d 772.

Two years after this apparent shift from the activism of the 1970s, in *Fernley v. Board of Supervisors of Schuylkill Township*, 509 Pa. 413, 502 A.2d 585 (1985), a four-member majority decided an issue unresolved since *Surrick*: it found the balancing test appropriate for de facto exclusion inappropriate for municipalities engaged in de jure bans, even if the municipality could demonstrate that it projected little or no growth in the future. Predictably, there were dissents, objecting both to the reformulation of the court's strategy and to the extreme remedy ordered by the majority: "remand . . . to the Court of Common Pleas for approval of appellants' proposed development [245 acres with garden apartments, town houses, and quadraplexes] unless the appellee can show that appellants' plan is incompatible with the site or reasonable, pre-existing health and safety codes and regulations." 509 Pa. 425, 502 A.2d 591.

Innovative legislative programs based on portions of the Mount Laurel Doctrine can also be found in California, in Orange County and San Francisco; in Montgomery County, Maryland, and in Hartford, Connecticut. Statutes in California and Connecticut establish guidelines for judicial review of local zoning decisions that deny permits for affordable housing. For example, California's statute places the burden on municipalities to demonstrate that exclusion is justified by legitimate planning needs. *California Government Code*, sec. 65589.5[d], 65589.5[h][2], and 65589.6 (St. Paul, Minn.: West, 1994). Connecticut also shifts the burden of demonstrating that substantial public interests outweigh the need for affordable housing. *Connecticut General Statutes Annotated*, sec. 8–30g (St. Paul, Minn.: West, 1994). It also follows Mount Laurel II in assigning all such appeals to a small number of judges. Ibid., sec. 8–30g[b].

Oregon's statewide planning system adopts portions of the Mount Laurel Doctrine although section 197.313 explicitly rejects affirmative duties to satisfy fair share requirements. *Oregon Revised Statutes*, sec. 5197-.005-.860 (Salem, Or.: Oregon Legislative Counsel Committee, 1994). Changes were also made to the Comprehensive Housing Affordability Strategy of HUD and the Section 8 Portability Policy partly as a result of the New Jersey experience. The tested allocation procedures of the New Jersey program are the model, among others, for the South Central (Connecticut) Regional Council of Governments, the Westchester Housing Implementation Commission, and the programs in Riverside, California. Cf. Burchell, Listokin, and Pashman, *Regional Housing Opportunities*. For an analysis of federal remedies, see Jones J. Hartnett, "Affordable Housing, Exclusionary Zoning, and American Apartheid: Using Title VIII to Foster Statewide Racial Integration," *New York University Law Review* 68 (1993): 89, 92–94, 111–14.

21. As Mount Laurel II put it, "Those regulations that do not provide the requisite opportunity for a fair share of the region's need for low and moderate income housing conflict with the general welfare and violate the state constitutional requirements of substantive due process and equal protection." Mount Laurel II, 92 N.J. 208–9, 456 A.2d 415.

22. *Warren*, 132 N.J. 39, 622 A.2d 1277 (emphasis in original).

23. *Warren*, 132 N.J. 31, 622 A.2d 1272 (citing *New Jersey Statutes Annotated* 52:27D-302a, 303). The act acknowledges the statutory scheme as incorporating constitutional obligations for regional considerations and planning concepts.

24. Two recent U.S. Supreme Court opinions question the validity presumption in cases involving the taking of property. Footnote 3 of Justice Scalia's opinion in *Nollan v. California Coastal Commission*, 483 U.S. 825, 836, 107 S.Ct. 3141, 3148 (1987), threatens to overturn the reasonable relationship test that has prevailed since Justice Sutherland's enunciation of it in *Village of Euclid v. Ambler Realty Co.*, 272 U.S. 365, 395, 47 S.Ct. 114, 121 (1926). And *Dolan v. City*

*of Tigard,* __ U.S. __, 114 S. Ct. 2309 (1994), reveals a court apparently ready to apply strict, in-depth reviews, at least in the field of developer exactions.

25. Mount Laurel I, 67 N.J. 159, 336 A.2d 717.

26. Politically, this is a precarious balance. It took COAH four years of highly difficult negotiations to convince the State Planning Commission to allow low- and moderate-income housing in prime agricultural and environmentally sensitive areas when properly safeguarded. This is a continuous battle, with towns seeking to use the SDRP as a shield against affordable housing. Some of this thinking has drifted into the new SDRP to carve out large areas as prime agricultural and environmentally sensitive areas, potentially a time bomb for both the administrative and judicial branches. It is bound to become an acid test for the court to make workable its own pronouncements.

27. See Charles M. Haar, "Regionalism and Realism in Land-Use Planning," *University of Pennsylvania Law Review* 105 (1957): 515.

28. *Kozesnik v. Township of Montgomery,* 24 N.J. 154, 131 A.2d 1 (1957). In *Rockhill v. Chesterfield Township,* 23 N.J. 117, 128 A.2d 473 (1956), it invalidated a zoning ordinance that was not in accordance with a comprehensive plan.

29. This course of events has influenced other states. The Mount Laurel experience has induced state legislatures across the nation to undertake a reconsideration of the blanket delegation of land-use powers to localities without mandating consideration of broader interests.

30. Mount Laurel I, 67 N.J. 175, 336 A.2d 725.

31. See, e.g., Robert D. Bullard, *Dumping in Dixie: Race, Class and Environmental Quality* (Boulder, Colo.: Westview, 1990).

32. Executive Order No. 12,898, *Federal Register* 59 (1994 microfiche): 7629. Cf. Vicki Been, "What's Fairness Got to Do with It? Environmental Justice and the Siting of Locally Undesirable Land Uses," *Cornell Law Review* 78 (1993): 1001.

33. See Elizabeth Deakin, "Growth Controls and Growth Management: A Summary and Review of Empirical Research," in David J. Brower, David R. Godschalk, and Douglas R. Porter, eds., *Understanding Growth Management* (Washington, D.C.: Urban Land Institute, 1989), 3.

34. *AMG Realty Co. v. Township of Warren,* 207 N.J. Super. 388, 447, 504 A.2d 692, 723–24 (1984). He went on to demolish the town's environmental argument:

> Defendants attempted to establish, through the testimony of an expert in waste water management, that the proposed projects would have a negative effect upon the Dead River and also that there was inadequate sewer capacity within the township to accommodate the projects. . . . Warren's expert pointed to the Wastewater Facility Plans affecting Warren . . . and the Water Quality Management Plans pertaining to Warren. . . . Both studies are planning tools designed to establish a blueprint well into the twenty-first century for avoiding water pollution. The plans are developed based on expected water flow which, in turn, is extrapolated from population projection. . . . [Based on them] defendant argues that the growth of the township is necessarily limited by the waste-

water allocation to Warren and the commitment Warren has made to its prospective users.

The reasoning is fallacious. The state population projections embody existing zoning patterns. In Warren's case and others, that zoning is exclusionary. (207 N.J. Super. 447–49, 504 A.2d 723–24)

35. Relying on Judge Morton I. Greenberg's opinion in *Albano v. Washington*, 194 N.J. Super. 265, 273, 476 A.2d 852, 857 (1984).

36. *Orgo Farms and Greenhouses, Inc. v. Township of Colts Neck*, 192 N.J. Super. 603, 471 A.2d 814 (1983).

37. *Urban League of Essex County v. Mahwah*, 207 N.J. Super. 169, 504 A.2d 66 (1984). In *Mahwah*, the court pointed out that "distance from water and sewerage connections, or lack of frontage on a public street, or location in the conservation area individually is not enough to preclude the granting of a compliance remedy." 207 N.J. Super. 283, 504 A.2d 125. Judge Serpentelli later noted that a project might be allowed even within a limited growth designation when it did "little or no violence" to environmental concerns or to the SDGP's growth management strategy. *J. W. Field, Inc. v. Township of Franklin*, 204 N.J. Super, 445, 465, 499 A.2d 251, 261 (1985).

38. In some contrast to *Orgo Farms and Greenhouses, Inc. v. Colts Neck*, 204 N.J. Super. 585, 499 A.2d 565 (1985), is *Allan-Deane Corp. v. Bedminster*, 205 N.J. Super. 87, 500 A.2d 49 (1985), which addresses underlying environmental distinctions not sufficient to favor one builder's remedy over another plaintiff. In *Allan-Deane*, the court said:

> The issue of whether a site may appropriately be included in the compliance package should not turn solely upon the question of its relative susceptibility to being sewered. Of course, if the proofs demonstrate that one site has very little likelihood of having the appropriate infrastructure provided to it and that another site is comparatively assured of having such facilities, those proofs cannot be overlooked. The evidence in this case does not support the conclusion that Dobbs is in any better position as it relates to sewer availability than any of the sites of the compliance package. In fact, the court must lean towards the conclusion that, as between the two plans, it is more likely the township plan will obtain approval and be implemented. (205 N.J. Super. 130, 500 A.2d 75)

As can be seen, the need for the trial judge to interact and engage in actual supervision meant detailed and exhaustive analysis of particular cases.

39. *AMG*, 207 N.J. Super. 449, 504 A.2d 724. The case was referred to the special master to ascertain whether the builders' projects were precluded by the unavailability of sewer capacity.

40. See *J. W. Field*, 204 N.J. Super. 445, 499 A.2d 251.

41. COAH has built on the judicial base, but with greater sensitivity to the natural setting and local sentiments by stressing the protection of prime agricultural and environmentally sensitive areas in reviewing designations of plans for new unit allocation purposes and by shaping growth into population centers such as villages, towns, and new regional centers. All this, necessarily, is in coordination with the State Planning Commission.

In determining need, municipalities can take into account the preservation of historically important architecture and sites. COAH has defined historic and architectural preservation as encompassing sites on the State Register of Historic Places, including all lands within a hundred-foot buffer area.

42. Much of the detailed environmental data was disposed of in hearings in front of special masters, although the evidence did play a role in several litigations. For example, the plaintiff, Allan-Deane Corporation, supported its ability to acquire the necessary planning permits by hiring a wastewater treatment expert who argued that a technology pioneered in South Africa could ensure water quality. (Currently, the township is using the system in place at the builder's remedy site.) Plaintiffs in both *Orgo Farms* and *J. W. Field* relied on a "development constraints" system developed by a University of Pennsylvania expert.

43. *Housing Act of 1949*, chap. 338, sec. 2, *Statutes at Large* 63 (1949): 413 (codified as amended in *U.S. Code* 42, sec. 1441 [1988]).

44. After the 1992 Los Angeles riots, a poll reported that 60 percent of the population felt that "too little has been done to improve the lot of blacks." "Giving Bush a Push," *Washington Post*, May 17, 1992, C1. It may be that social justice is only embraced until a personal commitment is required, but there is the possibility that the courts are acting more in consonance with popular belief than some people might believe.

45. See especially Paul M. Sniderman and Thomas Piazza, *The Scar of Race* (Cambridge, Mass.: Belknap Press, 1993), which relies on two of the largest academic surveys, the National Election Study and the General Social Survey.

46. Gunnar Myrdal, *An American Dilemma* (New York: Harper, 1944).

47. Mount Laurel II, 92 N.J. 209, 456 A.2d 415.

48. Ibid., 92 N.J. 212–13, 456 A.2d 417.

49. Conversation with Ethel Halley, daughter of Ethel Lawrence.

50. *Hills Development Co. v. Township of Bernards*, 103 N.J. 1, 24, 510 A.2d 621, 634 (1986). The court's warning in *Hills*/Mount Laurel III that it would reenter the picture should the agency created by the legislature prove ineffective indicates that the commitment to the creation of affordable housing remains. The immediate issue of the acceptance of the RCAs, however, shifted the doctrine's substantive vision. Though every municipality was still required to respond to regional housing shortages—by act of the legislature now held not to be constitutionally infirm—each no longer had to provide an appropriate variety and, at least as far as 50 percent of the obligation is concerned, choice of housing for "all categories of people who may desire to live within its boundaries." Mount Laurel I, 67 N.J. 179, 336 A.2d 728.

51. See Garry Wills, *Reagan's America: Innocents at Home* (Garden City, N.Y.: Doubleday, 1987).

52. See, e.g., Ronald Reagan, Inaugural Address, January 20, 1981, *Public Papers of the Presidents of the United States: Ronald Reagan, 1981* (Washington, D.C.: U.S. Government Printing Office, 1982), 2. "All of us need to be reminded that the Federal Government did not create the States; the States created the Federal Government."

53. Cf. Nicholas Lemann, *The Promised Land: The Great Black Migration and How It Changed America* (New York: Vintage, 1992), 343–58. The contrast-

ing view is expounded in Charles A. Murray, *Losing Ground: American Social Policy, 1950–1980* (New York: Basic Books, 1984). Cf. James Davison Hunter, *Before the Shooting Begins: Searching for Democracy in America's Culture War* (New York: Free Press, 1994).

54. This happened in the case of Judge Paul Garrity putting the Boston Housing Authority into receivership. See *NAACP v. Boston Housing Authority*, 723 F.Supp. 1554 (1989).

55. *Hills*, 103 N.J. 21, 510 A.2d 632.

56. A further interesting argument can be raised. The revised New Jersey land-use planning law requires a housing plan. If a locality does not include an affordable housing component as part of the comprehensive plan on which zoning must be based, it may find itself without the power to zone at all.

57. *The Federalist, No. 49*, 347. It is the legislative department, Madison added, that "is everywhere extending the sphere of its activity and drawing all power into its impetuous vortex." *The Federalist, No. 48*, 343.

58. For a less benevolent view of the agency, see Lamar, Mallach, and Payne, "Mount Laurel at Work," 1197.

59. The need for judicial support may extend to the State Planning Commission. Efforts to keep the SDRP current will be hampered by the budget constraints of the legislature and the state's perennial fiscal crisis.

60. See Joel Garreau, *Edge City: Life on the New Frontier* (New York: Doubleday, 1991); and Charles M. Haar and John Lindsay, *Business and the Revolution in Land Use Planning: New Private Sector Roles and New Suburban Forms* (Cambridge, Mass.: Lincoln Institute of Land Policy, 1987).

61. There has been virtually no change in the degree of residential segregation of African-Americans since 1970. See Douglas S. Massey and Nancy A. Denton, *American Apartheid: Segregation and the Making of the American Underclass* (Cambridge, Mass.: Harvard University Press, 1993). Nearly 30 percent—or nine million blacks—live in almost complete racial isolation, primarily in central cities.

# Acknowledgments _____

I AM especially grateful to the judges and special masters who took the time to share their experiences in the Mount Laurel litigations. The Council on Affordable Housing, notably its first director, Douglas Opalski, and the current directory, Shirley Bishop, were most helpful.

I have had the benefit of advice and suggestions from many sources. My long-time friend and colleague Jerold Kayden read through the book with meticulous care. Michael Wolf and Jerome Rose made substantial contributions. George Raymond helped with specific comments on the manuscript, as did Robert Burchell, Morton J. Horwitz, Larry Levinson, Peter Lewis, Ed McAmis, and Jeff Surenian. Special thanks are due to Theodore Cross for his insistence on simplification and clarification. My daughter, Susan Haar, was a good companion in a series of interviews with judges and special masters. Stephen Eisdorfer and Philip Caton afforded me the benefit of their reactions, as did the late judge, Lois Forer. My wife, Suzanne Keller, provided unique perspective and indispensable support.

I am indebted to the word processing division of Harvard Law School, Cheryl Frost, Colleen Murphy, Susan Salvato, Debbie Soares and Selena Tan, who worked through many drafts of the book. I benefited from the research skills and goodwill of several law school students, Sarah Cooleybeck, Cam Elliot, Ansley Samson, and Robyn Tarnofsky. Christiane Wollaston-Joury coordinated all the activities with her usual thoroughness and unfailing good humor.

Valuable suggestions came from Hilbert Fefferman, Zachary Karabell, Cynthia Rose, Jeanne Smoot, and Anita Summers.

Princeton University Press—Malcolm DeBevoise, Heidi Sheehan, and Sterling Bland—worked with admirable efficiency to bring this work to publication. Sarah St. Onge provided valuable editing skills. Travel expenses were funded by the Twentieth Century Fund and by the Federal National Mortgage Association.

I hope the work is worthy of all their efforts.

# Picture Credits